JESUS CHRIST SOLARPUNK

An Eco-Friendly Guide to Life

By

Tracy Carol Taylor

Tracy Taylor

JESUS CHRIST SOLARPUNK
Copyright © 2025 by Tracy Carol Taylor. All Rights Reserved.

No part of this publication may be reproduced, stored in a retrieval system, or transmitted in any way by any means, electronic, mechanical, photocopy, recording, or otherwise, without the proper permission of the author except as provided by USA copyright law.

Scripture quotations marked (KJV) are taken from the Holy Bible, King James Version, Cambridge, 1769. Used by permission. All rights reserved.

Scripture quotations marked (NIV) are taken from the Holy Bible, New International Version, NIV, Copyright © 1973, 1978, 1984 by Biblica, Inc. ™ Used by permission of Zondervan. All rights reserved worldwide.

The opinions expressed by the author are not necessarily those of Prince of Pages, Inc.

Published by Prince of Pages, Inc.
N. Carlin Springs Road | Arlington, VA 22203 USA
www.princeofpages.com
Cover design by Midjourney
Published in the United States of America
ISBN: 978-1-949252-48-4

Table of Contents

Introduction 7

Chapter 1: 14

In the Beginning: God's Creation and Our Role 14

Chapter 2: 26

The Garden Model: Living in Harmony with Nature ... 26

Chapter 3: 41

Divine Order in Creation and Energy 41

Chapter 4: 60

Stewardship of Resources...................................... 60

Chapter 5: 75

Love Thy Neighbor: Building Connected Communities 75

Chapter 6: 93

The Pyramid of Equality – Unity Under God 93

Chapter 7: 117

The Sabbath Principle: Rest and Renewal for the Earth 117

Chapter 8: 139

The Loaves and Fishes Principle: Multiplying Resources 139

Chapter 9: 168

City of Light: Designing for the Common Good 168

Chapter 10: 189

Seeds of Faith: Cultivating Hope in Difficult Times . 189

Chapter 11: 213
Renewing the Mind: Adopting a Christ-Centered Perspective 213

Chapter 12: 237
Prayer, Meditation, and Energy Flow 237

Chapter 13: 260
Living Water: Sustainable Practices for Daily Life ... 260

Chapter 14: 283
Sustainable Living Through Biblical Wisdom 283

Chapter 15: 311
Technology in Harmony with God's Design 311

Chapter 16: 336
Overcoming Giants: Facing Climate and Social Challenges 336

Chapter 17: 364
Be Strong and Courageous: Trusting God in a Changing World 364

Chapter 18: 391
The Garden of Humanity: Celebrating God's Diverse Creation 391

Chapter 19: 418
Let Your Light Shine: Spreading Hope Through Action 418

Chapter 20: 445
The Narrow Path: Choosing Faith Over Convenience 445

Chapter 21: 470

Salvation and Creation: Redemption for All Things . 470

Chapter 22: 496

The Green Communion: Salvation as Communal Restoration.. 496

Chapter 23: 508

Thy Kingdom Come: Envisioning a New Heaven and New Earth 508

Chapter 24: 524

Faith in Bloom: Living as New Creations 524

Conclusion: 543

Walking Forward in Light and Truth..................... 543

Bibliography 558

Tracy Taylor

Introduction

Welcome to a Bright, Green Future!

Have you ever looked at our world and thought, "Things could be so much better"? Maybe you've seen trash piling up, heard about animals losing their homes, or worried about all the smoke coming from factories. Perhaps you've wondered what the Bible might say about taking care of our beautiful planet.

Well, you're not alone! This book was written especially for you and your family.

Imagine a world where solar panels glitter on rooftops like diamonds catching the sun. Picture gardens bursting with vegetables and fruits growing between apartment buildings. Think about people sharing what they have, working together, and caring for God's amazing creation—all while following Jesus' teachings.

This isn't just a dream—it's called "Solarpunk," and it fits perfectly with what the Bible teaches us about being good stewards of Earth!

What This Book Is All About

The Bible tells us that God created this wonderful world and then trusted humans to take care of it. In Genesis 1:28-30, God gives us an important job: to be caretakers of the Earth and all its creatures. He didn't say, "Use everything up as fast as you can!" Instead, He invited us to be responsible gardeners of His creation.

This book explores how God's Word in the Bible—especially in the beautiful language of the King James Version—gives us a perfect blueprint for living sustainably and in harmony with nature. We'll discover that caring for creation isn't just a modern idea—it's been God's plan all along!

What in the World is "Solarpunk"?

If you're wondering what "Solarpunk" means, you're about to discover something amazing! Solarpunk is a vision of the future where people use renewable energy like solar power, grow food locally, reduce waste, build beautiful green and eco-friendly cities, and work together as communities. Solarpunk celebrates the beauty of nature alongside human creativity, believing we can tackle big challenges like climate change if we all pitch in. It's about building a world where everyone has what they need, where we repair and create things ourselves, and where our neighborhoods are designed to be both sustainable and wonderful places to live. It's optimistic and hopeful, focusing on solutions rather than problems.

Now, here's the exciting part—these Solarpunk ideas match up wonderfully with Biblical teachings! When Jesus taught us to love our neighbors, share with others, and not worry about storing up treasures on Earth, He laid the groundwork for exactly the kind of world Solarpunk imagines.

A God-centered Solarpunk life means:

Solarpunk principles beautifully align with Jesus's teachings and Biblical wisdom. When we care for God's Earth as a precious creation rather than resources to exploit, we honor the Creator who entrusted us as stewards of His wonderful world. Treating everyone with love and dignity reflects Jesus's command to "love your neighbor as yourself" and recognizes that all people bear God's sacred image. Using clean energy sources demonstrates respect for God's creation, much like Adam was called to tend to the Garden of Eden. Growing and sharing food in the community mirrors the early Christian church in Acts, where believers "had everything in common" and "gave to anyone who had need." Building communities where everyone has enough reflects God's heart for justice and provision, remembering how Jesus fed the multitudes and taught that the Kingdom of God belongs to those who care for the "least of these." In these ways, Solarpunk's vision of a harmonious, sustainable future resonates deeply with Christ's teachings of love, stewardship, and community.

Why the King James Bible?

You might wonder why we mention the King James Bible in this book. The beautiful, poetic language of the King James Version helps us see the wonder and majesty of God's creation in a special way. When it says, *"The heavens declare the glory of God; and the firmament sheweth his handywork"* (Psalm 19:1), we can almost hear the stars singing!

The King James Version also contains rich agricultural metaphors and detailed descriptions of how God's people were meant to live on the land—letting fields rest every seven years, caring for animals, and sharing harvests with those in need. These ancient instructions hold surprisingly modern wisdom for sustainable living!

The Big Ideas We'll Explore

Throughout our journey together, we'll discover amazing connections between faith and creation care:

Hope: The Bible is full of hope! God promises to make all things new (Revelation 21:5), and Solarpunk shows us practical ways to participate in this renewal.

Faith: True faith isn't just about what we believe—it's about how we live. Jesus called us to be *"doers of the word, and not hearers only"* (James 1:22).

Creation Care: God instructed humans to tend and keep the Garden (Genesis 2:15). In this lesson, we'll learn practical, fun ways your family can care for creation today.

Cooperative Living: The early Christians "*had all things common*" (Acts 4:32) and ensured everyone's needs were met. We'll see how modern communities are rediscovering this biblical principle.

How This Book Will Change Your Life

Are you ready for an adventure? This book isn't just filled with interesting ideas—it's a guidebook for transformation! By the time you finish reading, you'll:

See God's Word with fresh eyes, discovering verses about creation care you might have overlooked

Find simple, practical ways your family can live more sustainably

Feel empowered to make changes in your home, school, and community

Connect with like-minded believers who share your passion for creation care

Experience the joy that comes from living in harmony with God's design

Have lots of fun activities and projects to try with your family and friends!

Whether you're a curious kid, a teen looking for purpose, or a parent wanting to raise children with godly values in an increasingly complicated world, this book has something special for you.

So, grab your Bible, put on your thinking cap, and get ready to discover how God's ancient wisdom and modern sustainability can come together to create something beautiful. Let's watch our faith bloom as we learn to care for God's creation in new and exciting ways!

Are you ready? Let's begin our journey toward a brighter, greener future—exactly the way God intended it to be!

Chapter 1:

In the Beginning: God's Creation and Our Role

"And God Saw That It Was Very Good"

Imagine being able to watch the entire universe come to life! The stars bursting into existence like beautiful fireworks, oceans filling with shimmering blue water, and animals of every kind appearing—from tiny colorful frogs to enormous elephants with swinging trunks.

That's exactly what happened at the beginning of time, and the Bible gives us a front-row seat to this amazing show in the very first chapter of Genesis.

"In the beginning, God created the heaven and the earth." (Genesis 1:1)

With these powerful words, the most incredible story ever told begins. God spoke, and where there was nothing, suddenly, there was everything! Light chased away the darkness. Waters separated to make sky and sea. Dry land pushed up through the waves. Plants sprouted in an explosion of green. The sun, moon, and stars appeared to mark days and seasons. Fish filled the seas, birds soared through the air, and animals roamed across the land.

After each day of creation, God looked at what He had made and declared it "good." But on the sixth day, after creating humans, God looked at everything He had made and called it "very good" (Genesis 1:31). That's like getting an A+ on the ultimate report card!

Humans: God's Special Caretakers

On that sixth day of creation, something extra special happened. God decided to make creatures unlike any others—humans who would be made in His own image:

"And God said, Let us make man in our image, after our likeness: and let them have dominion over the fish of the sea, and over the fowl of the air, and over the cattle, and over all the earth, and over every creeping thing that creepeth upon the earth." (Genesis 1:26)

When God gave humans "dominion," He wasn't giving us permission to do whatever we wanted with the Earth. The word "dominion" in the Bible is more like being given an important job or responsibility. Think of it like this: if your parents put you in charge of a younger sibling while they make dinner, they're not saying you can boss your sibling around or take their toys! They're trusting you to be kind, helpful, and responsible.

That's exactly what God was doing when He gave humans dominion over creation. He was entrusting us with the care of His masterpiece—this beautiful planet with all its amazing plants and animals.

What Does It Mean to Be a Steward?

Being a steward means taking care of something that doesn't belong to you. A school librarian is a steward of all the books in the library. A park ranger is a steward of the forest and its wildlife. And humans are stewards of God's creation.

In Genesis 2:15, the Bible tells us that God placed Adam in the Garden of Eden "*to dress it and to keep it.*" The Hebrew words "abad" and "shamar" mean to serve, work, protect, and preserve. God didn't put Adam in the garden to use it up or destroy it, but to care for it and help it flourish!

When we understand that Earth isn't actually ours—it's God's—it changes how we treat it. We stop asking, 'What can I take from this?' and start asking, 'How can I care for this gift I've been given?'

Many Native American tribes lived by a profound philosophy of balance with the land. They saw themselves not as owners but as relatives of the natural world. They practiced thoughtful stewardship, taking only what was needed for survival while ensuring resources would remain for future generations.

When hunting, many tribes used every part of the animal—meat for food, hides for clothing and shelter, bones for tools—showing respect for the creature's sacrifice. When gathering plants, they often harvest selectively, leaving enough to regrow and sometimes replanting seeds to ensure continued abundance.

This relationship with the land was strengthened through ceremonies that expressed gratitude and reciprocity. Many tribes performed rituals to thank Mother Earth and the Creator before and after harvests or hunts. Some practiced controlled burns to manage forests, understanding that certain ecosystems needed periodic fires to stay healthy.

Their approach reflected a deep wisdom: that humans are part of nature's circle, not separate from it, and that our well-being depends on maintaining harmony with all living things.

Kindness to All Creation

God cares deeply about how we treat not just people but animals and all of nature. In Proverbs 12:10, the Bible tells us:

"A righteous man regardeth the life of his beast: but the tender mercies of the wicked are cruel."

This verse shows us that being good means caring properly for animals. Throughout the Bible, we see more examples of this care:

- God commanded that even work animals should rest on the Sabbath (Exodus 20:10)

- Farm animals were to be fed before their owners ate (Deuteronomy 25:4)
- Baby birds and their mothers were protected by special laws (Deuteronomy 22:6-7)
- Wild animals were given their own land and food sources (Psalm 104:10-11)

Even plants were to be treated with respect and care! Hebrew farmers were instructed to let their fields rest every seven years (Leviticus 25:4) and to leave the edges of their fields unharvested for the poor and for wildlife (Leviticus 19:9-10).

Activity Box: Creation Care Detective

Grab your Bible and look up these verses about God's care for creation: Job 38:25-27, Psalm 104:10-30, Matthew 6:26-30. In your notebook, write down or draw one surprising thing you learned about how God cares for plants, animals, or the Earth itself!

Solarpunk: A Vision That Matches God's Plan

Now that we understand God's original blueprint for how humans should relate to creation, let's talk about something exciting happening today called "Solarpunk."

Solarpunk is a movement that imagines a future where people live in harmony with nature, using clean energy like solar power, growing food locally, reducing waste, and working together as communities. It's bright, hopeful, and full of creative solutions to environmental problems.

Does that sound familiar? It should! Solarpunk's vision aligns beautifully with God's original plan for humans to be caretakers of creation.

Here are some ways Solarpunk reflects biblical values:

1. Harmony with Nature

Solarpunk: People design cities and homes that work with natural systems, not against them.

Bible: Adam and Eve lived in a garden, not a concrete jungle (Genesis 2:8-15).

2. Clean Energy

Solarpunk: Communities use renewable energy from the sun, wind, and water.

Bible: God provides sustainable resources that naturally renew themselves (Psalm 104:13-14).

3. Local Food

Solarpunk: People grow food in community gardens and share the harvest.

Bible: God's people were instructed to plant gardens and share their abundance (Leviticus 19:9-10, Jeremiah 29:5).

4. Reduced Waste

Solarpunk: Nothing is wasted; materials are reused or recycled.

Bible: Jesus instructed disciples to gather leftover food so nothing would be wasted (John 6:12).

5. Community Focus

Solarpunk: People work together and share resources for the common good.

Bible: The early church shared everything they had (Acts 4:32-35).

Twelve-year-old Mia shares: "When our church started a community garden based on biblical principles, I thought it would be boring. But it's become my favorite place! We grow vegetables for our food bank, and I've made friends with elderly people who teach me cool gardening tricks. Last week, Mrs. Rodriguez showed me how to save tomato seeds just like her grandmother taught her in Mexico!"

Why This Matters Today

Our beautiful planet Earth is facing some serious challenges right now:

- Pollution in our air, water, and soil
- Loss of forests and wildlife habitat
- Climate change affecting weather patterns
- Growing mountains of trash and plastic
- Species becoming extinct

As Christians who understand our God-given role as stewards, we have a special responsibility to address these problems. This isn't about politics or trends—it's about faithfulness to God's very first instructions to humanity!

Pastor James puts it well: "When we care for creation, we're not just being environmentalists—we're being obedient to God's command. We're showing gratitude for His gift of this incredible planet, and we're loving our neighbors by ensuring they have clean air, water, and soil."

Putting It Into Practice

So how can you—yes, YOU—start living out your role as a steward of God's creation? Here are some simple ideas to try this week:

For Kids:

- Start a nature journal to notice and appreciate God's creation
- Pick up litter in your neighborhood or local park
- Help plant and care for a garden at home or at school
- Turn off lights and water when not using them
- Learn to identify local plants and animals

For Families:

- Read Genesis 1-2 together and discuss God's view of creation
- Start a compost bin for food scraps
- Walk, bike, or use public transportation when possible
- Choose reusable items instead of disposable ones
- Visit a local farm or nature preserve to connect with nature

Remember, being a good steward isn't about being perfect—it's about making choices that honor God and care for His creation, one step at a time.

Looking Ahead

In the following chapters, we'll explore practical ways to live out your role as a steward of God's creation. We'll explore exciting Solarpunk ideas that align with biblical principles, learn from inspiring examples of Christians caring for creation, and discover how sustainable living can be an act of worship and faith.

As we end this chapter, take a moment to look around you. Every tree, flower, animal, and star belongs to God. He made them all, called them good, and trusted you to help care for them. What an amazing responsibility and privilege!

Family Discussion Questions:

1. What part of God's creation do you find most amazing or beautiful? Why?

2. How do you think God feels when seeing how humans treat His creation today?

3. What's one change our family could make this week to be better stewards of creation?

4. How might caring for creation be a way of sharing God's love with others?

Teacher's Corner: This chapter establishes the theological foundation for creation care by examining key texts from Genesis that define humanity's role as stewards rather than exploiters of creation. The dominion mandate is reframed through the lens of responsible caretaking, a concept readily accessible to young minds through familiar analogies.

For classroom application, consider taking students outdoors for a creation scavenger hunt, identifying examples of interconnectedness in natural systems. This experiential learning reinforces the biblical concept of creation's inherent value and humans' responsibility toward it. The Solarpunk framework provides a positive, solution-oriented approach that empowers rather than overwhelms young people when facing environmental challenges.

Chapter 2:

The Garden Model: Living in Harmony with Nature

Eden: God's Perfect Design

Have you ever planted a tiny seed and watched in wonder as it pushed through the soil, reaching for the sunlight? Or felt the cool squish of mud between your toes after a spring rain? If so, you've experienced just a small taste of what Adam must have felt in the very first garden—the Garden of Eden!

While we learned in Chapter 1 that God created the entire world and called it "very good," the Bible tells us that He did something extra special for humans. In Genesis 2:8, we read:

"And the LORD God planted a garden eastward in Eden; and there he put the man whom he had formed."

Imagine that! God Himself planted a garden specifically for humans to live in. This wasn't just any garden—it was perfect in every way, with crystal-clear rivers, fruit-bearing trees, and all kinds of amazing plants and animals. Eden was where heaven and earth overlapped, a place where humans could walk and talk with God while surrounded by His magnificent creation.

But God didn't place Adam in this paradise to lounge around all day! Genesis 2:15 tells us:

"And the LORD God took the man, and put him into the garden of Eden to dress it and to keep it."

The words "dress" and "keep" tell us something incredibly important about God's plan for humans. Even in a perfect world, we were meant to be gardeners! Adam's job was to tend, nurture, protect, and care for this beautiful place God had made.

God could have created a world that took care of itself completely, with no need for human help. But instead, He designed a world where humans and nature work together in partnership. That tells us something amazing—God wants us to be co-creators with Him!

What Eden Teaches Us Today

Eden isn't just a lovely story about the past—it's a blueprint for how we should live now! Even though sin has changed our world, God's original design still teaches us important principles for living in harmony with nature.

Eden Principle #1: Everything is Connected

In Eden, plants, animals, humans, and God all existed in perfect balance. Nothing was wasted, and everything had a purpose. Today, scientists call this "ecology"—the study of how living things relate to each other and their environment.

Eden Principle #2: Humans Are Caretakers, Not Conquerors

Adam wasn't told to bulldoze the garden and build a shopping mall! He was told to nurture what God had already made. This teaches us that development should work with nature, not against it.

Eden Principle #3: Gardens Provide for All Needs

Eden supplied food, beauty, an animal habitat, clean water, and a place for humans to work and play. When properly designed, modern green spaces can do the same!

Eden Principle #4: Work Can Be Joyful

Adam's work in the garden wasn't a punishment—it came before sin entered the world! Caring for creation can and should be satisfying and meaningful.

Activity Box: Eden Detective

Read Genesis 2:8-15 carefully and make a list of all the things mentioned in the Garden of Eden. What plants, waters, resources, and jobs can you find? How many purposes did the garden serve? Draw your own version of what you think Eden might have looked like!

Reimagining Our World Through Solarpunk Designs

Now, let's fast-forward to today. Our current world often looks very different from Eden. Many of us live in concrete cities, shop in giant stores, and rarely get our hands in the soil. But an exciting movement called Solarpunk is reimagining how we can return to something more like God's original design!

Solarpunk is a vision of a future where humans live in ways that heal rather than harm the Earth. Solarpunk designs blend beautiful architecture with lush gardens, clean energy, and strong communities. Here are some amazing examples of how Solarpunk designs are bringing back the Garden Model:

Vertical Forests

In Milan, Italy, an architect named Stefano Boeri designed apartment buildings called "Vertical Forests." These towers have terraces filled with hundreds of trees and thousands of plants! The trees provide shade, clean the air, create homes for birds and insects, and make the buildings beautiful. It's like living in a garden in the sky!

Urban Farms

In cities worldwide, people are turning vacant lots, rooftops, and even old factories into gardens that grow food. In Detroit, Michigan, urban farms now produce fresh vegetables for neighborhoods where grocery stores are scarce. In Singapore, a 'sky farm' on top of a shopping center grows more than 500 tons of vegetables every year!

Food Forests

Unlike regular orchards that grow just one type of fruit tree in straight rows, food forests mimic natural woodlands with many layers of useful plants. Tall fruit and nut trees create a canopy, with smaller berry bushes beneath them and herbs and vegetables growing at ground level. Everything works together just like in a natural forest, but it provides food for people, too!

Rainwater Harvesting

Many Solarpunk designs include beautiful systems for collecting rainwater from roofs and pavement. This water can be stored in underground tanks or decorative ponds and then used to water gardens during dry periods. Some buildings even have "living machines" that use plants to clean and filter water naturally!

Twelve-year-old Aiden shares: "Our school installed rain gardens that collect water from the roof. Before, all that water just went down storm drains, but now it waters native plants that attract butterflies and hummingbirds. We even get to help maintain them during science class!"

Jesus' Teachings on Simplicity and Generosity

When Jesus came to Earth, He often taught outdoors, using examples from nature to explain spiritual truths. He pointed to lilies, sparrows, seeds, and crops to help people understand God's love and wisdom. And many of His teachings connect perfectly with caring for creation!

In Matthew 6:19-21, Jesus said:

"Lay not up for yourselves treasures upon earth, where moth and rust doth corrupt, and where thieves break through and steal: But lay up for yourselves treasures in heaven, where neither moth nor rust doth corrupt, and where thieves do not break through nor steal: For where your treasure is, there will your heart be also."

This teaching helps us see that constantly buying and accumulating more stuff isn't the path to happiness. When we focus on having the newest phone, the trendiest clothes, or the biggest house, we're storing up "treasures on earth" that don't last and don't satisfy our hearts. In fact, they often become financial burdens.

Jesus encourages a simpler way of living that values relationships, kindness, and spiritual growth over material possessions. This simpler lifestyle is also much better for God's creation! When we buy less, we use fewer resources, create less waste, and often find ourselves more connected to the natural world around us.

Jesus also frequently taught about generosity and sharing with others. In Luke 3:11, John the Baptist (preparing the way for Jesus) instructed: "*He that hath two coats, let him impart to him that hath none; and he that hath meat, let him do likewise.*"

This spirit of sharing aligns perfectly with the Solarpunk vision of communities where neighbors share resources like tools, garden harvests, and rainwater. When we share, everyone can have what they need without excessive production straining the Earth's resources.

Practical Applications: Creating Your Own Eden

Are you excited to start bringing a little bit of Eden into your own life? Here are some practical ways you and your family can begin living more in harmony with nature:

1. Start a Garden (No Matter How Small!)

You don't need a huge yard to grow things. Even a few pots on a windowsill can become a mini garden! Try growing herbs like basil, mint, or cilantro—they're fairly easy to care for and can add fresh flavors to your meals.

If you have some yard space, consider converting part of your lawn into a vegetable garden or native plant habitat. Start small, with just a few square feet, and expand as you learn!

2. Create a Wildlife Habitat

God cares about all His creatures, not just humans! You can help local wildlife by:

- Putting up bird feeders or birdhouses
- Planting flowers that provide nectar for bees and butterflies
- Creating a small pond for frogs and beneficial insects
- Leaving a pile of branches and leaves in a corner of your yard as shelter for small animals

Ten-year-old Maya tells us: "I started a 'pollinator patch' in our yard with flowers that butterflies love. Now we see monarchs, swallowtails, and bees all summer long! Dad says we're helping God's creatures do their important work."

3. Harvest Rainwater

Place a rain barrel under your gutter downspout to collect rainwater for your garden. This free water will save your water bill and reduce runoff that can cause erosion. Some cities even offer discounted rain barrels to residents!

4. Go on a "Stuff Diet"

Challenge your family to buy less new stuff for a month. Instead, try:

- Borrowing books from the library instead of buying them
- Repairing broken items instead of replacing them
- Trading clothes or toys with friends when you want something new
- Making homemade gifts instead of store-bought ones

5. Create Community Green Spaces

Look for opportunities in your neighborhood or school to create shared gardens or green areas:

- Volunteer at a community garden
- Help plant trees with a local organization
- Ask if your school would allow students to create a garden on campus
- Work with your church to start a "Creation Care" team that plants flowers or vegetables on church grounds

Project Box: Mini Food Forest in a Box

Create a self-contained mini ecosystem that demonstrates the layers of a food forest! You'll need a clear plastic storage container with a lid (shoe-box-sized works well).

Layer 1: (Bottom): Small rocks for drainage

Layer 2: Potting soil mixed with compost

Layer 3: (Groundcover): Plant clover or mint seeds

Layer 4: (Herbs): Add small herb plants like thyme or oregano

Layer 5: (Shrubs): Place a small strawberry plant in one corner

Layer 6: (Tree): Plant a bean seed and give it a small trellis to climb

Water gently, place the lid on loosely, and put in a warm spot with indirect sunlight. Watch your mini food forest grow! This creates a miniature water cycle where plants release moisture that condenses on the lid and "rains" back down.

The Joy of Garden Living

Amazing things happen when we follow God's original plan by caring for creation and living more like gardeners! Families who embrace this lifestyle often report:

- More time spent together outdoors
- Healthier eating habits with fresh, homegrown food
- Reduced stress and anxiety as they connect with nature
- Stronger community bonds through shared gardens and harvests
- A deeper appreciation for God's intricate and beautiful creation
- More opportunities to share God's love with neighbors

Pastor Miguel, who leads a church with an urban garden ministry, shares: "When we started our community garden, we thought we were just growing vegetables. But we discovered we were actually growing relationships—with each other, our neighbors, and with God. Working in the soil reminds us of our connection to creation and Creator."

Looking Ahead

Our next chapter will explore how energy from the sun—the same light God created on Day One—can power our modern world in clean and sustainable ways. We'll discover how renewable energy connects to Biblical principles and how Nikola Tesla's fascinating discoveries about energy might teach us something about God's divine order in creation!

For now, remember that each small step toward garden living brings us closer to God's original design. Whether you're planting your first seed or redesigning your entire backyard as a food forest, you're participating in God's plan to restore harmony between humans and the rest of creation.

As you look around at the world this week, try to imagine it through God's eyes—not as resources to be consumed, but as a garden to be tended. How might that change the choices you make?

Family Discussion Questions:

1. If you could design your own garden, what would you include? What plants, features, or spaces would make it special?

2. What's one "Eden Principle" that you think our family could apply better in our home or yard?

3. How might growing some of our own food or sharing with neighbors help us better understand Jesus' teachings on simplicity and generosity?

4. What's your favorite way to spend time in nature, and how does it help you feel connected to God?

Teacher's Corner: This chapter builds upon the theological foundation established in Chapter 1 by exploring the specific model of Eden as God's intentional design for human-nature relationships. The garden metaphor provides an accessible framework for students to understand ecological principles while reinforcing the spiritual dimensions of creation care.

Consider supplementing this chapter with hands-on activities like seed starting or terrarium building to help students experience the joy and responsibility of nurturing and growing things. The Solarpunk examples offer excellent launching points for STEAM projects integrating Science, Technology, Engineering, Art, and Mathematics through sustainable design challenges.

For churches and Christian schools, the garden model offers rich opportunities for interdisciplinary learning: science (plant biology, ecosystems), history (agricultural practices through time), art (garden design), and of course, Biblical studies (examining all the garden references throughout Scripture).

Chapter 3:

Divine Order in Creation and Energy

The Wonderful Pattern of Three

Have you ever noticed how many important things come in threes? Think about it: morning, noon, and night divide our day. The Earth, sea, and sky make up our world. The beginning, middle, and end structure every good story. There is the past, the present, and the future.

This pattern of three isn't just a coincidence—it's woven into the very fabric of creation! And perhaps the most amazing "three" of all is how God reveals Himself to us: as Father, Son, and Holy Spirit—the Trinity.

"For there are three that bear record in heaven, the Father, the Word, and the Holy Ghost: and these three are one." (1 John 5:7, KJV)

The Trinity is one of Christianity's most beautiful and mysterious teachings. God is three distinct persons—Father, Son, and Holy Spirit—yet completely one God. It is like a perfect team, where each member has unique gifts but works in complete harmony with the others.

Think of water—it can exist as liquid water, solid ice, or steam vapor. Three different forms, but all H_2O. God is infinitely more complex than water, of course, but this gives us a tiny glimpse of how something can be both three and one at the same time.

The Trinity shows us that relationship and harmony are at the very heart of God. The Father, Son, and Holy Spirit have existed forever in perfect love and cooperation. Nothing in the Trinity is wasted or working against the others—it's a model of perfect energy and balance!

God's Creation Reflects This Divine Order

When God created the universe, He built these patterns of harmony and balance into everything! Scientists discover more of these amazing patterns every day:

The Earth's Water Cycle: Water evaporates from oceans, forms clouds, falls as rain, and returns to the sea—an endless, perfect cycle that provides fresh water for all life.

The Food Chain: Plants capture energy from the sun, animals eat plants, and when plants and animals die, they decompose to feed new plants—a beautiful cycle where nothing is wasted.

Seasons: Spring, summer, fall, and winter follow one another in perfect sequence, each playing its crucial role in the rhythm of life.

A kid named Isaac noticed this divine pattern in his backyard: "I've been keeping a nature journal, and I realized that the dandelions in our yard are like tiny solar panels! They collect sunlight, then birds eat their seeds, and the birds spread the seeds to grow new dandelions. It's like a tiny power plant God designed!"

The Light of the World

One of the most powerful images Jesus used to describe Himself is found in John 8:12:

"Then spake Jesus again unto them, saying, I am the light of the world: he that followeth me shall not walk in darkness, but shall have the light of life."

Light is essential for life. Plants need light for photosynthesis. Animals (including us humans!) need the food that plants make. We need light to see where we're going. Without light, our world would be cold, dark, and lifeless.

When Jesus calls Himself "the light of the world," He's telling us something profound—just as physical light sustains physical life, Jesus sustains our spiritual life! And just as the sun freely gives its energy to everyone on Earth, Jesus freely offers His love and salvation to all people.

Think about this: almost all energy on Earth comes from the sun. The food you eat? Plants grew it using sunlight. The fossil fuels that power cars? They're made from ancient plants and animals that got their energy from the sun long ago. Even the power that comes from wind and water comes from the sun, heating our atmosphere and driving weather patterns!

In a similar way, all spiritual energy comes from God. Every act of love, kindness, and goodness ultimately flows from Him—the source of all light and life.

Activity Box: Light Explorers

Try this simple experiment to see how energy from light can create movement!

You'll need:
- A small solar-powered toy or solar calculator
- A flashlight
- A notebook for observations

Step 1: Place the solar toy in direct sunlight. Observe what happens.

Step 2: Move it to shade. What changes?

Step 3: Shine the flashlight on the solar panel. Does it respond?

Step 4: Try different light sources around your house.

In your notebook, record which light sources worked best. How is this like our spiritual lives? When do you feel most energized by God's light?

Tesla's Amazing Number Discoveries

Nikola Tesla, born in 1856, was one of history's most brilliant inventors. He created technologies that help power our world today, including alternating current (AC) electricity, which powers your home!

Tesla was fascinated by patterns in mathematics and energy. He once said, "If you only knew the magnificence of the 3, 6, and 9, then you would have a key to the universe." What did he mean by this mysterious statement?

Tesla noticed that when you examine certain number patterns, especially in systems that flow in circles (like electricity), the numbers 3, 6, and 9 play special roles:

- If you keep doubling 1, you get: 1, 2, 4, 8, 16, 32, 64... and if you add the digits of each number together, the pattern is: 1, 2, 4, 8, 7, 5, 1... It cycles every six numbers.

- If you do the same with 3, you get: 3, 6, 12, 24, 48, 96... and when you add those digits: 3, 6, 3, 6, 12 (1+2=3), 15 (1+5=6) ... You always get 3 or 6!

- And the number 9 has an even more special property. Any number multiplied by 9, when you add its digits together, equals 9. Try it! 9×3=27 (2+7=9), 9×5=45 (4+5=9), 9×12=108 (1+0+8=9).

Isn't that amazing? Tesla saw these patterns as evidence of divine order in the universe—a hidden language showing that everything is connected in magnificent ways!

While not everyone agrees about exactly what Tesla meant about 3, 6, and 9, many Christians see a beautiful connection to the Trinity. Just as these three special numbers create patterns that govern mathematics and energy, the three persons of the Trinity create the pattern that governs all creation!

In Christianity, the numbers 3, 6, and 9 each carry special significance, though their importance varies:

The number three is deeply meaningful in Christian tradition. It represents the Holy Trinity—God the Father, God the Son (Jesus), and the Holy Spirit. The number three is used throughout the Bible in many important ways: Jesus rose on the third day after His crucifixion, Peter denied Jesus three times, and Jesus prayed three times in the Garden of Gethsemane. The number three often symbolizes divine completeness or perfection.

The number six is generally understood as representing mankind and human weakness. In Christian numerology, six falls short of seven (representing divine perfection). In Revelation, 666 is called "the number of the beast" and symbolizes evil or opposition to God.

The number nine appears less prominently in Christian symbolism. Some traditions connect it to the fruits of the Holy Spirit (though there are typically listed as nine fruits in Galatians 5:22-23) or associate it with divine completeness as 3×3. In some interpretations, Jesus died at the ninth hour of the day.

These numerical patterns add a rich layer of symbolism to Christian texts and teachings, showing how God's design appears even in mathematics.

One Pastor says, "Tesla glimpsed the mathematical poetry God wrote into creation. The universe operates by divine laws that are elegant and harmonious—not chaotic or random. When we discover these patterns, we see echoes of God's orderly mind!"

Renewable Energy: Tapping Into God's Provision

Now, let's connect all these ideas to something very practical: how we power our homes, schools, and communities!

For about 150 years, humans have mainly used fossil fuels like coal, oil, and natural gas for energy. These fuels formed over millions of years from the remains of ancient plants and animals. When we burn them, we release stored sunlight energy from long ago. But fossil fuels are limited—once we use them up, they're gone—and burning them creates pollution that harms God's creation.

Renewable energy works differently. Instead of using ancient, stored energy, renewable sources tap into the ongoing energy flows God built into creation:

Solar Power: Harvesting Light Directly

Solar panels capture sunlight and convert it directly into electricity—no pollution, no waste! The sun bathes Earth with enough energy daily to power human civilization for a year. By using solar power, we accept God's daily gift of energy rather than depleting stored resources.

Thirteen-year-old Emma shares this story: "My dad installed solar panels on our roof last year. He showed me on an app how much energy we're making each day. On sunny days, we make more electricity than we use, and it goes back to the grid to help our neighbors. It feels like we're sharing God's gifts!"

Wind Power: Harnessing the Breath of Creation

In Genesis 1:2, "*the Spirit of God moved upon the face of the waters*." Throughout the Bible, God's Spirit is compared to wind or breath. Wind turbines capture the energy of moving air, harvesting the movement God built into our atmosphere!

The Power of Water: The Flow That Never Stops

Hydroelectric dams and newer technologies like tidal generators capture the energy of flowing water—another endless cycle God designed. Jesus used water as a powerful metaphor for eternal life in John 4:14: "*But whosoever drinketh of the water that I shall give him shall never thirst; but the water that I shall give him shall be in him a well of water springing up into everlasting life."*

All these renewable energy sources share something important: they tap into the ongoing, abundant energy flows God created rather than depleting limited resources. They work with creation's patterns instead of disrupting them.

Real-Life Solar Stories: Communities Powered by Light

Around the world, Christians and Solarpunk communities are discovering the joy of powering their lives with renewable energy:

Sunshine Church in California

Pastor Rodriguez says, "Our church building needed a new roof, and we were facing high electricity bills. We prayed for wisdom, and a member suggested solar panels. At first, some people were skeptical, but then we realized that God provides the sunshine for free! Now, our solar array produces all the power we need, plus extra that we donate to families in need through our utility's community solar program. The money we save goes to our mission work in Mexico, where we've helped install solar panels on three orphanages!"

The New Light Village in Tanzania

In a remote part of Tanzania, a Christian nonprofit helped establish a "solar village" where 50 homes now have small solar panels and battery systems. Before this, families used dangerous kerosene lamps that caused respiratory problems and fire hazards.

Twelve-year-old Jabari from the village says, "Having solar lights changed everything for me. Now, I can study at night without my eyes hurting from the kerosene smoke. My little sister doesn't cough all night anymore. We can charge a cell phone so my mom can sell her handicrafts online. The pastor says we're using Jesus, the Light of the World, to improve our lives!"

The Garden Apartments in Portland, Oregon

This innovative housing community combines many of the ideas we've discussed. The buildings have solar panels, rainwater collection systems, and shared gardens where residents grow food together.

"We designed our community around the pattern of threes we see in creation," explains architect Sarah Chen. "Each building has three sections—living spaces, community spaces, and garden spaces. Energy flows from the sun to our panels to our homes. Water flows from the sky to our gardens to our tables. We tried to create a place where people can live harmoniously with God's creation rather than fight against it."

How Your Family Can Be Part of This Movement

Ready to bring some of these exciting ideas into your own life? Here are ways your family can tap into God's divine patterns of energy:

1. Start Simple: Be Energy Aware

Begin noticing where your home's energy comes from and how you use it. Make a chart tracking how many appliances, lights, and devices you use daily. Learn about your local power sources—is your electricity from coal, natural gas, nuclear, or renewables?

2. Reduce First

The easiest way to use more renewable energy is to need less energy overall! Challenge your family to reduce energy waste by:

- Turning off lights when leaving rooms
- Unplugging chargers when not in use
- Using natural light during the day instead of electric lights
- Hanging clothes to dry instead of using the dryer on sunny days

3. Try Solar on a Small Scale

You don't need a full roof of solar panels to start using the sun's energy:

- Use a solar charger for your phone or tablet
- Try solar-powered garden lights for your yard or walkway
- Build a simple solar oven for cooking (great science project!)
- Use a solar shower bag for camping trips

4. Advocate for Renewables

Talk to your church, school, or community leaders about renewable energy:

- Could your church install solar panels?

- Might your school incorporate solar education into science classes?
- Does your utility offer a "green power" option for your home?

Project Box: Build a Simple Solar Phone Charger

With help from an adult, you can build a basic solar charger!

You'll need:

- A small solar panel (5-10 watts, available at electronic stores or online)
- A USB charging controller (matches the solar panel output to what your phone needs)
- A small box or container
- Wire and basic tools

Many websites and videos offer step-by-step instructions for assembling these components safely. This project teaches electrical concepts, provides a useful device, and helps you connect to God's gift of solar energy!

Divine Patterns in Your Life

The divine order we've explored in this chapter—the Trinity, mathematical patterns, and renewable energy cycles—isn't just interesting information. It's an invitation to align your life with God's beautiful design!

When you choose to live in harmony with creation rather than exploiting it, you're honoring the Creator. When you value patterns of giving and receiving rather than taking and wasting, you're reflecting God's nature. And when you see God's light—both physical sunlight and Jesus, the Light of the World—as essential for life, you're growing in wisdom.

Dr. James Henderson, a Christian physicist, shares: "The more I study how energy works in creation, the more I'm amazed by God's genius. In physics, we learn that energy is never created or destroyed, only transformed from one form to another. This reminds me of God's eternal nature and how His love flows through creation in never-ending cycles of giving and receiving."

Looking Ahead

In our next chapter, we'll explore how God's instructions about not wasting resources—even something as simple as gathering leftover bread after feeding a crowd—can guide us in creating a world with less pollution and waste. We'll discover how "Thou Shalt Not Waste" is actually an important biblical principle with exciting modern applications!

For now, try to notice the patterns of three and the cycles of energy in your daily life. Where do you see God's harmony and balance? How might you better align your energy use with the divine order woven into creation?

As Jesus, our Light, said: *"Ye are the light of the world... Let your light so shine before men, that they may see your good works, and glorify your Father which is in heaven"* (Matthew 5:14-16).

Family Discussion Questions:

1. Where do you see patterns of three in creation around you? How might these reflect the Trinity?

2. If Jesus is the "Light of the World," how can we better reflect His light in our lives?

3. How could our family better use God's renewable energy through sun, wind, or water?

4. How does understanding the mathematics and science of creation help us appreciate God more?

Teacher's Corner: This chapter bridges spiritual concepts with scientific understanding in ways accessible to young minds. The Trinity serves as an entry point to explore patterns in nature, establishing a framework where faith and science complement rather than contradict each other. Tesla's mathematical observations provide a tangible connection between abstract number patterns and divine order that can inspire scientifically minded students.

For classroom application, consider incorporating STEM activities that demonstrate energy transformation and mathematical patterns. Solar projects offer excellent hands-on learning while reinforcing the theological concepts of stewardship and divine provision. The chapter intentionally presents renewable energy not as a political position but as a practical application of biblical principles—caring for creation, using God's gifts wisely, and considering future generations.

Parents and educators can use this chapter to help students recognize God's design in both Scripture and the natural world, fostering a worldview where faith informs scientific curiosity, and technological innovation serves creation care.

Chapter 4:

Stewardship of Resources

The Miracle of the Leftovers

Imagine being in a huge crowd—thousands of people gathered on a grassy hillside to hear Jesus teach. The sun is setting, stomachs are rumbling, and everyone is miles from the nearest town. What would happen next?

In Matthew 14, we find one of Jesus' most amazing miracles. With just five loaves of bread and two fish, Jesus fed over 5,000 people! Everyone ate until they were full—a true miracle of multiplication. But what Jesus did *after* the meal teaches us something just as important as the miracle itself:

"And they did all eat, and were filled: and they took up of the fragments that remained twelve baskets full." (Matthew 14:20)

Wait a minute—Jesus could create food from almost nothing, yet He instructed His disciples to gather all the pieces left over. Why would the Son of God, who could multiply food whenever He wanted, care about collecting leftovers?

This small detail reveals something powerful: Even in the midst of abundance, God values every resource and doesn't want anything to be wasted. Jesus demonstrated that being a good steward means appreciating and using wisely *everything* God provides—not just when something is scarce, but even when there seems to be plenty!

Jesus could have just made the leftovers disappear or told everyone not to worry about them. Instead, He specifically instructed His disciples to gather every piece. This shows us that nothing God provides should be treated as disposable or worthless.

God's Creation: A Zero-Waste Design

Have you ever watched a nature documentary or spent time observing your backyard ecosystem? If so, you might have noticed something remarkable: in nature, there is no such thing as "trash"!

In God's original design, everything serves a purpose, and nothing is wasted:
- Fallen leaves decompose to feed the soil
- Animal droppings fertilize plants
- Dead trees become homes for woodpeckers and insects
- Even animal carcasses provide food for scavengers and eventually return nutrients to the soil

This beautiful system reflects God's perfect wisdom. As Psalm 104:24 tells us:

"*O LORD, how manifold are thy works! In wisdom hast thou made them all: the earth is full of thy riches.*"

The apostle Paul reminded the Corinthians that "*God is not the author of confusion, but of peace*" (1 Corinthians 14:33) and that "*Let all things be done decently and in order*" (1 Corinthians 14:40). God's creation shows this divine order—cycles of growth, use, decomposition, and renewal that keep everything in perfect balance.

When we create things that cannot be reused or don't decompose naturally—like certain plastics that last for hundreds of years—we're disrupting God's orderly system. This disruption leads to pollution, habitat destruction, and waste that harms the beautiful world God entrusted to our care.

Activity Box: Nature's Recycling Detectives

Grab a magnifying glass and head outside to investigate how God designed nature to reuse everything! Look under fallen logs, examine composting leaves, or watch insects at work. In your notebook, draw or describe three examples of "nature's recycling system" you observe. How could these natural systems inspire how we handle our own resources?

The Problem with Our Throwaway Culture

Today, we live very differently from how people lived in Bible times. Back then, most people owned very few possessions and used them carefully. Clothes were mended, not thrown away when torn. Food scraps fed animals or enriched garden soil. Water was carried from wells or rivers, so every drop was valued.

Now, many of us live in what's called a "throwaway culture." We use something briefly, throw it away, and buy something new—often without thinking about where those discarded items end up.

Every year, each person in America throws away about 1,600 pounds of trash—that's roughly the weight of a cow! Much of this waste ends up in landfills (giant piles of trash buried in the ground) or, sadly, in our oceans, where it harms marine life.

Eleven-year-old Tyler noticed this problem while visiting his grandparents' lake: "I was excited to go swimming, but when we got to the beach, there was plastic trash everywhere. We spent two hours picking up bottles, food wrappers, and even old toys before we could swim. It made me wonder: if everyone took care of their own stuff, we wouldn't have to clean up messes like this."

Biblical Wisdom for Modern Waste Problems

The Bible gives us timeless wisdom that can help us address our modern waste challenges. Here are some principles we can apply today:

1. Value Everything God Provides

When the Israelites wandered in the desert, God provided manna—bread from heaven. But He gave specific instructions: gather only what you need for the day (Exodus 16:16-20). Those who gathered too much found that the extra rotted overnight.

This teaches us to take only what we need and to use what we take. Before buying something new, we can ask: "Do I really need this? Will I use it fully?"

2. Practice Sabbath for Resources

God commanded the Israelites to let their fields rest every seventh year (Leviticus 25:4-5). This practice—called the Sabbatical Year—allowed the soil to replenish its nutrients naturally.

Today, we can apply this principle by choosing products made from renewable resources and giving natural systems time to regenerate.

3. Care for the Vulnerable

Throughout Scripture, God instructs His people to care for those in need by sharing resources. In Leviticus 19:9-10, farmers were told not to harvest the edges of their fields but to leave them for the poor and the foreigners.

When we reduce waste and share resources, we ensure that God's bounty can support everyone, not just those who can afford to buy the most.

Become a Waste Warrior: Practical Steps for Kids and Families

Ready to follow Jesus' example of gathering up the fragments so nothing is wasted? Here are some exciting ways to start:

Composting: Turning "Trash" into Treasure

Composting is like having a tiny recycling factory right in your backyard! When you compost, you collect fruit and vegetable scraps, eggshells, coffee grounds, yard trimmings, and other organic materials. Over time, tiny organisms break these down into rich, dark soil that helps plants grow strong and healthy.

Thirteen-year-old Sophia started composting as a science project: "At first, I thought it would be gross, but now I think it's amazing! We put banana peels and apple cores in our compost bin, and a few months later, we have this super-rich soil for our garden. My mom's tomato plants that are grown in compost soil are twice as big as the ones in regular soil!"

Mini-Guide: Start Your Own Compost Bin

1. Find a container (a special compost bin, an old trash can with holes drilled in it, or even just a designated corner of your yard)

2. Add "browns" (dry leaves, newspaper, cardboard) and "greens" (fruit/vegetable scraps, coffee grounds, grass clippings)

3. Keep it slightly damp (like a wrung-out sponge)

4. Turn or stir it occasionally to add air

5. Be patient! In a few months, you'll have wonderful compost to help your plants grow.

Upcycling: Creative Transformation

Upcycling means taking something old or unwanted and transforming it into something new and useful. Unlike recycling (which breaks materials down), upcycling gives items a whole new purpose through creativity!

Some fun upcycling projects to try:

- Turn an empty pasta sauce jar into a pencil holder
- Transform an old t-shirt into a reusable grocery bag
- Use cardboard tubes from paper towels to organize cables
- Plant flowers in an old boot or broken teapot
- Create art from bottle caps or broken toys

Nine-year-old Marcus discovered upcycling during art class: "My teacher showed us how to make bird feeders from plastic bottles. Now, whenever we finish a bottle of juice or soap, I think, 'What could this become?' Last month, I made a robot from empty cereal boxes, and it won first prize in the school craft fair!"

Zero-Waste Heroes: Aiming for No Trash

Some families are taking stewardship to the next level by trying to produce zero waste. While that might sound impossible, it's incredible how close you can get by making simple changes:

The Five Rs of Zero-Waste Living:

1. **Refuse** what you don't need (like free promotional items or excessive packaging)

2. **Reduce** what you do buy (ask: "Do I really need this?")

3. **Reuse** items instead of buying disposables (water bottles, shopping bags, etc.)

4. **Recycle** what can't be refused, reduced, or reused

5. **Rot** (compost) your food scraps and yard waste

The Johnson family began their zero-waste journey after learning about plastic pollution at church. "We started small, just bringing reusable bags to the grocery store. Then, we added water bottles and coffee mugs. Now, three years later, our family of four produces only a small amount of trash every month! The kids have become the biggest advocates—they check packages at the store and remind us to bring containers for restaurant leftovers."

Stories of Stewardship: Kids Making a Difference

All around the world, young Christians are finding creative ways to be better stewards of God's resources:

The Lunch Box Revolution

Students at Grace Christian Academy noticed how much trash their school produced during lunch. With their teacher's help, they started a "Waste-Free Lunch" campaign, encouraging classmates to use reusable containers instead of disposable bags and wrappers. Within one month, they reduced their lunchtime waste by 85%!

Community Swap Shop

A youth group at First Baptist Church organized a quarterly "Swap Meet" where families bring items they no longer need (clothes, toys, books, sports equipment) and exchange them for things they can use. Nothing is sold—everything is shared freely. Leftover items are donated to a local shelter or orphanage.

Compost Crew

Middle-school students collect food scraps from neighborhood restaurants to feed their school garden's compost system. The garden produces vegetables for the school cafeteria and local food bank, creating a beautiful cycle of nourishment and care.

Small Changes, Big Impact

Maybe you're thinking, "I'm just one kid. How much difference can I really make?" Remember the story of the five loaves and two fishes! Jesus took one small boy's lunch and used it to feed thousands. In the same way, your small acts of stewardship—when blessed by God—can have an impact far beyond what you might imagine.

Every time you choose a reusable water bottle instead of a plastic one, you prevent hundreds of bottles from ending up in landfills over the course of a year. Each time you compost an apple core instead of throwing it away, you participate in God's perfect cycle of renewal. When you repair a torn shirt, instead of discarding it, you honor the resources and labor that went into making it.

Pastor Lee from New Hope Church says, "Stewardship isn't about being perfect—it's about being faithful with whatever God has entrusted to you. Every small choice to reduce waste is a way of saying 'thank you' to the Creator for His abundant gifts."

Project Box: Family Waste Audit

Challenge your family to collect and examine your trash for one week. Sort it into categories: food waste, packaging, paper, etc. What's the biggest source of waste in your home? Together, brainstorm three simple changes you could make to reduce your most common type of waste. Try implementing these changes for a month, then repeat the audit to see your progress!

Looking Ahead

In our next chapter, we'll move from caring for physical resources to caring for our most precious resource—each other! We'll explore how Jesus' command to "love thy neighbor" connects with the Solarpunk vision of supportive, sharing communities where everyone's needs are met.

For now, remember Jesus gathering those fragments after feeding the 5,000. Every resource—no matter how small or seemingly insignificant—matters to God. By caring for what He's given us and eliminating waste, we show our love for the Creator and for future generations who will inherit the Earth we leave behind.

Let's pray together: "Heavenly Father, thank you for providing everything we need. Help us to be wise stewards who gather up the fragments of Your blessings so that nothing is wasted. Open our eyes to see value in what others might discard and give us creative ideas for using resources in ways that honor You. Amen."

Family Discussion Questions:

1. What's one thing our family regularly throws away that might be reused, recycled, or composted instead?

2. How might Jesus' command to gather the leftover fragments apply to our lives today?

3. What's one "wasteful habit" you could challenge yourself to change this week?

4. How does reducing waste show love for God, for others, and for future generations?

Teacher's Corner: This chapter connects scriptural principles of stewardship with practical environmental education. By using Jesus' miracle of the loaves and fishes—familiar to most Christian children—as a springboard for discussing resource conservation, students can see how biblical values directly inform modern sustainability practices.

The activities suggested throughout the chapter incorporate multiple learning modalities: kinesthetic learning (composting, upcycling projects), analytical thinking (waste audit), observational skills (nature investigation), and creative expression (upcycling crafts). These varied approaches make the material accessible to different types of learners while reinforcing the core theological concept that careful stewardship of resources honors God's design.

For classroom application, consider implementing a classroom compost bin for snack scraps and using the resulting soil for a class garden. This provides a tangible, ongoing demonstration of nature's cycles while teaching responsibility and patience. The family waste audit could be adapted as a classroom activity, with students tracking different categories of waste generated during school hours and collaboratively developing solutions.

Chapter 5:

Love Thy Neighbor: Building Connected Communities

The Golden Rule of Neighborhoods

Have you ever been the new kid on the block? Or have you had a day when you really needed help with something? We all know that wonderful feeling when a neighbor notices and reaches out with kindness—whether it's bringing over cookies to welcome you, helping carry groceries when your arms are full, or just offering a friendly smile on a tough day.

Jesus knew how important neighbors are in our lives. When asked about the greatest commandments, He said something truly profound:

"Thou shalt love the Lord thy God with all thy heart, and with all thy soul, and with all thy mind. This is the first and great commandment. And the second is like unto it, Thou shalt love thy neighbour as thyself." (Matthew 22:37-39)

Think about that for a moment: Jesus placed loving our neighbors right after loving God—making it the second most important commandment in all of Scripture! Clearly, how we treat the people around us matters tremendously to God.

But what does it mean to "love thy neighbour as thyself"? It means treating others with the same care, respect, and kindness you'd want to receive. It means seeing their needs as important as your own. And in today's busy, sometimes disconnected world, it means making a special effort to build relationships with the people God has placed in your life—even when it might be easier to keep to yourself.

The First Christian Community: A Revolutionary Way of Living

The earliest Christians took Jesus' teaching about loving neighbors to an extraordinary level. In the book of Acts, we get a fascinating glimpse into how the very first Christian community lived after Jesus returned to heaven:

"And all that believed were together, and had all things common; And sold their possessions and

goods, and parted them to all men, as every man had need." (Acts 2:44-45)

Wow! Can you imagine sharing everything you own with your neighbors? These early Christians created a community where nobody went without while others had too much. They understood that everything they owned ultimately came from God, so they held their possessions with open hands, ready to share whenever someone needed them.

This wasn't just a nice idea—it was revolutionary! In the ancient Roman world, where the early church began, most people only looked out for their own families or social groups. The Christian practice of caring for everyone in their community—regardless of social status, ethnicity, or background—stood out like a bright light in a dark room.

Dr. Rivera, who studies early Christian communities, explains: "The early believers didn't just attend worship services together and then go back to their separate lives. They shared meals, resources, time, and talents. They created a new kind of extended family where everyone belonged, and everyone contributed what they could. This radical way of living made others curious about their faith—it was a powerful witness to God's love!"

Activity Box: Early Church Community Game

Gather some friends or family members and play "Early Church Resources." Each person starts with 5-10 small items (pencils, erasers, small toys, etc.). Take turns rolling a die. If you roll 1-2, Someone has a need! Choose someone to give one of your items to. 3-4: God provides! Everyone receives one new item. 5: Community project! Everyone contributes one item to the center and then decides together how to use these resources to help someone. 6: Persecution! The authorities confiscate some items, but the community shares what remains equally.

After playing, discuss: How did it feel to share resources? Was anyone worried about running out? How does this relate to the early church in Acts?

Solarpunk Communities: Ancient Wisdom for Modern Times

Let's fast-forward to today. Many neighborhoods in our modern world can feel isolated. Some people live next door to others for years without ever having a real conversation! We often drive from our houses to work or school and back again without creating meaningful connections with the people who live around us.

But an exciting movement called Solarpunk envisions a different way of living—one that actually looks a lot like the community values we see in the early church! Solarpunk imagines neighborhoods where:

- People know each other's names and needs
- Resources like tools, vehicles, and even extra food are shared rather than duplicated in every household.
- Energy from renewable sources like solar power is distributed fairly
- Green spaces are maintained together for everyone's benefit
- Skills and knowledge are exchanged freely
- Everyone contributes according to their abilities and receives according to their needs.

Twelve-year-old Zoe shares her experience: "Our neighborhood started a tool library where families can borrow tools instead of everyone buying their own. My dad borrowed a pressure washer to clean our driveway and then showed our elderly neighbor how to use it on her walkway. Now, we always talk to her, and she teaches me about the native plants in her garden. It's like we're actually neighbors now, not just people who live near each other!"

The Bible's Blueprint for Connected Communities

The Bible is filled with instructions about how to live well together in a community. These ancient teachings align perfectly with modern Solarpunk visions:

Share Resources Generously

"Give to him that asketh thee, and from him that would borrow of thee turn not thou away." (Matthew 5:42)

Jesus taught us to be generous and open-handed with what we have. This doesn't mean we give away everything without wisdom, but rather that we approach our possessions with a spirit of sharing instead of hoarding.

Care for Vulnerable Neighbors

"Learn to do well; seek judgment, relieve the oppressed, judge the fatherless, plead for the widow." (Isaiah 1:17)

Throughout Scripture, God shows special concern for those who might be overlooked or marginalized in society. A truly Christian community ensures everyone is included and cared for, especially those who might otherwise be forgotten.

Work Together for the Common Good

"Bear ye one another's burdens, and so fulfill the law of Christ." (Galatians 6:2)

When we help carry each other's burdens—whether that's lending a hand with yard work, providing a meal during illness, or offering emotional support during tough times—we're fulfilling Christ's law of love.

Cultivate Peace and Unity

"Behold, how good and how pleasant it is for brethren to dwell together in unity!" (Psalm 133:1)

God delights when His people live in harmony. This doesn't mean we all have to be the same or agree on everything, but we treat each other respectfully and work through conflicts with love and patience.

Real-Life Examples: Modern Communities Living Biblical Principles

These biblical principles aren't just nice ideas—they're being put into practice in exciting ways by Christians and Solarpunk communities around the world:

The Sharing Gardens in Oregon

The Jensen family started with a simple idea: use their large backyard to grow vegetables not just for themselves but for their entire neighborhood. They invited neighbors to help with planting, weeding, and harvesting—and to share in the bounty.

"At first, only a few people joined in," explains 14-year-old Mia Jensen. "But after the first harvest, when everyone got to take home fresh tomatoes and zucchini, more neighbors wanted to participate. Now, we have 15 families who take turns tending the garden. We've expanded to three yards on our block and grown enough vegetables to share with the local food pantry too! The best part is that I've met so many interesting neighbors I never knew before."

The Tool Library Movement

In cities across America, communities are creating lending libraries—not just for books but also for tools! Instead of every household buying rarely used items like pressure washers, ladders, or specialized kitchen equipment, neighbors can borrow these items when needed and return them for others to use.

Pastor Williams helped his church start a tool library in its community center: "We received tool donations from church members and local businesses. Now, anyone in the community can borrow what they need for home repairs or projects. It's saved people money, reduced clutter in homes, and created a hub where neighbors meet and often help each other with projects. One man came to borrow a drill and ended up finding four volunteers to help rebuild his porch after a storm damaged it!"

The New Day Co-Housing Community

In Colorado, twelve families created a co-housing neighborhood where each family has their own private home, but they share certain spaces and resources:

- A common house with a large kitchen and dining area for community meals (twice weekly)
- A workshop filled with tools everyone can use
- A community garden and orchard
- A playroom filled with toys for all the neighborhood children
- A playground and picnic area
- A guest apartment that any family can reserve when relatives visit

Eleven-year-old Jamal, who lives in the community, shares: "It's like having a huge extended family! There are always kids to play with, and I know all the adults by name. When my mom had surgery last year, different neighbors brought us dinner every night for two weeks. We do the same when other families need help. I can't imagine living any other way now."

Practical Ideas: Building Connected Communities Where You Live

Ready to strengthen connections in your own neighborhood? Here are some practical ideas that kids, families, and communities can try:

For Kids

1. **Create a Neighborhood Map**: Draw a map of your neighborhood and add neighbors' names as you meet them. Include notes about their interests or needs.

2. **Start a Little Free Library**: With your parents' help, set up a small weatherproof box where people can take or leave books for sharing.

3. **Organize a Neighborhood Cleanup Day**: Invite friends to help pick up litter in common areas or a nearby park.

4. **Deliver Welcome Baskets**: When new families move in, bring a small gift with a handwritten note introducing your family.

5. **Share Your Skills**: Are you good at math, crafts, or sports? Offer to teach younger kids in your neighborhood.

For Families

1. **Host a Block Party or Potluck**. Invite neighbors to gather in your yard, driveway, or local park. Keep it simple and have everyone bring something to share.

2. **Create a Neighborhood Directory**: Collect contact information (with permission) and emergency contacts for neighbors who want to be included.

3. **Start a Meal Train**: When a neighbor is dealing with illness, a new baby, or a loss, organize neighbors to provide meals.

4. **Establish a Neighborhood Social Media Group**: Create an online space where neighbors can share announcements, ask for help, or offer items they no longer need.

5. **Create a Community Garden**: Transform an unused lot or portion of yards into a shared garden space.

For Communities

1. **Develop a Skill-Share Program**: Create a system where people can exchange services based on their skills (like tutoring, minor repairs, haircuts, or language lessons).

2. **Start a Time Bank**. In a time bank, people exchange hours of service rather than money. For example, one hour of childcare equals one hour of home repair equals one hour of computer help.

3. **Create a Tool or Kitchen Equipment Library**: Collect donated or purchased items that each household can borrow rather than buy.

4. **Establish Community Workdays**: Schedule regular days where everyone pitches in on projects that benefit the whole neighborhood.

5. **Develop a Community Emergency Plan**: Work together to prepare for potential emergencies, knowing who has special needs, useful skills, or important resources.

Project Box: Neighborhood Connection Map

Create a visual map of your neighborhood that shows connections rather than just houses! You'll need:

- A large piece of poster board
- Colored markers
- Small sticky notes
- Photos or drawings of houses/apartments in your neighborhood

Step 1: Draw the basic layout of your neighborhood streets.

Step 2: Add pictures or drawings of each home.

Step 3: Use different colored lines to show connections:

- Red for sharing tools or resources
- Blue for helping with tasks/projects
- Green for sharing garden produce/plants
- Yellow for social connections/friendships
- Purple for skill-sharing/teaching

Add more lines to your map as you meet neighbors and build connections. Watch as the web of community grows over time!

The Ripple Effect of Loving Your Neighbor

When we follow Jesus' command to love our neighbors as ourselves, something beautiful happens—it creates a ripple effect that extends far beyond our immediate community.

Pastor Garcia says: "When we build strong, caring neighborhoods, we're not only making life better for ourselves and those around us. We're creating living testimonies that show God's love in action. People who might never enter a church building can experience Christ's love through a community that shares, cares, and bears one another's burdens."

Research shows that connected communities experience:

- Lower crime rates
- Better health outcomes
- Increased resilience during disasters or hardships
- Improved mental health and reduced loneliness
- Greater environmental sustainability through sharing resources

Thirteen-year-old Aiden noticed this change after his family helped start a community garden: "Before the garden, I only knew the names of two kids on our block. Now I know almost everyone! Last winter, when we had that big snowstorm and the power went out, nobody panicked because we were checking on each other. Some families had generators they shared, others had camp stoves to heat food, and Mr. Wilson, who has a wood stove, invited elderly neighbors to stay warm at his house. It wasn't just about vegetables—the garden taught us to look out for each other!"

Looking Ahead

In our next chapter, we'll explore how God's command for Sabbath rest applies not just to people but to the Earth itself. We'll discover how giving land, resources, and ourselves proper periods of rest and renewal is essential for sustainability and well-being.

For now, remember that Jesus placed "love thy neighbor" as the second greatest commandment for a reason. Our relationship with God is expressed through our relationships with those around us. When we build connected, caring communities, we create a small glimpse of heaven on earth—a place where everyone belongs, contributes, and is valued as a precious child of God.

As you go through this week, look for opportunities to strengthen the connections in your neighborhood. Each small act of kindness, each resource shared, and each moment spent really listening to a neighbor is a step toward the kind of community Jesus envisioned when He taught us to love our neighbors as ourselves.

Family Discussion Questions:

1. Who are the neighbors in our community that we know well? Who might we need to get to know better?

2. What resources or skills does our family have that we could share more generously?

3. How might our neighborhood change if more people practiced the kind of community described in Acts 2:44-45?

4. What's one specific action our family could take this week to strengthen community connections?

Teacher's Corner: This chapter bridges theological concepts with practical sociology to empower students to become active participants in community building. The parallels drawn between the early church in Acts and modern Solarpunk movements help students see how timeless biblical principles can be applied in contemporary contexts.

Consider supplementing this chapter with service-learning projects that allow students to practice community-building firsthand. The neighborhood connection map activity provides an excellent foundation for discussions about social networks, interdependence, and how communities function as ecosystems of relationship.

For church and school settings, this chapter offers opportunities to discuss the countercultural nature of the Christian community in both ancient and modern contexts. Students can explore how radical sharing and mutual care distinguished early Christians from their Roman contemporaries and how similar practices might positively distinguish modern Christian communities.

Jesus Christ Solarpunk

Chapter 6:

The Pyramid of Equality – Unity Under God

The Magnificent Pyramid

Have you ever seen a picture of the Great Pyramid of Giza in Egypt? It's one of the most amazing structures in the world—a perfect shape with four triangular sides that meet at a single point at the top. For thousands of years, people have marveled at pyramids, not just because they're impressive to look at, but because there's something special about their shape—strong, balanced, and pointing upward to the sky.

This chapter will explore something even more amazing than stone pyramids. We'll discover how God designed relationships between people to work like a beautiful pyramid of equality and unity, with God Himself at the highest point!

Imagine a triangular pyramid with three sides. Each side is equally important—if any one side were missing, the pyramid couldn't stand. In God's design for human relationships, we can think of this pyramid as having:

- One side that represents men
- One side that represents women
- One side that represents all the beautiful diversity of human culture
- And God at the apex (the top point), holding everything together in perfect balance

This pyramid model helps us understand something really important: in God's kingdom, all people have equal value and dignity. Yet, we each bring unique and wonderful gifts to create a complete picture of God's image on Earth.

Men: Leadership Through Service

In many cultures throughout history, men have often been taught that leadership means having power over others, giving orders, and being in control. But Jesus showed us a completely different way of thinking about leadership!

"Husbands, love your wives, even as Christ also loved the church, and gave himself for it." (Ephesians 5:25)

Think about that for a moment. How did Christ love the church? Did He demand to be served? Did He use His power to control others? Not at all! Jesus—the King of Kings—washed His disciples' feet, served the hungry, welcomed children, and ultimately gave His life for others.

This means that authentic God-honoring leadership for men isn't about being the boss or making all the decisions. It's about following Jesus' example of selfless service, protection, and sacrifice for others. True strength isn't shown by controlling people but by lifting them up, listening to them, and using whatever privileges you have to benefit those around you.

Twelve-year-old Miguel shares how he sees this in his own family: "My dad is definitely strong—he can fix our car and carry heavy stuff—but what I admire most is how he looks for ways to help others. He gets up early on Saturdays to drive elderly church members to the farmers' market. He listens to my mom's ideas about family decisions. And he told me that being a man isn't about being in charge, but about taking responsibility to care for the people God puts in your life."

1 Timothy, Chapter 3, verses 1-7 say it like this: *"This is a true saying, if a man desire the office of a bishop, he desireth a good work.*

² A bishop then must be blameless, the husband of one wife, vigilant, sober, of good behaviour, given to hospitality, apt to teach;

³ Not given to wine, no striker, not greedy of filthy lucre; but patient, not a brawler, not covetous;

⁴ One that ruleth well his own house, having his children in subjection with all gravity;

⁵ (For if a man know not how to rule his own house, how shall he take care of the church of God?)

⁶ Not a novice, lest being lifted up with pride he fall into the condemnation of the devil.

⁷ Moreover he must have a good report of them which are without; lest he fall into reproach and the snare of the devil.

⁸ Likewise must the deacons be grave, not doubletongued, not given to much wine, not greedy of filthy lucre;

⁹ Holding the mystery of the faith in a pure conscience.

¹⁰ And let these also first be proved; then let them use the office of a deacon, being found blameless.

¹¹ Even so must their wives be grave, not slanderers, sober, faithful in all things.

¹² Let the deacons be the husbands of one wife, ruling their children and their own houses well.

¹³ For they that have used the office of a deacon well purchase to themselves a good degree, and great boldness in the faith which is in Christ Jesus."

In this passage, Paul outlines the qualities needed for church leaders. A good leader should be of excellent character—honest, faithful in marriage, and clear-minded. They should also welcome others warmly into their homes and be skilled at explaining God's teachings.

Paul emphasizes that leaders shouldn't be people who drink too much, lose their temper, or argue constantly. Instead, they should be gentle and not focused on gaining wealth. How they guide their families shows how they'll care for God's church family.

Women: Strength and Wisdom

The Bible contains many powerful examples of women whose strength, wisdom, and courage made a tremendous difference in God's story. From Deborah, the judge who led Israel into battle, to Esther, who saved her people from destruction, to Priscilla, who taught theology and co-led the early church with her husband, Scripture shows us that women are vital leaders in God's plan.

One of the most beautiful descriptions of a woman's strength appears in Proverbs 31:10-31, which describes a woman of noble character whose value is "far above rubies."

"10 Who can find a virtuous woman? for her price is far above rubies.

11 The heart of her husband doth safely trust in her, so that he shall have no need of spoil.

12 She will do him good and not evil all the days of her life.

¹³ She seeketh wool, and flax, and worketh willingly with her hands.

¹⁴ She is like the merchants' ships; she bringeth her food from afar.

¹⁵ She riseth also while it is yet night, and giveth meat to her household, and a portion to her maidens.

¹⁶ She considereth a field, and buyeth it: with the fruit of her hands she planteth a vineyard.

¹⁷ She girdeth her loins with strength, and strengtheneth her arms.

¹⁸ She perceiveth that her merchandise is good: her candle goeth not out by night.

¹⁹ She layeth her hands to the spindle, and her hands hold the distaff.

²⁰ She stretcheth out her hand to the poor; yea, she reacheth forth her hands to the needy.

²¹ She is not afraid of the snow for her household: for all her household are clothed with scarlet.

²² She maketh herself coverings of tapestry; her clothing is silk and purple.

²³ Her husband is known in the gates, when he sitteth among the elders of the land.

²⁴ She maketh fine linen, and selleth it; and delivereth girdles unto the merchant.

²⁵ Strength and honour are her clothing; and she shall rejoice in time to come.

²⁶ She openeth her mouth with wisdom; and in her tongue is the law of kindness.

²⁷ She looketh well to the ways of her household, and eateth not the bread of idleness.

²⁸ Her children arise up, and call her blessed; her husband also, and he praiseth her.

²⁹ Many daughters have done virtuously, but thou excellest them all.

³⁰ Favour is deceitful, and beauty is vain: but a woman that feareth the Lord, she shall be praised.

³¹ Give her of the fruit of her hands; and let her own works praise her in the gates."

This biblical portrait hardly matches the limited roles that some cultures have tried to force women into throughout history! Instead, we see a multi-talented leader whose different strengths complement—not compete with—the men in her community.

Fourteen-year-old Sophia reflects: "When we studied Proverbs 31 in youth group, I was amazed by how active and strong this woman was. She wasn't just sitting at home—she was running businesses, helping the poor, and speaking with wisdom. Our youth pastor pointed out that different translations describe her as 'valiant,' 'virtuous,' and 'excellent'—the same Hebrew word used to describe mighty warriors in other parts of the Bible! That made me realize that being a godly woman means being brave and strong, not timid and weak."

God at the Apex: Bringing Everything Together

In our pyramid model, the most important point is at the top—God Himself, who created both men and women in His image and who brings unity to our diversity. As we read in Genesis 1:27:

"So God created man in his own image, in the image of God created he him; male and female created he them."

Notice something fascinating here: the full image of God isn't reflected in men alone or in women alone but in both together! This tells us that both masculine and feminine qualities reflect different aspects of God's character. God possesses both the strength and protection we might associate with masculinity and the nurturing compassion we might associate with femininity—and both are equally valuable and necessary.

When God is truly at the apex of our relationships, something beautiful happens. Instead of competing for power or struggling over who's in charge, men and women can appreciate each other's unique contributions and work together as equals under God's authority. This is similar to a football team, with both offense and defense doing their job to ensure that the team wins.

Pastor Williams explains this: "When we put God first in our relationships, we stop focusing on who has power over whom. Instead, we ask, 'How can we both use our different gifts to serve God and others?' This changes everything! Instead of a hierarchy where one person dominates, we create partnerships where different strengths complement each other—just like different instruments in an orchestra create more beautiful music together than any could alone."

Activity Box: Pyramid Building

In small groups, try this cooperative challenge: Using index cards or playing cards, build the tallest pyramid you can. The catch? Each person can only use one hand, and no one can give direct orders to others. You'll need to communicate, cooperate, and value each person's contribution to succeed!

After the activity, discuss: How did you have to depend on each other? Was anyone's contribution more important than others? How does this relate to our "pyramid of equality" under God?

Breaking Misconceptions: What Paul Really Taught

Sometimes, people misunderstand certain Bible passages, especially some of Paul's letters, thinking they teach that women should be subordinate to men. But when we look carefully at what Paul wrote, considering the cultural context and his other teachings, we discover something quite different!

For example, in Ephesians 5:21, just before the often-quoted verses about wives and husbands, Paul writes:

"Submitting yourselves one to another in the fear of God."

This mutual submission—everyone yielding to everyone else out of reverence for Christ—is the foundation for all Christian relationships! Then, Paul goes on to describe how this looks in different relationships. Yes, wives are called to respect their husbands, but husbands are called to love their wives sacrificially, "*[20] Giving thanks always for all things unto God and the Father in the name of our Lord Jesus Christ;*

[21] Submitting yourselves one to another in the fear of God.

[22] Wives, submit yourselves unto your own husbands, as unto the Lord.

[23] For the husband is the head of the wife, even as Christ is the head of the church: and he is the saviour of the body.

24 *Therefore as the church is subject unto Christ, so let the wives be to their own husbands in every thing.*

25 *Husbands, love your wives, even as Christ also loved the church, and gave himself for it;*

26 *That he might sanctify and cleanse it with the washing of water by the word,*

27 *That he might present it to himself a glorious church, not having spot, or wrinkle, or any such thing; but that it should be holy and without blemish.*

28 *So ought men to love their wives as their own bodies. He that loveth his wife loveth himself.*

29 *For no man ever yet hated his own flesh; but nourisheth and cherisheth it, even as the Lord the church:*

30 *For we are members of his body, of his flesh, and of his bones.*

31 *For this cause shall a man leave his father and mother, and shall be joined unto his wife, and they two shall be one flesh.*

32 *This is a great mystery: but I speak concerning Christ and the church.*

³³ Nevertheless let every one of you in particular so love his wife even as himself; and the wife see that she reverence her husband."

That's a much higher standard of selfless service than what's asked of wives!

In 1 Corinthians, Paul affirms that in marriage, the husband's body belongs to his wife just as the wife's body belongs to her husband (1 Corinthians 7:4)—a revolutionary statement of equality in a time when women were often treated as property!

Perhaps most importantly, Paul makes this powerful declaration in Galatians:

"There is neither Jew nor Greek, there is neither bond nor free, there is neither male nor female: for ye are all one in Christ Jesus." (Galatians 3:28)

This verse proclaims the radical equality of all people in God's kingdom—regardless of ethnicity, social status, or gender. While we maintain our wonderful differences, these differences no longer determine our value or limit our purpose in Christ's community.

In the ancient world, strict hierarchies determined everyone's place in society. Paul's teaching—that slaves and masters, men and women, and people of different ethnicities were all equal in Christ—was absolutely revolutionary! He wasn't reinforcing the cultural status quo but transforming it with the radical equality of God's kingdom.

Celebrating Cultural and Ecological Diversity

Our pyramid model of equality doesn't just apply to gender—it embraces all the wonderful diversity God created among humans and throughout the natural world! Just as a pyramid has many stones that all contribute to its strength and beauty, God's creation flourishes through diversity.

Human Cultural Diversity

God didn't make all humans identical—He delights in the magnificent variety of languages, traditions, arts, foods, and perspectives found among different cultures! Think of Revelation 7:9, which describes people *"of all nations, and kindreds, and people, and tongues"* standing before God's throne. Heaven itself will be multicultural and multiracial!

When we recognize that different cultures reflect various aspects of God's creativity, we can approach cultural differences with curiosity and respect rather than fear or judgment. We can ask, "What might God want to teach me through this different perspective?" instead of assuming our own cultural way is always best.

Eleven-year-old Zack from a multicultural church shares: "At our church's international festival, I tried foods from twenty different countries! Pastor Kim taught us that each culture gives us a slightly different picture of God. For example, Korean Christians emphasize community in ways that teach Americans about our connection to each other. In contrast, American traditions might emphasize individual relationships with God in ways that enrich other cultures. No one has the complete picture alone!"

Ecological Diversity

God's love of diversity extends beyond humans to the incredible variety in the natural world. Genesis tells us that God created plants and animals "according to their kinds" (Genesis 1:11-

12, 21, 24-25)—not just one type of plant or animal, but thousands of different species!

Scientists estimate there may be 8.7 million different species on Earth! Each plays a unique role in its ecosystem, just as each person plays a unique role in the human community. And the most stable, resilient ecosystems are those with the greatest biodiversity.

Solarpunk communities embrace this divine pattern by protecting and celebrating biodiversity. Instead of vast lawns with just one type of grass, they create diverse gardens with many plants supporting insects, birds, and other wildlife. Instead of relying on just one crop that could fail, they practice polyculture—growing many different food plants together to create resilient food systems.

Thirteen-year-old Leila's science project explored this connection: "I created two mini garden boxes—one with just lettuce, and one with lettuce, marigolds, basil, and carrots growing together. The diverse garden had fewer pest problems, and the plants actually grew better together than they did alone! It reminded me of how God designed both nature and human communities to thrive through diversity, not uniformity."

Living the Pyramid of Equality in Everyday Life

What does the pyramid of equality look like in practice? Here are some ways families, schools, churches, and communities can honor this biblical model:

At Home

• Families can make decisions together, valuing each person's input regardless of age or gender.

• Parents can model mutual respect, sharing responsibilities based on gifts and abilities rather than rigid gender roles.

• Children can learn that being a godly man or woman has more to do with character (kindness, integrity, service) than with stereotypical behaviors or interests.

Jason, age 12, noticed this at home: "My dad's actually a better cook than my mom, so he makes dinner most nights while mom (who's good with numbers) handles the family budget. They told me they each do what they're best at instead of what society expects. That makes sense to me!"

At School and Church

- Leadership teams can include diverse voices and perspectives
- Everyone's gifts can be recognized and utilized, regardless of gender or background
- Stories and examples can feature diverse heroes of faith—both men and women from various cultures who have served God in different ways

In Solarpunk Communities

- Decision-making can be collaborative, seeking consensus rather than top-down control.
- Different skills and perspectives are valued for their unique contributions.
- Resources and responsibilities are shared equitably
- Natural ecosystems are protected for their biodiversity

After studying these principles, Pastor Garcia's church transformed their approach: "We realized we weren't fully utilizing the gifts of everyone in our congregation. Our leadership team now includes men and women with different backgrounds and perspectives. Our community garden incorporates Native American companion planting wisdom alongside modern techniques. Our worship includes songs from different cultural traditions. We're stronger and more vibrant because we've embraced the fullness of God's diverse design!"

The Strength of Unity in Diversity

When we truly understand God's pyramid of equality, we discover something wonderful: unity doesn't mean uniformity! True unity happens when diverse people come together under God's leadership, each contributing their unique gifts toward a shared purpose.

Think about beautiful mosaic artwork made of many different colored tiles. From a distance, you see the complete picture. Up close, you appreciate how each different piece adds to the whole. The artwork would lose its beauty and depth if all the tiles were identical!

In the same way, when men and women of different cultures and backgrounds come together in partnership under God, we create a more complete picture of God's image than any one group could alone. We need each other's different perspectives and gifts to fully reflect God's multifaceted character and to accomplish His purposes in the world.

As Psalm 133:1 reminds us: *"Behold, how good and how pleasant it is for brethren to dwell together in unity!"* This God-honoring unity—where differences are celebrated rather than erased or ranked—brings our communities a special blessing and effectiveness.

Looking Ahead

In our next chapter, we'll explore another key principle from Scripture that has powerful implications for sustainable living: the Sabbath! We'll discover how God's command to rest regularly applies not just to people but to the land itself, providing a pattern for renewal and restoration that's essential for the health of both humans and ecosystems.

For now, remember that in God's kingdom, the pyramid of equality places God at the apex, with all people—regardless of gender, ethnicity, or background—standing on equal ground beneath Him. When we recognize every person's equal value and unique contributions, we create communities that better reflect God's character and fulfill His purposes on Earth.

Family Discussion Questions:

1. How have you seen different strengths and abilities in our family members complement each other?

2. What misconceptions about men's and women's roles have you encountered, and how do they compare with what we've learned from Scripture?

3. How might our family better celebrate and learn from people of different cultural backgrounds?

4. In what ways could our church or community better reflect the "pyramid of equality" we've discussed?

Teacher's Corner: This chapter addresses complex theological concepts regarding gender roles and equality in a way that is accessible to young readers while maintaining biblical integrity. The pyramid metaphor provides a visual framework that helps students conceptualize equality under God's authority without falling into either hierarchical subordination or the erasure of meaningful differences.

For classroom application, the cooperative pyramid-building activity offers an experiential learning opportunity that reinforces the concept of interdependence and equal value amid different contributions. This can be expanded into discussions about how diverse perspectives strengthen problem-solving in science, mathematics, and other academic disciplines.

The chapter intentionally balances its discussion of gender equality with broader applications to cultural and ecological diversity. This approach helps students make connections between biblical principles and contemporary environmental ethics. It also supports cross-curricular learning that bridges theological concepts with science, social studies, and character education.

Chapter 7:

The Sabbath Principle: Rest and Renewal for the Earth

A Divine Pause Button

Have you ever played a video game or watched a movie for so long that your eyes started to feel tired, and your brain got fuzzy? Or maybe you've worked on a difficult homework assignment and reached that point where nothing makes sense anymore. What did you need in that moment?

A break! A chance to rest, recharge, and return with fresh energy and a clear mind.

In His infinite wisdom, God knew that all of creation—including people, animals, and even the land—needs regular rest periods to thrive. That's why He established one of the most beautiful gifts in Scripture: The Sabbath.

"Remember the sabbath day, to keep it holy. Six days shalt thou labour, and do all thy work: But the seventh day is the sabbath of the LORD thy

God: in it thou shalt not do any work, thou, nor thy son, nor thy daughter, thy manservant, nor thy maidservant, nor thy cattle, nor thy stranger that is within thy gates." (Exodus 20:8-10)

This commandment is extraordinary! God didn't just tell people to take a day off—He included servants, visitors, and even animals in this mandate for rest. Every creature deserves time to recharge! And as we'll discover, this principle extends even to the land itself.

More Than Just a Day Off

The Sabbath isn't just about taking a break from work—though that's certainly part of it. It's about stepping out of the rush of everyday activities to remember what truly matters: our relationship with God, each other, and the created world around us.

Pastor Rodriguez explains it beautifully: "The Sabbath reminds us that we are not defined by what we produce or accomplish. We are valued by God simply because we exist as His beloved creation. When we pause our constant doing to simply be, we reconnect with this fundamental truth."

In our busy modern world, where we're constantly bombarded with messages telling us to do more, buy more, achieve more, and rush more, the Sabbath is a radical countercultural practice. It whispers, "Slow down. Rest. There is more to life than endless productivity."

Twelve-year-old Ethan shares how his family practices the Sabbath: "Every Sunday, we have a 'screen-free day.' No phones, tablets, computers, or TV. At first, I thought I'd hate it, but it's become my favorite day! We play board games, go hiking, read books, or just talk. I've gotten to know my little sister better because we actually play together instead of just sitting next to each other on our devices. And I sleep better on Sunday nights too!"

The Land Needs Rest Too!

The biblical concept of the Sabbath goes beyond just a weekly day of rest. In Leviticus 25:1-7, God gives an amazing instruction:

"Six years thou shalt sow thy field, and six years thou shalt prune thy vineyard, and gather in the fruit thereof; But in the seventh year shall be a sabbath of rest unto the land, a sabbath for the

LORD: thou shalt neither sow thy field, nor prune thy vineyard." (Leviticus 25:3-4)

The entire land was to rest every seventh year! Farmers were instructed not to plant crops but to let the fields lie fallow (unplanted). This practice, called the "Sabbatical Year," shows God's concern not just for human well-being but also for the health and restoration of the Earth itself.

Why would God command people to let their farmland rest for an entire year? Wouldn't that lead to food shortages? Actually, this ancient wisdom aligns perfectly with what modern agricultural science has discovered:

- Soil needs time to replenish its nutrients
- Fields that never rest become depleted and less productive over time
- Allowing natural vegetation to grow temporarily helps prevent erosion
- Pest cycles are disrupted when crop patterns change

God's instruction for a Sabbath year wasn't just a spiritual practice—it was a sophisticated land management technique that ensured sustainable food production for generations!

Mrs. Henderson, who teaches agricultural science and leads a church garden ministry, explains: "When we farm the same land year after year without rest, we're essentially withdrawing nutrients from the soil's 'bank account' without making any deposits. Eventually, that account runs dry. The Sabbath year allows natural processes to make deposits back into the soil, ensuring its long-term fertility."

Activity Box: Soil Sabbath Experiment

Try this simple experiment to see how rest affects soil health!

You'll need:

- Three small containers
- Soil from your yard or garden
- Fast-growing seeds (like radishes or beans)
- A sunny windowsill

Step 1: Fill all three containers with soil and plant the same number of seeds in each.

Step 2: Label them Container A, B, and C.

Step 3: Once plants are growing well, begin these treatments:

- Container A: Keep harvesting and immediately replanting new seeds
- Container B: After harvest, let soil rest for one week before replanting
- Container C: After harvest, let soil rest for three weeks before replanting

Continue this cycle and observe the differences in plant growth over time. Which soil produces the healthiest plants in the long run?

Permaculture: Modern Wisdom Meets Ancient Practice

Today, many sustainable farmers and gardeners practice a system called permaculture, which stands for "permanent agriculture." Permaculture designs mimic patterns found in natural ecosystems to create gardens and farms that are productive, resilient, and sustainable over the long term.

What's fascinating is how closely permaculture principles align with biblical Sabbath concepts! Here are some examples:

Crop Rotation

Instead of growing the same crop in the same place year after year (which depletes specific nutrients and attracts specialized pests), permaculture farmers rotate different types of plants through their fields. This gives the soil a kind of "partial Sabbath" from any one crop's specific demands.

Fourteen-year-old Maya explains how her family uses this technique: "In our garden, we have four main sections. Each year, we move our plant families to the next section—so where we grew tomatoes this year, we'll plant beans next year, then leafy greens, then root vegetables, and finally back to tomatoes in the fifth year. Dad says each plant family uses different nutrients and adds different benefits to the soil, so this rotation keeps everything in balance."

Cover Cropping

During rest periods, permaculture gardeners often plant "cover crops" like clover or buckwheat. These crops aren't harvested for food but instead are turned back into the soil to add nutrients—

especially nitrogen, which most food crops need in large amounts.

This practice mirrors the biblical instruction in Exodus 23:10-11, which says that during the Sabbath year, whatever grows naturally should be left "that the poor of thy people may eat: and what they leave the beasts of the field shall eat." The land produces, but in a different way, that ultimately benefits the soil.

Polyculture Instead of Monoculture

Rather than growing large areas of just one type of plant (monoculture), permaculture emphasizes diverse plantings (polyculture) where multiple species grow together in mutually beneficial relationships. This approach reduces pest problems and maximizes productivity while giving the soil a more balanced set of demands.

Pastor Kim, who leads a church permaculture project, sees spiritual symbolism in this practice: "Just as we learned in our last chapter that human communities thrive through diverse gifts working together, so too does God's creation flourish when diverse plants and animals interact in harmony.

Monoculture represents our human tendency to overly simplify and control; polyculture represents God's intricate web of interdependent relationships."

Sabbath Economics: Jubilee and Reset

The most dramatic expression of the Sabbath principle in Scripture comes from the Jubilee Year, described in Leviticus 25:8-55. After seven cycles of seven years (49 years total), the 50th year was declared a Jubilee—a super-Sabbath when:

- All debts were forgiven
- The land returned to its original family owners
- Slaves and prisoners were freed
- The land received rest

This extraordinary system prevented a few families from permanently accumulating wealth while others remained perpetually poor. It ensured that every family had access to productive land and that human communities, like the soil, received regular opportunities for rest and reset.

Dr. Washington, an economist and Christian sustainability advocate, explains: "God's Jubilee system recognized that without regular corrections, economic systems naturally trend toward inequality and exploitation—of both people and natural resources. The Jubilee year refreshed the entire community, preventing both ecological and economic collapse."

While Jubilee doesn't have many literal applications today, its principle—that both human society and natural systems need periods of restoration and rebalancing—remains profoundly relevant to our modern environmental and social challenges.

Slowing Down: The Gift of Intentional Living

Beyond specific agricultural practices, the Sabbath principle invites us to a fundamentally different relationship with time itself. In a world that worships speed, efficiency, and constant activity, choosing to slow down is a radical act of both faith and environmental stewardship.

When we rush through life, we:

- Use more disposable products for convenience

- Drive instead of walk or bike
- Choose fast food over home-cooked meals
- Miss opportunities to appreciate and protect the natural world
- Lose connection with our community and even with our own thoughts and feelings

Sabbath-inspired slower living invites us to:
- Choose quality over quantity
- Value relationships over productivity
- Create less waste by taking time for reusable options
- Notice the natural world around us
- Listen to God's voice in moments of quiet

Thirteen-year-old Zoe shares how her family practices intentional slowness: "Once a month, we have what Mom calls 'Pioneer Day.' We pretend we live in olden times—we cook from scratch over the fire pit in our backyard, play board games, read books aloud by lantern light, and try to do things the slow way. Last time, we made butter by shaking cream in a jar while telling stories. It took forever, but it tasted amazing! These days help us appreciate what we have and remind us that rushing isn't always better."

Solarpunk Communities: Building Rest Into Design

Solarpunk communities take the Sabbath principle seriously by designing neighborhoods, buildings, and systems that prioritize rest and renewal for both people and the natural world. Here are some examples:

Walkable Neighborhoods

By creating communities where daily needs are within walking distance, Solarpunk designs reduce the rush and stress of commuting while lowering pollution from vehicles. Slower transportation methods like walking and cycling create natural pauses in the day.

Community Work Patterns

Some Solarpunk communities organize work schedules so that essential services continue while ensuring everyone gets proper rest. They might arrange rotating Sabbath days so that different community members rest on different days or create shared work patterns that give everyone more leisure time.

Natural Building Cycles

Buildings and infrastructure follow natural rhythms. Maintenance and updates are planned according to seasonal patterns rather than constant construction. Materials are chosen for longevity rather than rapid replacement.

Circular Systems

Inspired by natural cycles of growth, rest, and renewal, Solarpunk communities design systems where "waste" from one process becomes input for another. Food scraps become compost for gardens, rainwater is collected for irrigation, and energy is stored during abundant periods for use during scarcity.

The New Eden Community in California incorporates these principles throughout its design. Resident Sarah Martinez explains: "We built rest into every aspect of our community. Our shared work schedule ensures everyone has adequate time off. Our gardens include sections that rest each season. Even our power systems incorporate rest—

our solar arrays collect excess energy during sunny periods so our generators can 'rest' at night and during cloudy days. Living this way feels more natural and sustainable for everyone."

Practical Steps: Bringing Sabbath Rest to Your World

Ready to incorporate the Sabbath principle into your life? Here are some age-appropriate ideas for kids, families, and communities:

For Kids

1. **Create a "Sabbath Box"**: Designate a special container where you put your electronic devices for a set period each week. Fill the time instead with outdoor exploration, creative projects, or meaningful conversations.

2. **Start a Slow Hobby**: Choose an activity that can't be rushed—like growing plants, learning an instrument, or creating art—and dedicate regular time to it.

3. **Practice Nature Observation**: Spend time each week sitting quietly in a natural setting, using all your senses to notice the details around you. Keep a journal of what you observe.

4. **Establish a "No Homework Day"**: Work with your parents and teachers to designate one day a week when you complete no homework, focusing instead on rest, family, and recreational activities.

For Families

1. **Create a Weekly Sabbath Rhythm**: Whether it's a traditional religious Sabbath or simply a designated "family day," establish a regular time when work stops and relationships take priority.

2. **Practice "Technology Sabbaths"**: Regularly disconnect from screens and digital devices as a family. Use the time for face-to-face connection, outdoor adventures, or creative projects.

3. **Incorporate Fallow Periods in Home Gardens**: If you grow food at home, designate sections that rest each season or year, using cover crops to restore soil health.

4. **Choose Quality Over Quantity**: Instead of filling schedules with endless activities, select fewer

commitments but engage in them more deeply and meaningfully.

For Communities

1. **Establish Community Sabbath Spaces**: Create parks, gardens, or gathering areas specifically designed for rest, reflection, and connection.

2. **Organize Work/Rest Cycles**: In community projects, build in regular breaks and celebrations, not just constant productivity.

3. **Practice Crop Rotation and Soil Rest** in community gardens and farms.

4. **Support "Slow Businesses"**: Patronize local establishments prioritizing quality, sustainability, and fair labor practices over rapid production and consumption.

Project Box: Create a Personal Sabbath Practice

Design your own mini-Sabbath practice with these steps:

Step 1: Choose a regular time (could be a full day, evening, or even just one hour per week).

Step 2: List activities that feel like work or obligation to you.

Step 3: List activities that bring you rest, joy, and connection with God, others, and creation.

Step 4: Create simple guidelines for your Sabbath time—what you'll set aside and what you'll embrace instead.

Step 5: Share your plan with your family and invite them to support or even join your practice.

Step 6: After trying your Sabbath practice for a month, reflect on how it has affected your life and relationships.

The Fruit of Rest: Unexpected Gifts of the Sabbath

When we honor the Sabbath principle—allowing ourselves, our communities, and the Earth regular periods of rest—we discover unexpected blessings:

Increased Productivity

Counterintuitively, regular rest actually improves our productivity during active periods! Studies show that workers who take proper breaks accomplish more than those who work continuously. Similarly, fields that experience fallow periods ultimately produce more abundant harvests over time.

Eleven-year-old Aiden noticed this in his schoolwork: "I used to try to power through my homework without breaks, but I'd get frustrated and make mistakes. Now, I use a timer and take a 10-minute break every 30 minutes—just looking out the window or stretching. I actually finish faster this way, and my work is better!"

Greater Creativity

Rest refreshes our minds and creates space for new ideas. Many of history's greatest insights and inventions have come during moments of relaxation rather than intense effort.

Deeper Relationships

Our connections deepen and strengthen when we slow down enough to truly be present with others. The Sabbath creates space for the conversations and shared experiences that build lasting bonds.

Ecological Health

Natural systems that receive appropriate rest periods—whether soil, water bodies, forests, or animal populations—demonstrate greater resilience, biodiversity, and long-term productivity.

Spiritual Growth

In the quiet spaces of Sabbath rest, we often hear God's voice more clearly. As Psalm 46:10 reminds us, sometimes we need to *"Be still, and know that I am God."*

Pastor Joanna, who leads workshops on Sabbath practices, shares: "When we create space for rest, we're making room for God to work in ways our constant activity might prevent. The Sabbath isn't primarily about what we don't do—it's about what becomes possible when we step back and allow God's restorative power to flow through our lives and communities."

Looking Ahead

In our next chapter, we'll explore how Jesus' miracle of multiplying loaves and fish teaches us about God's abundance and our role in wisely sharing resources. We'll also discover how the Solarpunk vision of shared economies reflects biblical principles of stewardship and community care.

For now, remember that the Sabbath principle—regular rest and renewal for people, communities, and the Earth—isn't an optional extra for those with spare time. It's a fundamental rhythm woven into creation by God Himself, essential for the health and flourishing of all living things.

As you go through this week, look for opportunities to incorporate moments of Sabbath rest into your life. Notice how these pauses affect your energy, your relationships, and your connection with God and creation. Just as God rested on the seventh day of creation and called it "very good," may your own experience of Sabbath rest reveal the goodness of God's design for a balanced, sustainable life.

Family Discussion Questions:

1. What activities feel most restful and renewing for each family member? How might we incorporate more of these into our weekly rhythms?

2. In what ways might our family benefit from a regular "Sabbath" practice—either religious or secular?

3. How could we apply the concept of "fallow periods" to areas of our life beyond gardening?

4. What's one thing our family could choose to slow down this week, and what might we gain by doing so?

Teacher's Corner: This chapter translates the biblical concept of the Sabbath into both ecological principles and practical life applications accessible to young learners. The connection between scriptural wisdom and contemporary environmental science reinforces the integration of faith and stewardship while providing a theological framework for sustainable practices.

For classroom application, the soil Sabbath experiment offers an excellent hands-on opportunity for students to observe the practical benefits of rest periods in natural systems. This could be expanded into a more comprehensive unit on soil health, decomposition, and nutrient cycles in a science curriculum.

Consider supplementing this chapter with discussions about time management and the impact of constant digital connectivity on young people's mental health. The Sabbath principle offers students a faith-based rationale for establishing healthy boundaries with technology and productivity demands—an increasingly important skill in today's fast-paced world.

Chapter 8:

The Loaves and Fishes Principle: Multiplying Resources

A Hungry Crowd and a Small Lunch

Imagine being part of an enormous crowd—thousands of people gathered on a grassy hillside, listening to Jesus teach all day long. The sun is beginning to set, stomachs are rumbling, and you are miles from the nearest village. There are no food trucks, convenience stores, or even a vending machine in sight! What would happen next?

This exact situation unfolds in one of Jesus' most famous miracles, told in John 6:1-14. The disciples were worried about the hungry crowd and suggested sending everyone away to find food. But Jesus had a different plan:

"When Jesus then lifted up his eyes, and saw a great company come unto him, he saith unto Philip, Whence shall we buy bread, that these may eat?" (John 6:5)

Philip quickly calculated that even eight months' wages wouldn't buy enough bread for everyone to have just a bite! Then Andrew discovered a young boy with a small lunch:

"There is a lad here, which hath five barley loaves, and two small fishes: but what are they among so many?" (John 6:9)

It seemed like nothing—just five small barley loaves (more like what we'd call rolls today) and two little fish. This tiny offering appeared completely inadequate in a crowd of over 5,000 people.

But then something extraordinary happened. Jesus took that seemingly insufficient lunch, gave thanks for it, and began distributing it to the people. Somehow, miraculously, that small amount of food multiplied until everyone in the crowd had eaten their fill—with twelve baskets of leftovers remaining!

This incredible story teaches us something powerful that we'll call the "Loaves and Fishes Principle": When we offer what we have—even if it seems small or inadequate—God can multiply it in amazing ways to meet needs beyond what we could imagine!

Beyond the Miracle: A Pattern for Sustainability

While this story shows Jesus' divine power to multiply resources miraculously, it also reveals a pattern that applies to how we steward Earth's resources today. Let's look at some key elements of this pattern:

1. Start with Gratitude for What You Have

Before multiplying the food, Jesus gave thanks for it. He didn't complain about how little there was; He expressed gratitude for what was available. Approaching Earth's resources with gratitude rather than a sense of entitlement or scarcity can help us see possibilities we might otherwise miss.

Eleven-year-old Nia shares how gratitude changed her perspective: "Last year, I really wanted a new bike. My parents suggested I try fixing up my old one first. I was disappointed until our neighbor, Mr. Lee, who loves restoring old things, offered to help. We spent Saturdays cleaning, oiling, fixing, and even customizing my bike with cool recycled decorations. Now, I love my bike even more than if I'd gotten a new one, and I learned tons of repair skills! Being thankful for what I had led to something better than what I thought I wanted."

2. Everyone's Contribution Matters

The miracle began with one boy willing to share his small lunch. What if he had kept it hidden, thinking it wouldn't make a difference? The entire miracle hinged on his willingness to offer the little he had.

In our world today, it's easy to think, "I'm just one person—what difference can I make?" But the Loaves and Fishes story reminds us that significant change often begins with small individual actions that inspire others and create ripple effects throughout communities.

3. Sharing Creates Abundance

In Jesus' miracle, food multiplied when it was shared. This reflects a profound truth about resources: hoarding often leads to waste, while thoughtful sharing can create surprising abundance.

Pastor Rivera explains it this way: "When we clutch tightly to 'our' resources, fearing we won't have enough, we often end up with exactly that—not enough. But when we open our hands and share wisely, we frequently discover there's more than enough for everyone. I've seen this principle at work in our church community garden. Individual families couldn't maintain large gardens on their own, but by sharing the work and the harvest, we all eat better than we could alone."

4. Nothing Is Wasted

After everyone had eaten their fill, Jesus instructed the disciples to "*Gather up the fragments that remain, that nothing be lost*" (John 6:12). Even in the midst of miraculous abundance, Jesus demonstrated careful stewardship of resources.

This teaches us that true sustainability isn't about generating endless resources to waste but about using what we have wisely and avoiding waste at every step.

Activity Box: Resource Multiplication Challenge

In small groups, try this creative challenge: Each person brings one random household item (like a rubber band, paper clip, empty bottle, etc.). Together, brainstorm as many useful things as possible that could be made by combining these items. Then, choose one idea and actually create it! You'll be amazed at how your "inadequate" resources multiply when combined with creativity and teamwork.

Modern Loaves and Fishes: Sustainability Success Stories

All around the world, communities are applying the Loaves and Fishes Principle to create surprising abundance from seemingly limited resources. Here are some inspiring examples:

The Sharing Garden Movement

In Portland, Oregon, neighbors transformed seven small, disconnected yard spaces—each too small for effective gardening alone—into a network of specialized growing areas connected by a path. One yard with full sun grows tomatoes and peppers; a shadier yard grows leafy greens, another hosts fruit trees, and so on.

"Separately, our yards were too small to grow much," community organizer Ms. Chen explains. "But something amazing happened when we thought of them as one distributed garden. We grow three times more food than if each had tried gardening independently! Now twenty-five families eat from this network, and we have enough excess to donate to our local food pantry every week."

Tool Libraries

Rather than every household buying rarely used tools that sit idle most of the time, communities are creating tool-lending libraries where members can borrow what they need when needed.

The North Portland Tool Library started with just a few donated items in a church basement. Today, it has over 3,000 tools and serves more than 5,000 community members! By sharing these resources, the community "multiplies" the usefulness of each tool while reducing waste and saving money.

Thirteen-year-old Marco volunteered there last summer: "It's amazing to see how many different projects get completed with the same tools. Last Saturday, I checked a ladder out to someone painting their house, and when it came back, it went to someone installing solar lights and then to someone rescuing a cat from a tree! Instead of three ladders sitting unused most of the time, one ladder helps dozens of people each month."

Seed Saving Networks

Traditional farmers have practiced seed saving for thousands of years—keeping seeds from their best plants to grow the following season. Today, seed libraries and exchanges are reviving this practice, allowing gardeners to share varieties adapted to local conditions.

Rocky Mountain Seed Alliance began with just a few packets of heirloom seeds. Now, they coordinate hundreds of gardeners who grow, save, and exchange thousands of seed varieties. These seeds are adapting better to local conditions with each growing season, creating food security that doesn't depend on purchasing new seeds yearly.

"It's like the miracle keeps happening season after season," explains Grandmother Rose, an elder who teaches seed saving. "The original seeds multiply into plants, which create hundreds more seeds, which grow into thousands more plants in countless gardens. From just a handful of seeds, entire communities can feed themselves for generations!"

Solarpunk Resource Multiplication

The Solarpunk movement creatively embraces the Loaves and Fishes Principle, blending traditional wisdom with modern innovation. Here are some examples of how Solarpunk communities multiply resources:

Circular Systems

Rather than the linear "take-make-waste" model of our current economy, Solarpunk designs create circular systems where "waste" from one process becomes a resource for another.

The Harmony Eco-Village in New Mexico demonstrates this beautifully. Kitchen scraps feed worms in a vermiculture system, producing rich fertilizer for the community garden. Graywater from sinks and showers irrigates fruit trees. Solar panels generate electricity, and their shade creates cool areas for gathering. Even human waste is composted in special systems to eventually create safe soil for non-food plants.

"Everything has multiple uses here," explains resident Sophia Jackson. "When you stop thinking of things as having just one purpose and then becoming trash, you discover amazing connections. Our resources multiply because we've designed our systems to mimic nature's cycles, where nothing is ever truly wasted."

Skill Sharing and Time Banking

Solarpunk communities recognize that knowledge and skills are resources that actually increase when shared! Through workshops, apprenticeships, and formal teaching, valuable abilities spread throughout the community.

Some communities use "time banking" systems, where people exchange hours of service rather than money. For example, one hour of childcare equals one hour of computer help equals one hour of home repair. This system values everyone's time equally while multiplying the community's total capacity to meet needs.

Twelve-year-old David participated in his community's summer skill-share program: "I taught people how to make friendship bracelets, and in exchange, I learned bicycle repair, basic coding, and how to bake bread! The cool thing is, now I'm teaching my friends bike repair, too, so the knowledge keeps spreading. It's like the loaves and fishes of skills!"

Energy Sharing Networks

Solar panels produce abundant energy during sunny days but none at night. Some communities are creating microgrids that allow neighbors to share excess energy with each other, multiplying the effectiveness of each installation.

In Brooklyn, NY, a neighborhood microgrid allows residents with solar panels to sell excess electricity directly to neighbors instead of back to the utility company. This keeps energy local, builds community relationships, and makes renewable energy more accessible to everyone—including those who can't afford their own panels.

Library of Things

Some communities expand beyond books and tools by creating "Libraries of Things," where members can borrow kitchen appliances, camping gear, party supplies, musical instruments, and other occasionally needed items.

"Our Library of Things started with donations of items people had sitting unused in their closets and garages," explains librarian Mr. Patel. "Now we have over 500 items that community members can borrow instead of buy. One bread maker now serves 30 families instead of sitting unused in 30 separate kitchens! The money people save by borrowing instead of buying gets reinvested in our community in other ways."

Biblical Wisdom for Resource Multiplication

The loaves and fishes miracle isn't the only place where Scripture teaches principles of resource multiplication. Throughout the Bible, we find wisdom for creating abundance through wise stewardship:

The Principle of the Harvest

"Be not deceived; God is not mocked: for whatsoever a man soweth, that shall he also reap." (Galatians 6:7)

This verse reminds us that one seed, when planted, can produce a plant bearing dozens, hundreds, or even thousands of new seeds. We participate in creation's multiplication system by sacrificing immediate consumption (eating the seed) and investing in the future (planting it).

The Principle of Generosity

"Give, and it shall be given unto you; good measure, pressed down, and shaken together, and running over, shall men give into your bosom. For with the same measure that ye mete withal it shall be measured to you again." (Luke 6:38)

Jesus teaches that generosity creates a cycle of abundance. When we give freely, we often receive even more in return—not always in the same form, but in ways that meet our needs and bring joy.

The Principle of Righteous Stewardship

"His lord said unto him, Well done, thou good and faithful servant: thou hast been faithful over a few things, I will make thee ruler over many things: enter thou into the joy of thy lord." (Matthew 25:21)

In the Parable of the Talents, Jesus teaches that those who wisely steward what they've been given will be entrusted with more, no matter how small the gift seems. This applies not just to money but to all the resources God has placed in our care.

Practical Applications: Multiplying Resources in Your Life

Ready to apply the Loaves and Fishes Principle in your own life? Here are practical ideas for kids, families, and communities:

For Kids

1. **Start a Skill-Share Club**: Gather friends and take turns teaching each other things you know how to do—whether it's jump rope tricks, drawing techniques, or computer skills.

2. **Create a Book Exchange**: Instead of letting read books sit on shelves, organize a system with friends to trade books you've finished, multiplying everyone's reading options.

3. **Plant Seeds from Fruits You Eat**: The next time you enjoy an apple, orange, or watermelon, save a few seeds and try

planting them. Watch how one piece of fruit can potentially grow into a plant that produces many more!

4. **Make "New" Art Supplies from Recyclables**: Collect items headed for the recycling bin and transform them into art materials—cardboard tubes become stamping tools, bottle caps become mosaic pieces, and food containers become paint holders.

Nine-year-old Luis shares: "I started collecting the cardboard tubes from paper towels and toilet paper. My friends thought I was weird until I showed them how to make awesome marble runs with them! Now, ten of us collect them, and we built this massive marble course in our after-school program that's way cooler than anything we could buy at a store."

For Families

1. **Organize a Neighborhood Swap Meet**: Host a gathering where families bring good-quality items they no longer need and exchange them for things they can use.
2. **Start a Meal-Sharing Rotation**: Coordinate with a few other families to cook larger batches of meals and share them, reducing the number of times each family needs to cook while increasing variety.
3. **Create a Family Upcycling Challenge**: Before throwing something away, challenge family members to brainstorm at least three potential new uses for it.
4. **Plant a Giving Garden**: Dedicate a section of your garden specifically for growing food to share with neighbors or local food banks.

For Communities

1. **Start a Community Composting System**: Collect food scraps from multiple households to create rich soil for community gardens, multiplying the fertility of your local food system.

2. **Create a Skill Inventory**: Survey community members to identify the diverse skills, tools, and resources available, then create systems for sharing these assets.

3. **Establish a Community Solar Program**: Work together to install solar panels that benefit multiple households, making renewable energy more accessible to everyone.

4. **Organize a "Repair Café"**: Host events where people with repair skills help fix broken items that might otherwise be

discarded, extending the useful life of community resources.

Project Box: Create a Resource Multiplication Map

Draw a diagram of your home, school, or neighborhood, and identify potential resource loops where "waste" from one activity could become input for another. For example: food scraps → compost →, garden →, more food. Challenge yourself to find at least five potential loops! List what would be needed to close the loop and start multiplying resources for each one.

The Miracle Continues: Your Part in God's Multiplication System

The Loaves and Fishes miracle didn't happen in isolation—it required a boy willing to share his lunch, disciples ready to distribute it, and a crowd open to receiving this unexpected gift. God performed the multiplication, but humans participated in the process.

Similarly, creating sustainable abundance today involves both divine provision and human participation. We can't multiply resources through magical thinking or wishful environmentalism, but when we align our actions with God's principles of stewardship, sharing, and wise design, we often discover "multiplier effects" that create surprising abundance.

Pastor James explains: "God has built multiplication systems into creation—seeds that produce hundredfold harvests, water that cycles endlessly through evaporation and rain, forests that regenerate after fire. Our job isn't to create these systems but to discover them, protect them, and align our human activities with their patterns. When we do this—when we stop working against creation's design and start working with it—we participate in ongoing miracles of multiplication."

The Loaves and Fishes Principle reminds us that scarcity often has more to do with distribution and stewardship than with absolute limits. While Earth's resources are indeed finite, God's design includes a remarkable capacity for renewal and abundance when those resources are managed according to divine wisdom.

A Christian environmental scientist, Dr. Michelle Wilson puts it this way: "The question isn't whether we have enough—it's whether we're wise enough to use what we have according to God's patterns. When we shift from an extractive mindset of 'take, make, waste' to a stewardship mindset of 'receive, multiply, share,' we discover that apparent scarcity often transforms into surprising sufficiency."

Looking Ahead

In our next chapter, we'll explore what Scripture and Solarpunk visions tell us about creating beautiful, functional cities that work with nature rather than against it. We'll discover how the biblical vision of the New Jerusalem offers inspiration for designing communities that foster both human flourishing and ecological health.

For now, remember the boy with his small lunch of five loaves and two fish. He couldn't possibly feed the multitude alone, but by offering what he had—as inadequate as it seemed—he participated in one of Jesus' most amazing miracles. In the same way, each of our small actions to share resources, reduce waste, and create sustainable systems may seem inadequate alone, but when blessed by God and combined with others' efforts, they can multiply to meet needs far beyond what we might imagine.

Family Discussion Questions:

1. What "small lunches" (resources or abilities) has God given our family that could be shared to benefit others?

2. Where do we see waste in our household that could be transformed into a resource for something else?

3. What's one area where we could practice sharing instead of individual ownership to multiply the usefulness of our resources?

4. How might God be inviting us to participate in "resource multiplication" in our community?

Teacher's Corner: This chapter uses the familiar biblical story of loaves and fishes as an entry point to explore principles of resource multiplication and circular economy concepts. For classroom application, consider supplementing the chapter with specific local examples of resource-sharing initiatives in your community. The Resource Multiplication Challenge activity can be expanded into a more extensive STEAM project in which students design and prototype solutions to specific resource challenges.

The biblical foundation provides a values-based framework for sustainability practices that extends beyond mere utility to encompass stewardship, generosity, and community care. This approach helps students see environmental action not as a political position but as an expression of faith principles. For Christian education settings, consider connecting this chapter with service-learning opportunities where students can practice the Loaves and Fishes Principle through community projects that multiply resources for those in need.

Chapter 9:

City of Light: Designing for the Common Good

The Shining City in the Sky

Have you ever dreamed about what the perfect city would look like? Maybe it would have sparkling clean streets, beautiful parks filled with birds and butterflies, friendly neighbors who know each other by name, and homes where everyone has exactly what they need to live comfortably. No pollution, no traffic jams, no dark alleys—just a place where people and nature thrive together in harmony.

Guess what? The Bible actually describes a city very much like this! In the book of Revelation, John shares an amazing vision of a city called the New Jerusalem. This heavenly city represents God's perfect plan for how communities could live:

"And I John saw the holy city, new Jerusalem, coming down from God out of heaven, prepared as a bride adorned for her husband. And I heard a

great voice out of heaven saying, Behold, the tabernacle of God is with men, and he will dwell with them, and they shall be his people, and God himself shall be with them, and be their God." (Revelation 21:2-3)

As John describes this marvelous city, one detail stands out as especially wonderful:

"And the city had no need of the sun, neither of the moon, to shine in it: for the glory of God did lighten it, and the Lamb is the light thereof." (Revelation 21:23)

Imagine a city so filled with God's presence that it doesn't even need streetlights or lamps! Divine light illuminates every corner, creating a place of perfect safety, clarity, and beauty. There are no shadows where harmful things can hide, no dark places that feel scary or dangerous—just radiant light everywhere.

While we can't create cities that literally glow with God's visible glory (at least not yet!), this heavenly vision gives us a blueprint for what our earthly communities could strive toward. What if we designed our neighborhoods, towns, and cities to reflect some of these divine qualities—bringing a little bit of heaven down to earth?

The New Jerusalem: God's Solarpunk City

When we look closely at the details of the New Jerusalem, something fascinating emerges—this heavenly city shares many features with what modern Solarpunk communities are trying to create! Let's explore some of these connections:

1. Built for Relationship, Not Isolation

The New Jerusalem is designed with the community at its center. God's presence dwells right in the middle of the city, accessible to all (Revelation 21:3). The city isn't divided into wealthy neighborhoods and poor ones—all residents have equal access to its treasures and resources.

Eleven-year-old Maya noticed this pattern in her church's study of Revelation: "I realized the New Jerusalem isn't like cities today where some neighborhoods have parks and good schools while others don't. Everything good in God's city is shared equally with everyone who lives there. No one is left out!"

2. Abundant Natural Elements

Though it's clearly a city with buildings and streets, the New Jerusalem incorporates stunning natural features. A crystal-clear river flows through its center, lined with fruit trees that produce a harvest every month (Revelation 22:1-2). These trees aren't just decorative—they provide "healing for the nations," showing that nature plays a vital role even in this perfect urban environment.

3. Beautiful, Sustainable Materials

The city is constructed from materials that last forever—precious stones, crystal, and gold so pure it's transparent like glass (Revelation 21:18-21). They suggest a place built with extraordinary care and craftsmanship, using the finest materials that never need replacement or create waste.

4. Designed for Walking

The New Jerusalem is described as a perfect cube or square, with gates on all sides and streets laid out in an orderly pattern. John carefully measures the city, showing that it's designed with thoughtful proportions and scale. Though enormous in its heavenly dimensions, its layout suggests a place where people can easily walk from one area to another.

5. Safe and Inclusive

The city's gates *"shall not be shut at all by day: for there shall be no night there"* (Revelation 21:25). This openness symbolizes both safety (no need for locked gates) and welcome to all who come in peace. The healing leaves of the trees are "for all nations," showing God's desire for diverse peoples to find health and home there.

Pastor Kim, who studies urban theology, explains: "The New Jerusalem isn't just a far-off heaven disconnected from our earthly concerns. It's God's vision for what the human community could be—a place of justice, beauty, sustainability, and flourishing for all. When we work to create more equitable, green, and connected cities today, we're actually participating in God's redemptive vision for creation."

Activity Box: Design Your Neighborhood of Light

Grab a large piece of paper and drawing supplies. Imagine you're designing a neighborhood inspired by the New Jerusalem! Include:

1. Places for people to gather and build community
2. Natural elements like gardens, trees, and water
3. Homes for various types of families
4. Ways for people to travel without cars
5. Spaces that serve the community's needs

After creating your design, share it with family or friends and explain how your neighborhood reflects God's love for people and creation.

Solarpunk Cities: Bringing the Vision Down to Earth

The Solarpunk movement envisions cities and towns that harmonize human needs with ecological health—communities that work with nature rather than against it. These visions align beautifully with the biblical values we've explored throughout this book:

Walkable Neighborhoods

In Solarpunk cities, everything you need for daily life—schools, grocery stores, parks, libraries, and workplaces—is within a comfortable walking distance of your home. Streets are designed primarily for people, not cars, making neighborhoods safer, quieter, and more connected.

Thirteen-year-old Elijah shares his experience: "My family moved from the suburbs, where we had to drive everywhere, to a walkable neighborhood near downtown. Now I can bike to school, walk to the library, and get ice cream with friends without asking my parents for a ride. I've met so many more neighbors just by being out walking instead of inside a car. It feels like we're actually part of a community now!"

Green Infrastructure

Rather than covering the earth with concrete and then building separate systems to manage rainwater, Solarpunk designs incorporate nature directly into infrastructure. Rain gardens capture stormwater, green roofs grow food and provide insulation, and wetlands clean water naturally while providing a habitat for wildlife.

In Portland, Oregon, some neighborhoods have transformed traditional storm drains into mini gardens called "bioswales" that filter rainwater naturally. "These aren't just functional—they're beautiful," urban planner Ms. Rodriguez explains. "Children walking to school get to see butterflies visiting flowers and birds catching insects, all while learning how nature can clean water better than any machine we could build."

Community-Centered Spaces

While modern cities often prioritize commercial spaces like shopping malls, Solarpunk designs emphasize community gathering places: public plazas, shared gardens, outdoor performance areas, and multi-use community centers where people can connect and collaborate.

The town of Florence, Massachusetts, transformed an abandoned factory into a community hub with workshops, art studios, a tool library, a community kitchen, and an indoor winter garden. "This space belongs to everyone," explains community organizer Mr. Chen. Whether you're taking a free class, sharing a meal, fixing your bicycle, or just enjoying the indoor garden during winter, the message is that you belong here."

Integrated Food Systems

Food doesn't magically appear in grocery stores—it needs to be grown somewhere! Solarpunk cities bring food production back into neighborhoods through community gardens, food forests in parks, rooftop farms, and even edible landscaping along streets. This reduces the energy needed to transport food long distances while connecting people more directly to their food sources.

Renewable Energy Independence

Solar panels on rooftops, small wind turbines, and innovative energy storage systems allow Solarpunk neighborhoods to generate their own clean power. Some communities create "microgrids" that can operate independently from the main power grid during emergencies, making neighborhoods more resilient.

Real-Life Examples: Communities Bringing the Vision to Life

All around the world, communities are already implementing elements of this vision, creating places that reflect both biblical values and Solarpunk ideals:

The Village of Possibility in Tennessee

This Christian Intentional Community was founded by five families who wanted to create a neighborhood that better reflects their simplicity, sustainability, and community values. They purchased 30 acres of former farmland and designed a pedestrian-focused village with shared green spaces, small homes clustered in groups, and a community center that serves as both church and gathering space.

"We wanted our physical environment to support, not hinder, our Christian witness," explains co-founder Sarah Martinez. "How could we truly love our neighbors if we never saw them because we were always in our cars? How could we care for God's creation while living in ways that destroyed it? Our village isn't perfect, but it helps us live more consistently with our beliefs."

Children thrive in this environment, and they are free to play outdoors safely with minimal supervision. Twelve-year-old Noah shares: "My favorite thing is that I can visit friends or go to the community garden without asking for a ride. And everybody knows everybody, so if I need help, there's always someone nearby who cares about me."

The Light of Creation Church in Seattle

When this urban congregation needed to renovate their aging building, they decided to transform it into a model of creation care. They installed solar panels that generate more electricity than the church uses, planted rain gardens to manage stormwater naturally, and converted their parking lot into a community garden and outdoor gathering space.

"We realized our building itself could be a witness to God's love for creation," explains Pastor Williams. "Now we host tours for other churches and community groups, showing how buildings can be designed to give back to the environment rather than just taking from it. And our congregation has grown because people are drawn to a faith community that puts its values into visible action."

The Taita Hills Eco-Village in Kenya

This Christian community developed a village model that combines traditional wisdom with modern sustainable technology. Homes built from local materials like stone and sustainable timber are arranged around shared courtyards where families cook and socialize together. Solar panels power lights and phone charging, while carefully designed water systems capture rainfall from tin roofs, filter it naturally, and store it for the dry season.

"Our village shows that sustainable living isn't just for wealthy countries," explains community leader Joseph Mwangi. "By combining our grandparents' knowledge about building with local materials with new technologies like solar power, we've created a community that honors both our Creator and our cultural heritage."

In the community school, children in the village learn traditional skills alongside modern subjects. "I'm learning how to grow drought-resistant crops from my grandmother and how to install solar panels from our community engineers," says fourteen-year-old Naomi. "Our village gives us the best of both worlds."

Creating Cities of Light: Practical Steps for Kids and Communities

Ready to help transform your own community into a place that better reflects God's vision? Here are some practical ideas for different age groups:

For Kids

1. **Create a Neighborhood Map**: Draw a map of your neighborhood showing all the places you can reach by walking or biking. Are there important things (like grocery stores or libraries) missing? Share your observations with adults who might help address these gaps.

2. **Start a School Garden**: Work with teachers and administrators to create a garden on school grounds that can provide food, habitat for pollinators, and outdoor learning opportunities.

3. **Organize a Walking School Bus**: Gather friends who live nearby to walk to school together,

perhaps with a parent volunteer as a "driver." This will reduce car trips while building community!

4. **Become a Local Expert**: Learn about the native plants, animals, and natural features of your area. Share this knowledge with friends and family to help them connect more deeply with your local environment.

Ten-year-old Jason took this approach: "I became really interested in the creek behind our school. I researched what animals lived there and learned that certain insects can tell you how clean the water is. Now I lead creek explorations for younger kids, and we're working with the city to improve the habitat along the banks."

For Families

1. **Choose Walkable Living When Possible**: When deciding where to live, prioritize neighborhoods where daily needs can be met without driving. If moving isn't an option, identify ways to walk or bike for some trips instead of automatically taking the car.

2. **Transform Your Yard**: Convert part of your lawn into a native plant garden, vegetable beds, or

mini food forest that provides habitat and food while requiring less water and maintenance than grass.

3. **Support Local Businesses**: To strengthen your neighborhood economy and reduce transportation costs, patronize stores and services within walking distance of your home.

4. **Host Neighborhood Gatherings**: Use your front yard, porch, or driveway for community-building events like block parties, game nights, or skill-sharing workshops.

For Churches and Communities

1. **Audit Your Property**: Evaluate church grounds and buildings for sustainability opportunities, such as solar installation, rainwater harvesting, native plant landscaping, or community garden space.

2. **Advocate for Better Design**: Participate in local planning processes to support pedestrian-friendly streets, mixed-use zoning, public transportation, and green infrastructure in your community.

3. **Create Third Places**: Develop gathering spaces that aren't homes or workplaces—community living spaces where people can connect with each other without spending money. Churches can open their buildings during the week for this purpose.

4. **Form Creation Care Teams**: Establish groups focused specifically on helping your congregation or community implement more sustainable practices and designs.

Project Box: Community Vision Walk

Organize a walk around your neighborhood with friends or family, looking specifically for possibilities to make it more like the "City of Light" we've discussed. Bring notebooks to record:

- Spaces that could become community gardens or gathering places
- Buildings that could benefit from solar panels or green roofs
- Streets that could be made safer for walking and biking
- Natural features that could be restored or enhanced

After your walk, create a vision board showing how these spaces could be transformed, and share it with community leaders or organizations that can help make these visions a reality.

Bringing Heaven Down to Earth

The biblical vision of the New Jerusalem isn't just about a distant future—it's an invitation to bring elements of God's perfect city into our present communities. When we design our neighborhoods and cities to foster connection, care for creation, and equitable access to resources, we're allowing little glimpses of heaven to break through into our everyday lives.

Pastor Garcia explains it this way: "Jesus taught us to pray, 'Thy kingdom come, Thy will be done on earth as it is in heaven.' That prayer isn't just spiritual—it's practical! We're asking God to help us create communities on Earth that reflect heavenly values: peace, justice, beauty, and harmony between people and creation."

As we've explored throughout this book, the Solarpunk vision offers exciting possibilities for answering that prayer in tangible ways. By reimagining how we design our human habitats—from individual homes to entire cities—we can create places that nurture both human flourishing and ecological health.

Thirteen-year-old Sofia shares how this vision inspires her: "When we studied Revelation in Sunday School, I used to think the New Jerusalem was just about heaven after we die. But now I understand it's also a blueprint for how we could live right now. I want to become an architect who designs buildings and neighborhoods that help people connect with each other and with nature. Maybe I can help build a little piece of God's city right here!"

Looking Ahead

In our next section, we'll explore how these external changes—in our homes, communities, and cities—connect with internal transformation. We'll discover how cultivating hope, renewing our minds, and growing spiritually are essential parts of living a truly sustainable life aligned with God's purposes.

For now, take some time this week to notice your community's design. What elements already reflect the City of Light we've discussed? What could be improved to better serve the common good? Remember that every garden planted, every solar panel installed, and every neighborhood gathering organized is a small step toward bringing a bit of heaven down to earth—a glimpse of God's shining city becoming visible in our world today.

Family Discussion Questions:

1. What aspects of our neighborhood help us connect with neighbors, nature, and God? What aspects make these connections more difficult?

2. If Jesus were designing our town or city, what might He do differently to help people love God and love their neighbors more effectively?

3. What's one small change our family could make to our home or yard that would better reflect the values of the New Jerusalem?

4. How might our church property be used in ways that better serve our community and care for creation?

Teacher's Corner: This chapter combines eschatological concepts with practical urban design principles, helping students connect their faith with tangible community development. The New Jerusalem serves as both a theological framework and an inspirational model for addressing contemporary challenges of urban sustainability.

Consider using the Community Vision Walk as a service-learning project for classroom application. Students can document their findings using photography or video, present their observations to local officials, and potentially implement small-scale improvements as a class. This provides experiential learning about civic engagement while reinforcing the theological concept that Christians are called to be agents of redemptive transformation in their communities.

The emphasis on walkable neighborhoods also creates opportunities for cross-curricular connections with health education (benefits of physical activity), mathematics (calculating distances and mapping), and social studies (community planning processes). Students can analyze how community design affects different populations, particularly considering accessibility

Tracy Taylor

for children, elderly individuals, and people with disabilities—an important aspect of designing for the common good.

Chapter 10:

Seeds of Faith: Cultivating Hope in Difficult Times

The Tiniest Giant

Have you ever held a seed in your palm and really looked at it? Something so small you might accidentally blow it away with a single breath. Something that looks so plain, so ordinary, that you might easily overlook it.

Yet inside that tiny speck lies an astonishing secret—the complete instructions for building a plant that might grow taller than your house, live for hundreds of years, and produce thousands more seeds just like itself! A mighty oak tree, a sprawling apple orchard, a field of golden wheat—all begin as humble seeds that most people would barely notice.

Jesus knew the amazing power of seeds. That's why He used them to teach one of His most important lessons about faith:

"And Jesus said unto them, Because of your unbelief: for verily I say unto you, If ye have faith as a grain of mustard seed, ye shall say unto this mountain, Remove hence to yonder place; and it shall remove; and nothing shall be impossible unto you." (Matthew 17:20)

Mustard seeds are tiny—about the size of the period at the end of this sentence. Yet Jesus said even faith that small could move mountains! This doesn't mean we can literally rearrange geography with our thoughts. Rather, Jesus was teaching that authentic faith, no matter how small it might seem at first, contains tremendous power to transform our lives and the world around us.

Just like a seed contains everything needed to grow into a mature plant when placed in good soil, even the smallest beginning of faith can grow into a powerful force for change when nurtured properly.

Twelve-year-old Zach discovered this when his family moved to a new city: "I felt so alone and scared at my new school. I prayed every morning, just a simple 'God, please help me get through today.' It didn't feel like much—definitely not mountain-moving faith! But each day got a little better. I found the courage to join the science club, where I made my first friend. Now, eight months later, I have a great group of friends, and I'm even helping other new kids feel welcome. My tiny prayers grew into something bigger than I could have imagined."

Hope in a Troubled World

We won't pretend that everything in our world is perfect. You've probably heard about serious problems like climate change, pollution, species extinction, and social injustice. These challenges can sometimes feel overwhelming, especially for young people who wonder what kind of world they'll inherit.

It's normal to feel worried, sad, or even angry when thinking about these problems. In fact, caring deeply about the Earth and its creatures is a sign that you understand God's heart for creation! Throughout Scripture, we see that God values the natural world He made and calls humans to care for it responsibly.

But God doesn't want us to be paralyzed by fear or despair. Instead, He offers us a special kind of hope—not wishful thinking that ignores problems but grounded confidence that God is still at work in our world. He invites us to partner with Him in healing and restoration.

Pastor Rivera explains it this way: "Biblical hope isn't about pretending everything is fine when it isn't. It's about believing that no matter how big the problems are, God is bigger. And it's about trusting that when we align our actions with God's purposes for creation, amazing transformation becomes possible."

This is where faith, like a mustard seed, comes in. We don't need to have all the answers or feel completely confident all the time. We simply need to plant our small seeds of faith in good soil—taking whatever steps we can, however modest they might seem, trusting that God can multiply their impact beyond what we could accomplish alone.

Solarpunk: Vision of Practical Hope

Throughout this book, we've explored Solarpunk's vision of a future where humans live in harmony with nature, using clean energy, sustainable agriculture, and compassionate communities to address environmental challenges. What makes Solarpunk special isn't just its creative ideas but its fundamentally hopeful approach.

Unlike some environmental messages that focus mainly on doom and gloom, **Solarpunk says, "Yes, we face serious problems—but we also have the creativity, technology, and wisdom to address them!"** It envisions a future worth working toward, not just a catastrophe to avoid.

This positive vision aligns beautifully with biblical hope, which always balances honest recognition of problems with confidence in God's redemptive purposes. As Romans 8:19-21 tells us, all of creation is waiting eagerly for complete restoration—and we get to participate in bringing glimpses of that restoration into the present!

Thirteen-year-old Maya shares: "When we studied climate change in school, I felt really scared and sad. But then our science teacher introduced us to Solarpunk ideas and showed us real communities already putting them into practice. We visited a neighborhood that installed community solar panels and started a bike-sharing program. Seeing real people making positive changes helped me feel hopeful instead of helpless. Now I'm working with friends to start a pollinator garden at our school—it's small, but it's something we can actually do right now."

Biblical Stories of Against-All-Odds Hope

The Bible is filled with stories of people who faced seemingly impossible situations yet held onto hope and saw incredible transformation. These stories remind us that God specializes in bringing new life from what appears dead or hopeless:

Noah's Ark: Preserving Life Amid Destruction

When the world faced catastrophic floods, Noah's faithful obedience in building the ark—despite years of ridicule from neighbors—preserved the precious diversity of Earth's creatures. From that small remnant of saved species, the entire planet was repopulated! In the same way, conservation efforts that protect endangered species today might seem small compared to the scale of extinction, but they preserve crucial biodiversity for future regeneration.

The Exodus: Freedom From Bondage

The Israelites endured generations of slavery in Egypt, a situation that must have seemed permanent and hopeless. Yet Moses' simple act of obedience—approaching Pharaoh with nothing but a staff and God's promises—led to the liberation of an entire nation. Today's efforts to address environmental injustice, where poor communities often bear the worst effects of pollution, might seem daunting, but they can lead to similar liberation.

Ruth and Naomi: Rebuilding From Loss

After losing their husbands and their security, Ruth and Naomi had every reason to despair. Yet Ruth's faithful decision to glean leftover grain from the fields—a small act of determined survival—eventually led to finding a new home, a new family, and even a place in the lineage of King David and eventually Jesus! Small acts of faithful stewardship today might similarly yield outcomes we can't yet imagine.

David and Goliath: Confronting Giant Problems

Young David faced a literally giant problem in Goliath—a warrior so intimidating that an entire army cowered in fear. With five smooth stones and immense courage, David accomplished what seemed impossible. Today's environmental "Goliaths" might seem equally intimidating, but with God's help, even young people armed with determination and creative solutions can make a tremendous difference!

Eleven-year-old Tyler found inspiration in this story: "When our class learned about plastic pollution in the ocean, I felt like we were facing a Goliath problem. But then I remembered David didn't try to fight the same way as everyone else—he used the skills he had. So, I started thinking about what I'm good at: making videos. I created a series about reducing plastic use that our school shared online. It might not solve the whole problem, but it's my smooth stone to throw at the giant!"

Real Stories of Hope and Transformation

All around the world, people of faith are planting seeds of hope that are growing into remarkable examples of healing and renewal. These stories show us what becomes possible when we combine mustard seed faith with practical action:

The Greening of Detroit

After decades of industrial decline left Detroit with thousands of vacant lots, a coalition of churches, community groups, and residents began planting urban gardens in these empty spaces. What started as a few small plots has blossomed into over 1,600 urban farms and gardens producing fresh food in former "food deserts. " These farms and gardens create beautiful green spaces where there was once only abandonment and bring neighbors together across generational and racial divides.

Pastor James of Eastside Community Church witnessed this transformation firsthand: *"Do not merely listen to the word, and so deceive yourselves. Do what it says.* — James 1:22. Twenty years ago, the vacant lot next to our church was a dumping ground for trash and a magnet for trouble. When we first suggested turning it into a garden, people laughed. 'Nothing good can grow here,' they said. But a small group of church members and neighbors had faith to try anyway. They cleared trash, brought in compost, and planted those first seeds. Today, that garden feeds 50 families, hosts community gatherings, and has inspired seven more gardens within walking distance. What looked dead has come spectacularly alive!"

The Return of the Elwha River

For over a century, the Elwha River in Washington State was blocked by two massive dams that decimated once-abundant salmon runs and devastated the indigenous Klallam tribe's way of life. After decades of seemingly hopeless advocacy, the dams were finally removed in 2011-2014. Scientists predicted it might take 30 years for salmon to return in significant numbers.

Instead, within just a few years, thousands of salmon were swimming upriver again. Native plants reclaimed exposed riverbanks, and wildlife returned to the recovering ecosystem. The Klallam tribe resumed cultural practices that had been impossible for generations.

"It's like witnessing a resurrection," explains tribal elder Margaret Williams. "For so long, we kept the memory of the free-flowing river and its salmon alive through our stories, even when it seemed impossible they would ever return. Now, our grandchildren are catching salmon in places their grandparents never could. It teaches us that healing is possible, even after a century of damage, if we have the faith to remove what blocks the river's natural flow."

Green Belt Movement in Kenya

When Wangari Maathai looked at the deforested hillsides of Kenya, she didn't see only environmental degradation—she saw an opportunity for transformation. Starting with just a few women planting tree seedlings in their backyards, she launched the Green Belt Movement in 1977. Despite facing ridicule, political opposition, and even arrest, Maathai persevered.

Today, over 51 million trees have been planted, restoring watersheds, preventing soil erosion, and providing sustainable income for thousands of families. Maathai later received the Nobel Peace Prize for her work connecting environmental conservation with democracy, peace, and women's rights—all growing from those first small seeds planted in faith.

Eden Project: Transformation from Destruction

In Cornwall, England, an abandoned China clay pit—a massive, barren crater left from mining—has been transformed into the Eden Project, a spectacular series of dome greenhouses containing plants from around the world. What was once a wasteland is now a center for environmental education that teaches half a million visitors annually about biodiversity and sustainability.

The project's founder, Tim Smit, explains: "When we first proposed building a world-class garden in what was essentially a moonscape, people thought we were mad. But we believed that even the most damaged places could be regenerated with enough imagination and determination. The Eden Project now stands as a physical embodiment of hope—proof that places and systems we think are beyond repair can actually become sources of new life and learning."

Planting Your Own Seeds of Hope

Ready to plant your own seeds of faith and hope? Here are some practical ways you can begin, no matter your age or circumstances:

For Kids

1. **Start a Hope Journal**: Record examples of environmental healing and positive change you discover through research or personal observation. On discouraging days, read through your collection of hope stories for inspiration.

2. **Create Resilience Art**: Make artwork that shows the transformation from damaged to healed landscapes or that depicts your vision of a sustainable future for your community. Share your art with others to spread hope visually.

3. **Form a Hope Club**: Gather friends who share your concerns about the environment but focus on sharing success stories and creating

positive projects rather than just discussing problems.

4. **Plant Literal Seeds**: Nurture a small garden, even if it's just a few plants in containers. Watching seeds grow into flourishing plants provides a tangible reminder of how small beginnings can yield beautiful results.

Ten-year-old Leila took this approach: "After a science lesson at school, I was really worried about disappearing bees. My mom helped me plant a pollinator garden in our yard with flowers that attract bees and butterflies. It's amazing to see how many insects visit even our small garden! Now, our neighbors are starting pollinator patches, too. It's like our little garden is spreading hope throughout the neighborhood."

For Families

1. **Create a Family Hope Chest**: Collect items that symbolize your family's environmental values and hopes for the future. Include seeds, photos of places you want to protect, articles about positive environmental changes, and notes about your family's actions.

2. **Adopt a Hope Practice**: Choose a regular action that nurtures hope, like sharing a positive environmental news story at dinner each week, praying together for creation care efforts, or celebrating "hope holidays" by planting trees on Earth Day or Arbor Day.

3. **Connect with Hope Communities**: Find a congregation, neighborhood group, or online community that balances honest recognition of environmental challenges with faithful, hopeful action. Surrounding yourself with others who share your concerns and determination makes sustainable hope possible.

4. **Make Hope Visible**: Post Bible verses about hope and renewal in visible places around your home. Add images of environmental restoration projects or Solarpunk artwork to remind your family that positive futures are possible.

For Communities

1. **Host a "Seeds of Hope" Festival**: Organize a community event featuring success stories of environmental restoration, workshops on

sustainable practices, seed exchanges, and art activities that envision positive futures.

2. **Create a Community Story Map**: Document places in your neighborhood that have been successfully restored or protected, along with the stories of people who made it happen. Make this map available online or as a walking tour to inspire others.

3. **Establish Hope Scholarships**: If your church or community organization offers scholarships, consider creating some specifically for young people pursuing education in environmental restoration, sustainable design, or related fields.

4. **Commission Hope Murals**: Transform blank walls into visual stories of environmental healing and community resilience. Public art can transform a neighborhood's narrative from despair to possibility.

Project Box: Personal Seed Faith Project

Choose an environmental concern that feels overwhelming to you. Then follow these steps:

Step 1: Research successful examples of people addressing this specific issue. Find at least three stories of positive change or restoration related to your concern.

Step 2: Identify one small, concrete action you can take this week related to this issue. Remember—mustard seed size is enough!

Step 3: Take that action and document it with a photo or journal entry.

Step 4: Share your action and how it connects to your faith with at least one other person.

Step 5: Reflect on how taking this small step affected your feelings about the larger issue. Did doing something, however small, shift your perspective from helplessness toward hope?

When Hope Feels Hard

Sometimes, despite our best efforts, hope can feel elusive. Environmental news can be discouraging, progress can seem painfully slow, and our individual actions might feel insignificant compared to global challenges. If you're struggling to maintain hope, here are some gentle suggestions:

Remember That Feeling Sad Shows You Care

Environmental grief—feeling sorrow about damage to the natural world—is a healthy response showing your heart is aligned with God's love for creation. Allow yourself to feel these emotions without judgment, knowing they come from a place of love.

Look for the Helpers

As Mr. Rogers famously advised during scary times: "Look for the helpers. You will always find people who are helping." In every environmental challenge, there are people working tirelessly for healing and positive change. Their faithfulness can renew our hope when our own feels depleted.

Embrace "Hope as a Discipline"

Civil rights activist and scholar Mariame Kaba teaches that hope isn't just a feeling but a discipline we practice even when we don't feel particularly hopeful. By choosing hopeful actions even during discouraging times, we gradually strengthen our capacity for sustainable hope.

Rest in God's Bigger Story

While we're responsible for doing our part, ultimately, creation's redemption is God's work, not solely ours. When you feel overwhelmed, it's okay to rest in the knowledge that God is working purposes far beyond what we can see or accomplish alone.

Pastor Garcia offers this encouragement: "Sometimes the most faithful thing we can do is plant our tiny seeds and then rest, trusting God with their growth. Faith means doing what we can while remembering that the final outcome rests in God's hands, not ours. This balance keeps us from both passivity and burnout, allowing us to sustain hope for the long journey."

Seeds That Surprise Us

One of the most amazing things about seeds is how they often surprise us, growing in unexpected ways or places. A crack in a sidewalk somehow nurtures a determined dandelion. A forgotten packet of seeds sprouts years after we thought it had lost its vitality. A tree species thought extinct is rediscovered in a remote canyon.

In the same way, our seeds of faith and hopeful action often yield surprising results—blossoming in ways we couldn't have predicted and producing fruit far beyond our original planting.

Dr. Emma Thompson, a Christian conservationist, shares this perspective: "In twenty years of restoration work, I've learned that ecosystems often have remarkable resilience we didn't anticipate. Areas we thought would take decades to recover sometimes show significant healing within just a few years when given the right conditions. This reminds me of Jesus' parable, in which the Sower is surprised when seeds yield thirty, sixty, or a hundred times what was planted. Both nature and God's kingdom often work through exponential, not just linear, growth—giving us reason for authentic hope even when challenges seem enormous."

Fourteen-year-old Michael discovered this principle through his school's environmental club: "We started a simple plastic recycling campaign, just trying to get kids to use the right bins. But it expanded in ways we never expected. Parents got involved and started a plastic-free lunch challenge. Then, the principal worked with the district to replace plastic utensils with compostables in all schools. Now, we're partnering with a company that turns plastic waste into building materials for affordable housing. Our tiny seed idea just kept growing and branching in amazing directions!"

Looking Ahead

In our next chapter, we'll explore how renewing our minds—changing how we think about ourselves, our possessions, and our relationship with creation—is an essential part of living sustainably. We'll discover how biblical wisdom about simplicity, contentment, and finding our identity in Christ rather than in consumption can free us to live more joyfully with less environmental impact.

For now, remember Jesus' teaching about mustard seed faith. You don't need to solve all the world's environmental problems single-handedly. You simply need to plant your small seeds of faithful action and nurture them with prayer, community support, and perseverance. Then watch with wonder as God brings growth beyond what you could have imagined!

As Isaiah 55:10-11 reminds us:

"For as the rain cometh down, and the snow from heaven, and returneth not thither, but watereth the earth, and maketh it bring forth and bud, that it may give seed to the sower, and bread to the eater: So shall my word be that goeth forth out of my mouth: it shall not return unto me void, but it shall accomplish that which I please, and it shall prosper in the thing whereto I sent it."

God's purposes for healing and restoring creation will ultimately prevail. What an amazing privilege it is to participate in this work by planting our mustard seeds of faith and hope!

Family Discussion Questions:

1. What environmental challenges make you feel worried or discouraged? Where do you see seeds of hope related to those same issues?

2. How might God be inviting our family to plant "mustard seeds" of positive action, even if they seem small compared to the problems?

3. When have you witnessed something small grow into something surprisingly significant?

4. What Bible stories of hope and restoration especially encourage you when facing difficult situations?

Teacher's Corner: This chapter addresses eco-anxiety and climate grief that many young people experience, providing a theological framework for hope without dismissing legitimate concerns. The mustard seed metaphor offers an accessible entry point for discussing complex concepts of faith, agency, and divine partnership in creation care.

For classroom application, consider supplementing this chapter with a "Seeds of Hope" bulletin board where students can post environmental success stories they discover through research or media. This ongoing collection provides visual reinforcement of the chapter's key message that positive change is possible and already happening.

The Personal Seed Faith Project can be expanded into a more comprehensive service-learning initiative. Students document their

211

projects and reflect on the practical outcomes and spiritual/emotional impact of moving from concern to concrete action. This approach integrates academic learning with character development and civic engagement, helping students become not only knowledgeable about environmental challenges but also equipped with the emotional and spiritual resources to address them with resilience and hope.

Chapter 11:

Renewing the Mind: Adopting a Christ-Centered Perspective

The Battle for Your Brain

Have you ever noticed that your mind sometimes feels like a busy playground filled with competing voices? Some voices whisper, "You need that new game to be happy!" while others suggest, "Maybe you could share what you already have." Some voices insist, "Everyone else has this, so you should too!" while quieter ones might ask, "But do I really need it?"

Every day, your amazing brain processes thousands of messages from advertisements, social media, friends, family, and your own inner thoughts. It's like having a super-powerful computer that's constantly running multiple programs at once! But unlike a computer, you can decide which programs to keep running and which ones to close.

In the book of Romans, the Apostle Paul gives us a powerful instruction about how to manage our mental "programs":

"And be not conformed to this world: but be ye transformed by the renewing of your mind, that ye may prove what is that good, and acceptable, and perfect, will of God." (Romans 12:2)

What does it mean to be "conformed to this world"? It means letting the world around us squeeze us into its mold—accepting without question the messages our culture sends about what we should want, how we should live, and what will make us happy.

Think of it like a cookie cutter that tries to shape every person into the same pattern: Buy more stuff! Bigger is better! Newer is always an improvement! You need this to be cool! Success means having lots of things!

But God invites us to something much more exciting—a transformation that happens when we renew our minds! This isn't just thinking positive thoughts or trying harder. It's about letting God's perspective reshape how we see everything:

ourselves, other people, our possessions, and our relationship with the created world.

Philippians 4:8 says, *"Finally, brethren, whatsoever things are true, whatsoever things are honest, whatsoever things are just, whatsoever things are pure, whatsoever things are lovely, whatsoever things are of good report; if there be any virtue, and if there be any praise,* **think on these things**.*"*

Twelve-year-old Marcus discovered this while scrolling through social media: "I kept seeing all these ads for cool sneakers, and everyone at school was talking about them. I felt like I NEEDED those shoes to fit in. However, during youth group, we talked about Romans 12:2 and how God wants us to think differently. I realized I was letting advertisements tell me what was important instead of God. When I prayed about it, I felt peaceful about wearing my regular sneakers and using the money I saved to help with our church's community garden project instead. It felt like my brain got an upgrade!"

The Consumer Treadmill vs. Kingdom Values

One of the biggest ways our minds get "conformed to this world" is through consumer culture—the constant message that buying new things will make us happy, solve our problems, and help us belong.

Think of it as a treadmill: You get something new and feel happy for a little while. But that happiness fades quickly, and soon, you're looking for the next new thing to buy. The treadmill keeps going faster and faster, but no matter how much you get, you never reach a destination of true contentment.

This consumer treadmill is exhausting not only for us, but it is also devastating for God's creation. Manufacturing all those products uses vast amounts of resources and energy, creating pollution and waste. Most of these items are designed to be replaced quickly rather than built to last, adding to our growing mountains of trash.

Jesus taught a completely different way of thinking about possessions and happiness:

"*Lay not up for yourselves treasures upon earth, where moth and rust doth corrupt, and where thieves break through and steal: But lay up for yourselves treasures in heaven, where neither moth nor rust doth corrupt, and where thieves do not break through nor steal: For where your treasure is, there will your heart be also.*" (Matthew 6:19-21)

When we renew our minds according to Jesus' teaching, we step off the consumer treadmill and discover the freedom of Kingdom values:

Consumer Treadmill Values:
- More is always better
- Newer is always an improvement
- Your worth depends on what you own
- Happiness comes from purchasing
- Nature is just raw material for products
- The goal of life is the accumulation of stuff

Kingdom Values:
- Enough is enough
- Well-made and durable is better than disposable

- Your worth comes from being God's beloved creation
  - Joy comes from relationships and purpose
  - Nature is God's masterpiece to be cherished
  - The goal of life is to love God and others

Pastor Kim explains: "Renewing our minds isn't about feeling guilty for having things. It's about freedom from the exhausting pursuit of more and more. When we see our possessions as gifts to be grateful for and tools for serving others rather than as the source of our identity and happiness, we experience the joy and contentment God wants for us."

Activity Box: Advertising Detective

For one day, carry a small notebook and write down every advertisement you notice—on billboards, websites, apps, packaging, clothing logos, etc. At the end of the day, count them up and ask:

- What messages did they send about what would make me happy?
- How did they try to make me feel dissatisfied with what I already have?

- Which ads appealed to my desire to fit in or be cooler?
- How might these messages conflict with what God says about me and what truly matters?

Mindfulness: Paying Attention to God's Presence

One powerful way to renew our minds is through the practice of mindfulness—being fully present and aware in each moment instead of constantly rushing to the next activity or distraction. While mindfulness has become popular in our culture today, Christians have been practicing forms of sacred awareness for thousands of years!

Jesus Himself modeled this careful attention to the present moment. Notice how He observed flowers and birds to teach about God's care (Matthew 6:26-30). See how He gave full attention to the people He encountered, even when His disciples tried to rush Him along. Listen to how He invited His followers to "consider the lilies" and notice God's presence in ordinary things.

When we practice Christ-centered mindfulness, we:

1. **Slow down enough to notice God's gifts all around us**. The brilliant colors of a sunset, the refreshing coolness of the water, the comforting smile of a friend—all these simple pleasures can be missed when we rush through life on autopilot.

2. **Become aware of our thought patterns and redirect them**. When we catch ourselves thinking, "I need a new phone to be happy," or "I'll never have enough," we can gently bring our thoughts back to God's truth: "I am already loved and valuable," and "God provides what I truly need."

3. **Make more intentional choices rather than reacting out of habit**. Instead of automatically reaching for our devices when bored or automatically buying something new when feeling down, we can pause and ask, "What would truly nurture my soul right now? What would honor God and care for creation?"

Thirteen-year-old Sophia discovered this practice during a nature walk with her youth group:

"Our leader asked us to be completely silent for ten minutes and just notice everything around us with all our senses. At first, I thought it would be boring, but then I started hearing birds I'd never noticed before. I felt the wind on my skin and smelled pine trees. I even spotted a tiny wildflower growing through a crack in a rock! It made me realize how many amazing things God creates that I usually miss because I'm busy looking at my phone. Now I try to take 'noticing walks' regularly, and it helps me feel peaceful and grateful instead of always wanting more stuff."

Solarpunk Simplicity: Less Stuff, More Life

Remember the Solarpunk vision we've been exploring throughout this book? One of its core values is simplicity—the idea that a good life doesn't require endless consumption and accumulation of stuff but rather thoughtful choices about what truly matters.

Solarpunk imagines communities where people:

- **Value quality over quantity**, choosing fewer but better-made items that last longer and create less waste

- **Share resources like tools and vehicles** instead of everyone needing to own everything individually
- **Find joy in creating rather than just consuming**, developing skills to make, grow, repair, and repurpose things
- **Design spaces that encourage connection** rather than isolating people with their individual possessions
- **Celebrate experiences and relationships** over accumulating more stuff

These Solarpunk values beautifully align with biblical wisdom! Jesus taught His followers to travel light (Luke 10:4), to share generously with those in need (Luke 3:11), and to find treasure in relationships with God and others rather than in material possessions (Luke 12:15).

The early Christians put these values into practice in remarkable ways:

"And all that believed were together, and had all things common; And sold their possessions and goods, and parted them to all men, as every man had need." (Acts 2:44-45)

While we might not live exactly like the early church today, their example reminds us that Christians have always challenged the "more is better" mindset of the surrounding culture.

Fourteen-year-old Aiden and his family embraced this simplicity after a challenging conversation: "Last year, our basement flooded, and we lost a bunch of stuff. At first, I was really upset about my damaged games and books. But then my dad asked an interesting question: 'Have you even thought about any of these things in the past six months?' I realized I hadn't! Most of it had just been sitting in boxes, unused. That made us rethink how much we really need. Now, before buying something new, we ask if it will truly add value to our lives or just take up space. Our house feels more peaceful with less clutter, and we have more money to share with others and support causes we care about."

Practical Mind Renewal: Exercises for New Thinking Patterns

Renewing your mind isn't something that happens overnight—it's more like building muscle through regular exercise. Here are some practical ways to strengthen your "mind renewal muscles":

For Kids

1. **Gratitude Scavenger Hunt**: Take a walk around your home or neighborhood with a notebook. Try to find and write down 20 things you're thankful for that you didn't pay for—like sunlight through a window, a cool breeze, a funny joke with a friend, or a beautiful tree. This helps train your brain to notice abundance that doesn't come from shopping!

2. **Media Fast Challenge**: Try going 24 hours without social media, video games, or television—activities often filled with consumer messages. Keep a journal of what you notice about your thoughts and feelings during this time.

3. **"Do I Really Need This?" Practice**: When you feel the urge to buy something, pause and ask: "Do I really need this, or just want it? Will it still matter to me in a month? Could I borrow or share instead of buying my own?" These questions help develop discernment.

4. **Creation Connection Time**: Spend 15 minutes each day simply observing and enjoying nature—whether that's watching clouds, caring for a plant, or listening to birds. This builds appreciation for God's gifts that can't be bought or sold.

Ten-year-old Leo tried this last practice: "I started sitting under this big oak tree in our yard for 15 minutes before dinner each day. At first, I was bored, but then I started noticing things. Like how the leaves move differently depending on the wind, the different birds that visit, and even a family of squirrels that has a nest there! Now it's my favorite part of the day, and I don't even bring my phone with me anymore."

For Families

1. **Contentment Conversations**: During family meals, take turns sharing something you already have that you're grateful for, a skill you're developing, or a relationship you value. This counters the culture's message that you always need something new.

2. **Alternative Gift Traditions**: Reimagine celebrations like birthdays and Christmas to emphasize experiences, handmade gifts, or charitable giving alongside or instead of store-bought presents.

3. **"Enough" Inventory**: As a family, discuss what "enough" looks like in different categories—clothes, toys, electronics, furniture, etc. Create guidelines for when something truly needs to be replaced versus when the desire for "new" is driving the purchase.

4. **Sacred Pause Practice**: Before making non-essential purchases, agree to a waiting period (perhaps 24 hours for small items, a week for larger ones). Use this time to pray, consider alternatives, and assess whether the purchase aligns with your family's values.

For Communities

1. **Mindful Consumption Workshops**: Host gatherings where people can learn practical skills for simplifying, such as creating capsule wardrobes, establishing toy libraries, or setting up neighborhood tool-sharing systems.

2. **"What Could Be Different?" Visioning**: After watching a film or reading a book, discuss how the characters' relationship with material possessions affects their happiness. How might their stories be different if they embraced Kingdom values around consumption?

3. **Sabbath Economics Study**: Explore biblical teachings about the Sabbath, the Jubilee, and economic practices that prioritize relationship and enoughness over accumulation. Discuss how these principles might be applied in today's context.

4. **Faith-Based Simplicity Challenges**: Create community challenges like "30 Days of Using What You Have" or "Buy Nothing Month," with regular gatherings to share experiences, struggles, and insights.

Project Box: Mind Renewal Jar

Create a special jar filled with Bible verses and positive thought prompts to replace consumer-driven thinking. Here's how:

You'll need:
- A clean jar with a lid
- Colored paper cut into small strips

- Pens or markers

On each strip of paper, write either:

- A Bible verse about contentment, God's provision, or true treasure
- A question that encourages mindful thinking (e.g., "What's something beautiful you noticed today?" or "How could you creatively use something you already have?")
- A simple action that aligns with Kingdom values (e.g., "Repair something instead of replacing it" or "Share something you own with someone else")

Whenever you notice your thoughts being pulled toward materialism or discontentment, draw a strip from your jar and reflect on it. This simple practice interrupts unhelpful thought patterns and plants seeds of renewed thinking!

Digital Mindfulness: Renewing Your Mind in a Screen-Filled World

Our digital devices can be wonderful tools for learning, connecting, and creating. But they can also become powerful shapers of our minds—often in ways that push us toward conformity with consumer culture rather than transformation by God's values.

Dr. Anderson, a Christian psychologist studying technology's effects on young people, explains: "The average teenager sees thousands of advertisements daily, many disguised as content from friends or influencers. These ads aren't just selling products—they're selling a worldview where happiness comes from consumption, status comes from owning the right things, and nature exists primarily as a source of materials for human use. This directly contradicts God's perspective on what truly matters."

Here are some ways to practice digital mindfulness:

1. Create Sacred Screen-Free Zones and Times

Designate specific spaces (like bedrooms or dinner tables) and times (like the first hour after waking or the hour before bed) as completely screen-free. This allows your mind to connect with God, others, and creation without digital interruption.

2. Use Technology Intentionally, Not Reflexively

Before picking up your device, pause and ask: "Why am I reaching for this right now? What am I hoping to gain? Is there something else that might better meet my actual need?" This simple practice helps you become a mindful user rather than a passive consumer of technology.

3. Curate Your Digital Environment

Just as you wouldn't welcome someone into your home who constantly tried to make you feel inadequate or always tried to sell you things, be selective about what voices you allow into your digital spaces. Unfollow accounts that fuel comparison or discontent and seek out content that aligns with Kingdom values.

4. Practice Digital Sabbaths

Consider taking regular breaks from all screens—perhaps one day each week or one weekend each month—to reset your attention and reconnect with God, people, and the natural world in unmediated ways.

Twelve-year-old Mia shares how this has helped her family: "Every Sunday, we have a 'Digital Sabbath' where all our devices go in a basket until Monday morning. The first few times were HARD—I felt so bored and kept reaching for my phone out of habit! But now I actually look forward to it. We play board games, go hiking, read books, or just talk. I've noticed I sleep better those nights, and I don't feel that weird, anxious feeling of always needing to check for notifications. It's like my brain gets to rest and remember what's actually important."

When Minds and Hearts Align: The Joy of Enough

Something beautiful happens as we practice renewing our minds according to God's perspective rather than consumer culture. We begin to experience the genuine contentment that comes from having "enough" rather than always craving "more."

The Apostle Paul described this transformed mindset in his letter to the Philippians:

"Not that I speak in respect of want: for I have learned, in whatsoever state I am, therewith to be content. I know both how to be abased, and I know how to abound: every where and in all things I am instructed both to be full and to be hungry, both to abound and to suffer need. I can do all things through Christ which strengtheneth me." (Philippians 4:11-13)

Note that Paul says he has "learned" to be content—it wasn't automatic or instant, but a process of training his mind to see things differently.

This contentment isn't about forcing yourself to be happy with less than you need. It's about discovering that your needs are simpler than consumer culture led you to believe and that your deepest longings—for meaning, belonging, and purpose—can't be satisfied by purchasing more stuff.

Pastor Rodriguez puts it this way: "True contentment comes when what we have aligns with what we truly value. When our minds are renewed according to Christ's perspective, we naturally desire different things—meaningful relationships, connection with creation, opportunities to serve others, and time to enjoy God's presence. And these treasures are available to everyone, regardless of financial resources."

Thirteen-year-old Emma experienced this shift during a power outage: "We lost electricity for three days after a big storm. At first, I was freaking out—no internet, no TV, no video games! But by the third day, something weird happened. I found myself actually enjoying the simpler pace. My family played cards by candlelight, we had long conversations, and I spent hours reading and drawing. When the power came back on, I felt oddly disappointed! That experience helped me realize how much of what makes me happy doesn't require electricity or buying things."

Looking Ahead

In our next chapter, we'll explore practical ways to apply this renewed mindset to our relationship with water, which is both a physical resource essential for life and a spiritual metaphor for God's refreshing presence.

Remember that renewing your mind isn't about forcing yourself to think positive thoughts or depriving yourself of things you enjoy. It's about freedom—being transformed by God's perspective so you can experience the genuine joy and contentment that comes from aligning your life with what truly matters.

As you go through this week, try to notice when your thinking is being "conformed to this world" through consumer messages. Gently redirect your thoughts toward God's truth, practicing the mindful awareness of His presence and provision all around you. Like a seed that grows slowly but steadily, these small moments of mind renewal will gradually transform how you see yourself, your possessions, and your place in God's creation.

Family Discussion Questions:

1. When have you felt pressure to buy something in order to be happy or fit in? How did that experience make you feel?

2. What's something you own that brings you genuine joy or serves a meaningful purpose in your

life? What makes it valuable to you beyond its price tag?

3. If Jesus lived in your neighborhood today, what do you think His approach to possessions, technology, and consumption would be?

4. What's one habit or practice our family could adopt to help us be more mindful of God's presence and less caught up in consumer culture?

Teacher's Corner: This chapter addresses environmental stewardship's cognitive and spiritual dimensions, recognizing that sustainable behaviors must be rooted in transformed thinking. For classroom application, consider implementing "mindful moments" throughout the school day—brief pauses for students to notice their surroundings, practice gratitude, or reflect on a scripture verse related to contentment or creation care.

The concept of "enough" provides rich opportunities for cross-curricular connections with mathematics (calculating ecological footprints), social studies (comparing consumption patterns across cultures and historical periods), and language arts (analyzing advertising messages). The digital mindfulness section is particularly relevant for today's students, who navigate complex media environments from an early age.

This chapter intentionally avoids shame-based approaches to consumption, instead emphasizing the freedom and joy found in aligning with Kingdom values. For Christian educators, this provides a foundation for discussing simplicity as a positive spiritual discipline rather than merely a restrictive set of rules. It helps students discover the liberating power of "enough" in a culture that constantly demands "more."

Chapter 12:

Prayer, Meditation, and Energy Flow

The Invisible Connection

Have you ever stood outside during a thunderstorm and felt the electric tingle in the air just before lightning strikes? Or placed your hand near (but not touching!) a speaker playing music and sensed the tiny vibrations flowing through the space between? Maybe you've walked into a room where people were arguing and immediately felt the tension, even though no one was speaking at that moment?

Our world is filled with amazing invisible connections—energy flowing all around us that we can't see with our eyes but can sometimes feel with our hearts and minds. Energy flows through electricity in our homes, radio waves carrying music through the air, and even the thoughts and feelings that pass between people who care about each other.

In this chapter, we'll explore something truly wonderful: how prayer and meditation can tap into these invisible energy flows, connecting us more deeply with God, creation, and each other. We'll also discover how one of history's most brilliant scientists, Nikola Tesla, understood some fascinating patterns in energy that might help us think about our spiritual practices in new ways!

Tesla's Amazing Discoveries About Energy

Nikola Tesla was an extraordinary inventor who lived from 1856 to 1943. He created technologies that help power our world today, including alternating current (AC) electricity that probably lights up your home right now! But beyond his practical inventions, Tesla had fascinating insights about the nature of energy, frequency, and vibration.

Tesla once said: "If you want to find the secrets of the universe, think in terms of energy, frequency, and vibration." He discovered that everything in our world—from the tiniest atom to the largest planet—vibrates at specific frequencies, creating patterns and rhythms that connect in surprising ways.

One of Tesla's most intriguing observations involved the numbers 3, 6, and 9, which he noticed created special patterns in mathematics and energy systems. He reportedly said: "If you only knew the magnificence of the 3, 6, and 9, then you would have a key to the universe."

While scientists are still exploring exactly what Tesla meant by this statement, many people have found these number patterns fascinating, especially when we consider how the number 3 appears throughout creation and Scripture:

- Morning, noon, and night divide our day
- Past, present, and future organize our time
- Body, mind, and spirit form our complete selves
- And most wonderfully, Father, Son, and Holy Spirit reveal God's nature!

Pastor Williams explains: "Tesla observed mathematical patterns that showed how energy flows in cycles and connections. While he approached this from a scientific perspective, we can see something similar in our spiritual lives. Prayer and Scripture create energy flows between us and God, and when we align ourselves with God's patterns, we experience harmony instead of discord."

The Word: Vibrations of Creation

The Gospel of John begins with one of the most powerful statements in all of Scripture:

"In the beginning was the Word, and the Word was with God, and the Word was God." (John 1:1)

This verse tells us something extraordinary: God's creative power operates through His Word. When God speaks, reality itself vibrates in response! Think about it:

"And God said, Let there be light: and there was light." (Genesis 1:3)

God didn't use hands or tools to create the universe—He spoke it into existence! His words carried creative energy that transformed nothingness into everything we see around us.

In Hebrew thinking, words weren't just symbols or sounds—they contained actual power and essence. When God named something, He wasn't just labeling it. He was defining its very nature and purpose. This is why names were so important in Bible times and why God sometimes changed people's names (like Jacob to Israel) when their purpose changed. Jacob's story is in Genesis Chapter 32.

This understanding gives us a new appreciation for spoken prayer and Scripture reading. When we speak God's words aloud, we're not just making sounds. We are releasing vibrational energy that carries meaning and power! The Bible itself tells us:

"So shall my word be that goeth forth out of my mouth: it shall not return unto me void, but it shall accomplish that which I please, and it shall prosper in the thing whereto I sent it." (Isaiah 55:11)

Twelve-year-old Sophia experienced this during a difficult time at school: "I was really nervous about a big presentation, so my mom suggested I read Psalm 56:3 out loud every morning: *'What time I am afraid, I will trust in thee.'* At first, I felt silly talking to my empty bedroom, but after a few days, something changed. Speaking the words aloud made them feel more real than just reading them silently. By the day of my presentation, I could still feel nervous butterflies, but underneath was this calm confidence that God was with me. It was like the words had become part of me!"

Activity Box: Sound Vibration Experiment

Try this simple experiment to see how sound creates physical vibrations!

You'll need:
- A clear plastic bowl or container
- Plastic wrap
- A rubber band
- 1-2 tablespoons of salt or sugar
- A metal spoon

Step 1: Stretch the plastic wrap tightly over the bowl and secure it with the rubber band.

Step 2: Sprinkle the salt or sugar evenly across the plastic wrap surface.

Step 3: Hold the metal spoon near (but not touching) the plastic wrap and tap it firmly or strike it against something metal.

Step 4: Watch how the salt or sugar granules jump and form patterns from the sound vibrations!

This demonstrates that sound isn't just something we hear—it creates physical movement and patterns in the world around us. In a similar way, our prayers and spoken Scripture send energy patterns into the world, though these spiritual vibrations are too subtle for our eyes to see!

The Power of Prayerful Meditation

Prayer is one of the most amazing gifts God has given us—direct communication with the Creator of the universe! But sometimes, our prayers can become rushed or routine. We might rattle off a quick "Thank you for this food, amen" before dinner without really connecting our hearts to God.

That's where meditation comes in—not the kind that empties your mind, but the kind that fills it with God's presence and truth. Biblical meditation means focusing deeply on God's Word, letting it sink from your mind into your heart until it begins to transform how you think, feel, and live.

King David understood this practice well:

"O how love I thy law! it is my meditation all the day." (Psalm 119:97)

"Let the words of my mouth, and the meditation of my heart, be acceptable in thy sight, O LORD, my strength, and my redeemer." (Psalm 19:14)

When we combine prayer (speaking to God) with meditation (reflecting deeply on God's Word), we create a complete energy circuit. God's truth flows into us through Scripture, and our response flows back to God through prayer. This sacred rhythm aligns us with God's vibrations of love, truth, and creativity.

Pastor Garcia explains, "Think of prayer meditation like tuning a musical instrument. If you've ever heard an orchestra tune-up, you know how chaotic it sounds at first—each instrument playing its own note. But once they all tune to the same frequency, beautiful harmony becomes possible. In the same way, prayer meditation tunes our hearts to God's frequency, allowing us to live in harmony with His purposes."

The 3-6-9 Prayer Routine

Remember those special numbers 3, 6, and 9—that Tesla found so significant in the patterns of energy? Some Christians have created a simple prayer routine based on these numbers to help them maintain spiritual connection throughout their day. This isn't a magic formula or secret code—just a practical rhythm that many find helpful for staying spiritually aligned.

Here's how the 3-6-9 Prayer Routine works:

3 Minutes of Morning Scripture (Beginning the Day)

Start your day with just three minutes of reading Scripture aloud. This doesn't have to be many verses—even a single verse read thoughtfully can set the tone for your entire day. The key is to speak the words aloud, allowing their vibrations to enter your mind and your body. As you read, imagine God's truth creating ripples of light and energy that flow through you and out into your day.

Fourteen-year-old Micah shares: "I used to check my phone first thing every morning, but now I keep my Bible by my bed and read just a few verses aloud before my feet hit the floor. It's only three minutes, but it's like setting the background music for my whole day. Even when things get crazy later, I can still hear those words echoing in my mind."

6 Moments of Mindful Prayer (Throughout the Day)

Six times during your day—perhaps once every 2-3 hours—pause for just a moment of mindful connection with God. This doesn't require closing your eyes or saying formal prayers (though you can if circumstances permit). It might be as simple as taking three conscious breaths while thinking, "God, I remember You are with me right now."

These brief pauses interrupt the chaotic frequencies of busy life and realign you with God's presence. They're like spiritual "reset buttons" that prevent you from being completely absorbed in the world's patterns and rhythms.

Eleven-year-old Leila discovered this practice during her school day: "My teacher doesn't know it, but when we transition between subjects, I use that moment to silently say 'Thank you, God' for something specific. Sometimes, it's just 'Thanks for helping me understand that math problem' or 'Thanks for my friend who shared her snack.' It only takes seconds, but it helps me notice God's presence even in ordinary school moments."

9 Minutes of Evening Reflection (Ending the Day)

Before bed, spend nine minutes in reflective prayer—reviewing your day with God, expressing gratitude, seeking guidance, or simply resting in God's presence. This longer period allows for deeper connection and helps transition your mind and spirit from the day's activities to restful sleep.

In many cultures, the number nine has traditionally symbolized completion or fulfillment. Ending your day with this practice helps you feel complete, releasing anything unresolved into God's capable hands.

Project Box: Create Your 3-6-9 Prayer Journal

Design a simple journal to support your 3-6-9 prayer routine!

You'll need:

- A notebook or journal (or create one from folded paper)
- Colored markers or pencils

- Stickers or decorative elements (optional)

Create three sections:

1. Morning Scripture: Write down short verses you might want to read during your 3-minute morning time.

2. Mindful Moments: Note simple phrases or breath prayers for your six daily pauses.

3. Evening Reflections: Create a template with prompts like "Today I'm grateful for...", "I felt God's presence when...", and "Tomorrow I need God's help with..."

Personalize your journal with colors and designs that bring you joy, making it a special place for connecting with God through the 3-6-9 rhythm.

Nikola Tesla, Energy, and the Trinity

One of the most fascinating connections between Nikola Tesla's observations and Christian faith involves the number three. Tesla recognized that the number three (along with its multiples six and nine) created special patterns in energy systems. Similarly, Christianity reveals God as the Trinity—Father, Son, and Holy Spirit—three persons in perfect unity.

This divine pattern of three-in-one appears throughout creation:

- Water exists as liquid, solid (ice), and gas (vapor)—three forms of one substance
- Time flows as past, present, and future—three aspects of one continuity
- Space extends in length, width, and height—three dimensions of one reality

Dr. Elizabeth Chen, both a physicist and Christian theologian, explains: "Nikola Tesla observed these mathematical patterns without necessarily connecting them to faith. However, as Christians, we can see in these patterns that they reflect the Creator's nature. The Trinity isn't just a theological concept—it's the fundamental pattern of relationship woven into the fabric of creation itself."

When we practice prayer-meditation with awareness of these patterns, we participate in the energy flow of God's triune nature. The Father's creative power, the Son's redeeming love, and the Spirit's sustaining presence flow through us and back to God in a continuous circuit of grace.

Energy Flow in Creation Care

This understanding of prayer, vibration, and energy has profound implications for how we care for God's creation. If everything in the universe vibrates with energy that ultimately flows from God, then our relationship with the natural world takes on new significance.

When we pray for the healing of damaged ecosystems, bless our gardens, or express gratitude for the beauty of a forest or ocean, we're participating in restoring proper energy flow between humans and the rest of creation.

The Solarpunk communities we've explored throughout this book intuitively understand this connection. Many incorporate regular practices of gratitude, blessing, and mindful attention alongside their practical sustainability efforts. They recognize that technological solutions alone aren't enough—our inner relationship with creation matters just as much as our outer actions.

Thirteen-year-old Rain shares how her family combines prayer with their garden work: "Every spring, when we plant our garden, we have a blessing ceremony. We read Genesis 1:11-12 where God commands plants to grow and bear seeds, and then we each say a prayer of thanks for the soil, seeds, sun, rain, and the people who will eventually eat the food. Mom says it reminds us that we're not really 'making' the garden grow—we're just cooperating with God's energy that's already flowing through creation."

Practical Applications: Energy-Aware Prayer Practices

Ready to experience the energy flow of prayer meditation in your own life? Here are some age-appropriate practices for kids, families, and communities:

For Kids

1. **Scripture Sound Waves**: Choose a short Bible verse and experiment with speaking it in different ways—whispered, sung, chanted, or spoken with different emotions. Notice how each approach creates a different feeling or vibration in your body and the space around you.

2. **Prayer Walking**: Take a slow, mindful walk through a natural area. With each step, silently or softly, say one word of thanks for something you

notice (Tree... Bird... Cloud... Friend...). Feel how your prayers connect you with each part of God's creation.

3. **Breath Prayer Rhythms**: Learn simple breath prayers that match your breathing pattern. As you inhale, think or whisper, "God is," and as you exhale, "with me." Try different phrases that are meaningful to you, allowing your breath and prayer to create a harmonious rhythm.

4. **Creation Conversation**: Find a quiet spot in nature and imagine having a conversation with something non-human—a tree, stream, or animal. First, tell it something you appreciate about it. Then quietly "listen" for what it might say back to you about its Creator. This isn't about actually hearing voices but using your imagination to connect more deeply with God through His creation.

Nine-year-old Marco tried this last practice: "I sat by this huge old oak tree in the park and told it I liked how strong and tall it was. Then I closed my eyes and tried to imagine what the tree might say back. In my mind, I heard, 'I've been standing here praising God with every leaf for a hundred years—

would you like to join me?' It made me think about how all creation constantly worshipped God, even when humans are too busy to notice!"

For Families

1. **Sound Bath Scripture Reading**: Take turns reading favorite Bible passages aloud while family members lie down with eyes closed, simply receiving the vibrations of the words without trying to analyze their meaning. Afterward, share what you felt or experienced during the reading.

2. **3-6-9 Family Rhythm**: Adapt the 3-6-9 routine for family life. Read a verse together at breakfast (3), pause for a brief moment of gratitude before each meal and at bedtime (6), and spend a few minutes sharing highlights and challenges before evening prayers (9).

3. **Energy Blessing Circle**: Stand in a circle holding hands. One person begins by speaking a blessing or prayer for the person to their right. The person receives the blessing and then passes it on to the next person. Imagine God's love flowing through the circle like electricity in a circuit.

4. **Creation Care Prayers**: Before undertaking environmental activities like gardening, recycling, or conservation projects, gather for prayer, acknowledging God as the source of all energy and life. This will connect your physical actions with a spiritual purpose.

For Communities

1. **Prayer Labyrinths**: Create temporary or permanent prayer labyrinths in church yards or community spaces. These walking paths help people experience prayer as a physical journey with patterns and rhythms that reflect life's spiritual energy flows.

2. **Sound Healing Services**: Host worship gatherings that incorporate sustained tones from singing bowls, chimes, or humming alongside Scripture reading and prayer. These vibrations can help people experience God's presence in new ways that transcend intellectual understanding.

3. **3-6-9 Community Challenge**: Invite community members to practice the 3-6-9 prayer routine for 21 days (3×7), providing support materials and gathering periodically to share

experiences. This creates both individual and collective energy alignment.

4. **Sacred Ecology Workshops**: Offer learning experiences that connect scientific understanding of energy and ecosystems with spiritual practices of prayer and Scripture meditation, helping people see creation care as both practical and mystical.

The Dance of Energy: Science and Faith Together

Some people believe that science and faith are opponents in a battle for truth. But what if they're actually dance partners in a beautiful exploration of God's created order? Tesla's scientific insights about energy, frequency, and vibration don't contradict our faith—they offer us new metaphors and models for understanding how God's Spirit might move in and through our world.

When Jesus explained spiritual truths, He often used examples from the physical world that people could see and touch—seeds growing, bread rising, water flowing. He knew that the visible world provides windows into invisible realities. In the same way, modern scientific understandings of energy and vibration can deepen our appreciation for spiritual practices like prayer and Scripture meditation.

Dr. James Washington, both a pastor and a physicist, shares: "Nikola Tesla was correct that energy flows in patterns throughout the universe. Where he saw mathematical principles, we as Christians can recognize the fingerprints of a Creator who designs with beautiful precision. Our prayers don't operate by magical formulas, but they do align us with the fundamental energy patterns God has woven into creation—patterns of giving and receiving, speaking and listening, flowing out and returning home."

Looking Ahead

In our next chapter, we'll explore how the natural element of water—essential for all life—serves as both a physical resource to be stewarded and a spiritual metaphor for God's refreshing, cleansing presence. We'll discover practical water conservation techniques alongside the deeper meaning of Jesus' promise to be "living water" for our souls.

For now, remember that prayer isn't just words disappearing into the air. When you pray and meditate on Scripture, you participate in the vibrant energy flow between Creator and creation. Your words, thoughts, and intentions create ripples that extend far beyond what you can see, connecting you with God's own rhythms of renewal and restoration for both people and the planet.

As you practice the 3-6-9 prayer routine or other spiritual disciplines this week, pay attention to how they affect your energy levels, your awareness of God's presence, and your connection to the created world around you. Like Tesla discovering invisible patterns in the universe's energy systems, you might begin to notice the subtle yet powerful ways that prayer creates harmony between your life and God's eternal purposes.

Family Discussion Questions:

1. Have you ever felt a place's "energy" or atmosphere change after prayer or worship? What was that experience like?

2. How might speaking God's Word aloud create different effects than just reading silently to yourself?

3. Where do you see patterns of three in creation that might reflect God's Trinitarian nature?

4. What time of day do you feel most connected to God? How might the 3-6-9 rhythm help you maintain that connection throughout your day?

Teacher's Corner: This chapter bridges scientific and spiritual understandings of energy in ways that honor both domains while maintaining theological integrity. For classroom application, the sound vibration experiment offers a hands-on demonstration of how invisible energy creates visible effects—a powerful metaphor for prayer that respects children's concrete thinking while inviting them into deeper spiritual awareness.

While this chapter discusses Tesla's observations about numerical patterns, it carefully avoids numerology or magical thinking. Instead, it uses these patterns as helpful memory devices and structural frameworks for prayer practices. The 3-6-9 routine offers a developmentally appropriate approach to spiritual disciplines that acknowledges children's need for concrete, time-bound practices while introducing them to contemplative traditions.

Consider supplementing this chapter with simple sound experiments using tuning forks, water, or string instruments to further demonstrate how vibrations create patterns, resonance, and harmony—all rich metaphors for spiritual alignment with God's purposes. The creation care connection emphasizes that our prayer practices aren't merely personal spiritual exercises but participate in God's ongoing work of cosmic restoration.

Chapter 13:

Living Water: Sustainable Practices for Daily Life

The Magic of Water

Splash! Drip-drop! Whoosh! Water is one of the most amazing substances on our planet—have you ever stopped to really think about it? This incredible liquid can transform from solid ice to flowing water to invisible vapor. It can carve mighty canyons and nurture the tiniest seed. Every living thing on Earth depends on water, from the tallest redwood tree to the smallest bacteria. Even you are mostly water—about 60% of your body!

But water isn't just physically essential—it's also spiritually significant. Throughout the Bible, water symbolizes God's presence, cleansing, renewal, and life-giving power. From the waters of creation in Genesis to the river of life in Revelation, water flows through Scripture just as it flows through our world.

In a famous conversation with a woman at a well, Jesus made an extraordinary statement about water that connects physical thirst with spiritual longing:

"Whosoever drinketh of the water that I shall give him shall never thirst; but the water that I shall give him shall be in him a well of water springing up into everlasting life." (John 4:14)

What an amazing promise! Jesus offers "living water" to satisfy our deepest spiritual thirst. This beautiful metaphor also reminds us how precious physical water is and how important it is to care for this gift that sustains all life on our planet.

In this chapter, we'll explore the wonder of water from both spiritual and practical perspectives. We'll discover how Jesus' promise of living water can refresh our souls while also learning practical ways to conserve and protect the physical water that sustains our bodies and our world. Get ready to dive into the amazing world of water!

Jesus: The Source of Living Water

When Jesus spoke about "living water," people in His time would have immediately understood the reference. In a hot, dry region like ancient Israel, the difference between stagnant water and flowing, "living" water was significant. Stagnant water in cisterns could become contaminated and taste stale, while fresh, flowing spring water was clean, cool, and life-giving.

But Jesus wasn't just talking about physical water. He was offering something much deeper—a spiritual connection with God that would satisfy the soul's deepest longings. Throughout Scripture, God is described as the source of life-giving water:

"For my people have committed two evils; they have forsaken me the fountain of living waters, and hewed them out cisterns, broken cisterns, that can hold no water." (Jeremiah 2:13)

"O LORD, the hope of Israel, all that forsake thee shall be ashamed, and they that depart from me shall be written in the earth, because they have forsaken the LORD, the fountain of living waters." (Jeremiah 17:13)

Jesus' conversation with the Samaritan woman at the well reveals something wonderful about God's character. While others avoided this woman because of cultural and religious differences, Jesus engaged with her directly, offering her living water that would forever quench her spiritual thirst. This shows us that God's refreshing presence is available to everyone, regardless of background or status.

Twelve-year-old Mia from Arizona reflects: "When I first read the story about Jesus and the woman at the well, I was confused about what 'living water' meant. But then my youth pastor explained that it's like this: if you drink normal water, you'll get thirsty again soon. But Jesus gives us a kind of spiritual water that keeps filling us up from the inside. I think about this when I'm feeling lonely or sad—I can pray and ask Jesus to fill me with His living water, and it helps me feel peaceful again."

This spiritual understanding of water also deepens our appreciation for physical water. When we recognize water as a sacred gift that reflects

God's provision and sustaining presence, we're more likely to value and protect it rather than take it for granted or waste it.

Activity Box: Water Meditation

Find a quiet place and pour a glass of clean water. Hold it carefully in your hands and consider these questions:

- Where did this water come from? What journey did it take to reach you?
- How many ways did you use water today? How would your life be different without it?
- As you take a sip, feel the water refreshing your body. How might Jesus' living water refresh your spirit in a similar way?
- Say a simple prayer of thanks for both physical water and the living water Jesus offers.

Our Water Planet: A Precious Resource

Earth is often called the "Blue Planet" because about 71% of its surface is covered with water. From space, our world appears as a beautiful blue marble swirled with white clouds. With so much water visible from space, it might seem like we have an endless supply!

But here's a surprising fact: only about 3% of Earth's water is freshwater that people can use, and most of that is locked up in ice caps and glaciers. Less than 1% of all Earth's water is available freshwater in lakes, rivers, and underground aquifers. This tiny fraction must support all human needs—drinking, farming, manufacturing—plus the needs of every freshwater ecosystem!

Today, many regions face water challenges:

- **Water Scarcity**: About 1.1 billion people worldwide lack access to clean water. By 2025, two-thirds of the world's population may face water shortages.

- **Water Pollution**: Industrial waste, agricultural runoff, and improper waste disposal contaminate precious water supplies.

- **Climate Change**: Shifting weather patterns are causing more droughts in some regions and flooding in others, making water availability less predictable.

- **Wasteful Practices**: In regions with abundant water, people often use far more than they need, and up to 50% of the water is lost through leaky pipes, inefficient appliances, and careless habits.

Thirteen-year-old Jamal shares his experience: "My state has had serious droughts for years. When I was little, our lawn turned brown because of water restrictions, and we had to take super-short showers. It made me realize water isn't something we can take for granted. My family started collecting rainwater and reusing 'gray water' from our sink to water plants. Now, even when we're not in a drought, we still treat water as precious."

As Christians who value God's creation and care about future generations, we have a special responsibility to be wise stewards of water resources. The good news is that each of us can make a significant difference through our daily choices and habits!

Rainwater: Catching Heaven's Gift

One of the most ancient and effective water conservation practices is rainwater harvesting, which involves collecting and storing rainwater for later use. This practice has existed throughout history and across cultures, including in the Bible, where cisterns (underground tanks) were used to store precious rainwater in dry regions.

Rainwater harvesting has many benefits:

- It reduces demand on municipal water supplies
- It decreases stormwater runoff that can cause erosion and flooding
- It provides water that's naturally soft and free of chemicals
- It connects us directly to the water cycle, helping us appreciate this amazing natural process

Today's rainwater harvesting systems range from simple rain barrels to complex collection systems. Here's how you and your family can start harvesting this gift from above:

Simple Rain Barrel Setup

A basic rain barrel system collects water from your roof through downspouts. Here's how to create one (with adult help):

1. **Get a Food-Grade Barrel**: Look for a 55-gallon food-grade plastic barrel (often available from car washes or food processing companies).

2. **Prepare the Barrel**: Clean it thoroughly and drill a hole near the bottom for a spigot (like a garden hose faucet).

3. **Add Overflow Protection**: Drill a hole near the top and attach a hose that will direct excess water away from your home's foundation when the barrel fills.

4. **Create a Debris Filter**: Cut a hole in the lid and cover it with a fine mesh screen to keep out leaves, insects, and debris.

5. **Position the Barrel**: Place it on a stable, level platform (cinder blocks work well) under a downspout.

6. **Modify the Downspout**: Either cut the downspout or use a diverter to direct water into your barrel.

One inch of rain falling on a 1,000-square-foot roof can yield approximately 600 gallons of water! Even a single rain barrel can capture enough water to significantly reduce your garden watering needs.

Eleven-year-old Sofia's family installed a rain barrel system: "My dad and I set up two rain barrels connected to each other. We painted them with cool nature designs, so they look nice in our yard. Now, when we need to water our vegetable garden, we use rainwater instead of the hose. During a big rainstorm, it's amazing how fast they fill up! It feels like we're getting a free gift every time it rains."

Advanced Collection Systems

For those looking to harvest more rainwater, more sophisticated systems might include:

- **Multiple Connected Barrels**: Linking several barrels to increase storage capacity.
- **Underground Cisterns**: Large underground tanks storing hundreds or thousands of gallons.
- **First-Flush Diverters**: Devices that divert the first few gallons of rainwater (which might contain more contaminants from the roof) away from the storage tank.
- **Pumps and Filtration**: These systems allow rainwater to be used for more purposes, including indoor non-potable uses like toilet flushing.

Some Solarpunk communities have designed beautiful, integrated rainwater systems that are both functional and artistic. These include spiral gardens with central collection ponds, sculptural water features that clean and aerate stored water, and living walls fed by rainwater that provide both beauty and food!

Project Box: Create a Miniature Rain Garden

Rain gardens help slow, filter, and absorb rainwater. Try making this mini version!

You'll need:

- A shallow container with drainage holes (like a plant saucer or small plastic tub)
- Small rocks or gravel
- Soil
- Small plants that like occasional wetness (ask at a garden center for recommendations)
- A watering can

Step 1: Place rocks in the bottom of your container.

Step 2: Add soil on top of the rocks, creating a slight depression in the middle.

Step 3: Plant your water-friendly plants in the soil.

Step 4: Place your mini rain garden where it will catch some rainfall or gently pour water from a watering can to simulate rain. Watch how the water collects in the depression, slowly filters through the soil, and eventually drains out the bottom.

This demonstrates how full-size rain gardens work to manage stormwater while providing habitat and beauty!

Every Drop Counts: Water Conservation at Home

Beyond harvesting rainwater, there are many ways we can be more mindful of our water use in daily life. These practices honor the preciousness of water and ensure that future generations will have access to this vital resource.

In the Bathroom

The bathroom accounts for about 60% of indoor water use in most homes! Here's how to reduce that:

- **Check for Leaks**: A single dripping faucet can waste 3,000 gallons per year! Place a few drops of food coloring in your toilet tank. If color appears in the bowl without flushing, you have a leak.

- **Shower Smarter**: Take shorter showers (try setting a 5-minute timer) and install a low-flow showerhead. Turn off the water while lathering.
- **Sink Sense**: Turn off the tap while brushing your teeth or washing your face. This simple habit can save hundreds of gallons monthly.
- **Flush Less**: Follow the rhyme: "If it's yellow, let it mellow; if it's brown, flush it down." Depending on your toilet's age, each flush uses 1.6-5 gallons.

Fourteen-year-old Daniel tried a conservation experiment: "For science class, I decided to measure how much water our family uses in a week. I was shocked to find that leaving the water running while brushing teeth wasted about 5 gallons per person daily! We all committed to turning off the tap, and our water bill actually went down the next month. It was cool to see how one small change made a real difference."

In the Kitchen

From cooking to cleaning, kitchens use lots of water:

- **Fill Dishwashers**: Running full loads of dishes is more efficient than washing by hand or doing partial loads.
- **Use Basin Method**: When washing dishes by hand, fill one basin with soapy water and another with rinse water instead of running the tap continuously.
- **Save Cooking Water**: Water used to cook pasta or steam vegetables contains nutrients and can water plants once it cools.
- **Keep Drinking Water in the Fridge**: Running the tap until it gets cold wastes several gallons. Instead, fill a pitcher and refrigerate it.

In the Yard

Outdoor watering can account for 30-70% of residential water use:

- **Water Deeply but Infrequently**: This encourages deeper root growth and more resilient plants. Morning is best to reduce evaporation.
- **Use Drip Irrigation**: These systems deliver water directly to plant roots with minimal waste.

- **Mulch Gardens**: A two-to-three-inch layer of mulch reduces evaporation and helps soil retain moisture.
- **Plant Native Species**: Plants adapted to your local climate often require less supplemental water once established.
- **Rethink Your Lawn**: Consider replacing part or all of your grass lawn with water-wise plants, a vegetable garden, or a natural meadow.

Activity Box: Become a Water Detective

Investigate your home's water use with this fun activity:

Step 1: Make a list of all the ways your household uses water in a typical day.

Step 2: For one day, carry a small notebook and tally every instance of water usage that you notice.

Step 3: Identify three ways your family could reduce water consumption.

Step 4: Present your findings and suggestions to your family. Could you challenge yourselves to implement these changes for two weeks?

Step 5: If possible, compare your water bill before and after making these changes.

Gray Water: Using Water Twice

When you wash your hands or take a shower, the water that goes down the drain isn't dirty enough to require full treatment—it's just "gray" rather than clear. This "gray water" can be reused for certain purposes, extending the value of each gallon and reducing overall water consumption.

Simple gray water practices include:

- **Bucket in the Shower**: Place a bucket in the shower to catch water while you wait for it to warm up. The clean water can be used for houseplants or outdoor gardens.
- **Laundry to Landscape**: In some areas, it's legal and practical to divert washing machine water directly to landscape irrigation through special hoses and filters.
- **Sink-to-Toilet Systems**: Some eco-homes have sinks mounted on toilet tanks, so hand-washing water fills the tank for the next flush.

Mrs. Garcia, who teaches environmental science, explains: "Gray water reuse mimics what happens in natural water cycles—water is used multiple times as it travels through ecosystems.

When we reuse water, we participate in this beautiful cycle God designed, where nothing is wasted, and everything serves multiple purposes."

Solarpunk Communities: Water Wisdom in Action

Throughout this book, we've explored how Solarpunk communities reimagine sustainable living. Here's how some of these communities approach water stewardship:

The Water Village in Portugal

In a small Portuguese town, residents transformed their water systems using both ancient wisdom and modern technology. Rooftops collect rainwater, while artistic bioswales along streets filter runoff into underground cisterns. Nearly 80% of the community's water needs are met through harvested rainwater, and all household gray water flows through beautiful plant-filled filtration gardens before returning to groundwater.

"Our grandparents knew how to value water," explains community founder Maria Santos. "They had sayings like 'Clear water is worth gold.' We're combining their wisdom with new technology to create closed-loop water systems where every drop serves multiple purposes before returning to the earth."

The Urban Oasis Project in Arizona

In Phoenix, Arizona—one of America's driest cities—a neighborhood association transformed a vacant lot into a water-harvesting demonstration site. Curved earthworks catch rainwater during infrequent storms, slowing it and allowing it to soak into the soil instead of running off. Desert-adapted fruit trees and native plants now thrive in what was once barren ground, creating a green oasis that serves as both a community garden and an educational center.

Twelve-year-old Aiden, who volunteers at the site, shares: "We've calculated that our half-acre site captures about 100,000 gallons of rainwater annually that used to just flow into storm drains! Now that water grows pomegranates, figs, and dates that we share with the neighborhood. It's amazing what happens when you work with nature instead of against it."

The Church of Living Waters

A church in Seattle redesigned their property to demonstrate creation care through water stewardship. They removed half their parking lot and replaced it with permeable paving that allows rainwater to soak through rather than run off. Rainwater from the roof flows into a series of beautiful rain gardens that spell out "LIVING WATER" when viewed from above. These gardens filter pollutants, reduce flooding, and create habitat for birds and beneficial insects.

"We wanted our physical building to reflect our theology," explains Pastor Williams. "Jesus is the living water, and we are called to be good stewards of physical water too. Visitors often come just to see our water systems, giving us opportunities to share about environmental stewardship and Jesus' offer of spiritual living water."

Spiritual Practices: Connecting Water and Faith

The powerful metaphor of Jesus as living water can inspire spiritual practices that deepen both our faith and our appreciation for physical water:

Baptismal Remembrance

In baptism, water symbolizes cleansing, new life, and participation in Christ's death and resurrection. Create a simple practice of touching your forehead each morning while praying: "Thank you, Jesus, for being my living water today. Help me remember my baptism and live as your new creation."

Blessing Everyday Water

Before drinking a glass of water, say a brief blessing: "Thank you, God, for the gift of water that sustains all life. May I never take it for granted, and may all people have access to clean water."

Scripture Water Meditation

Choose a Bible verse about water (like John 4:14, Isaiah 44:3, or Revelation 22:17) and reflect on it while observing water in some form—a stream, rainfall, or even just water flowing from a faucet. Consider how the physical properties of water illuminate the spiritual truth in the verse.

Thirteen-year-old Leila shares her experience: "During a youth retreat, our leader had us sit beside a stream and read Psalm 42:1—*'As the hart panteth after the water brooks, so panteth my soul after thee, O God.*' Then we stayed quiet for five minutes just watching the water and thinking about what it means to truly thirst for God. It made the verse so much more real to me, and now whenever I see a stream or river, I remember that my soul needs God just like my body needs water."

Looking Ahead

In our next chapter, we'll explore how facing environmental challenges requires courage and faith, similar to what David needed when confronting Goliath. We'll discover biblical principles for approaching seemingly insurmountable problems with confidence in God's power and presence.

Remember that Jesus offers living water that satisfies our deepest spiritual needs. As we experience this refreshing spiritual reality, may we also become better stewards of the physical water that sustains all life on our beautiful blue planet. Every time you take a drink, turn on a faucet, or feel the blessing of rain, let it remind you of both the practical value of water conservation and the spiritual promise of Christ's living water flowing within you.

Family Discussion Questions:

1. Where have you experienced water today? How would your life be different without easy access to clean water?

2. What's one water conservation practice our family could adopt this week?

3. When Jesus spoke of offering "living water," what do you think He meant? How have you experienced this spiritual water in your own life?

4. What's the connection between valuing Jesus as our spiritual living water and caring for physical water in creation?

Teacher's Corner: This chapter bridges scriptural metaphor with practical environmental stewardship, helping students connect spiritual concepts and tangible actions. The water metaphor provides an accessible entry point for discussing both theological concepts (Jesus as living water) and environmental principles (water conservation).

For classroom application, consider conducting water audits of your school building or implementing simple rainwater harvesting for a school garden. These hands-on activities provide experiential learning opportunities while reinforcing the chapter's core message that water is both spiritually significant and physically precious.

The activities suggested throughout the chapter incorporate multiple learning styles—kinesthetic learning (water experiments), visual learning (observing water systems), and reflective practices (water meditations). This multisensory approach helps students internalize both the scientific concepts of water conservation and the spiritual symbolism of water in Scripture.

Chapter 14:

Sustainable Living Through Biblical Wisdom

Seeds of Truth: The Parable of the Sower

Have you ever planted a seed and watched with wonder as it pushed through the soil, unfurling its first tiny leaves toward the sunlight? There's something almost magical about planting—taking a small, seemingly lifeless speck and witnessing it transform into a towering sunflower, a juicy tomato, or a fragrant herb. It's one of nature's most amazing miracles!

Jesus knew the power of seeds and soil to teach important lessons. That's why He shared one of His most famous stories—the Parable of the Sower:

"Behold, a sower went forth to sow; And when he sowed, some seeds fell by the way side, and the fowls came and devoured them up: Some fell upon stony places, where they had not much earth: and

forthwith they sprung up, because they had no deepness of earth: And when the sun was up, they were scorched; and because they had no root, they withered away. And some fell among thorns; and the thorns sprung up, and choked them: But other fell into good ground, and brought forth fruit, some an hundredfold, some sixtyfold, some thirtyfold." (Matthew 13:3-8)

While Jesus used this story primarily to explain how people receive God's Word differently, it also contains remarkable wisdom about caring for the earth! Every gardener knows that successful growing depends on understanding the relationship between seeds and soil—just as Jesus described nearly 2,000 years ago.

This chapter will explore how biblical wisdom, especially from parables like the Sower, offers profound guidance for sustainable living today. We'll discover connections between ancient agricultural knowledge and modern organic gardening, learn how to harness the sun's energy wisely, and explore how communities can balance self-sufficiency with mutual support—just as God intended!

The Good Earth: Organic Gardening and Biblical Wisdom

The Parable of the Sower reveals several key insights about successful growing that align perfectly with modern organic gardening principles:

1. Soil Health Is Everything

In Jesus' parable, the same seed produced completely different results depending on the soil quality. The seed on the path couldn't even take root, the seed in rocky soil couldn't develop strong roots, and the seed among thorns was choked out, but the seed in good soil produced an abundant harvest.

Modern organic gardeners deeply understand this principle: Healthy soil creates healthy plants. Instead of relying on synthetic fertilizers that simply feed plants, organic methods focus on building living soil full of beneficial microorganisms, earthworms, and natural nutrients.

Twelve-year-old Miguel from New Mexico shares his gardening experience: "My grandpa taught me that you don't feed the plant, you feed the soil, and the soil feeds the plant. We make compost from kitchen scraps and fallen leaves, and our garden soil gets better every year. Last summer, our tomato plants grew taller than me!"

2. Working With Nature, Not Against It

Notice that in Jesus' parable, the Sower didn't try to change the seeds' fundamental nature or force them to grow in poor conditions. Instead, the lesson focuses on providing the right environment for natural growth.

Organic gardening follows this same wisdom—working with nature's systems rather than fighting against them. This includes:

- **Companion Planting**: Growing plants together that help each other, like planting basil near tomatoes to improve flavor and repel pests.
- **Natural Pest Management** involves encouraging beneficial insects, such as ladybugs and praying mantises, to control harmful bugs instead of using toxic chemicals.

- **Crop Rotation**: Changing what grows in each garden area yearly to prevent soil depletion and disease buildup.

These approaches mirror God's design for creation, where diverse plants and animals work together in balanced ecosystems.

3. Patience and Observation

Another subtle lesson from the parable is the importance of observation and patience. The Sower had to understand different soil conditions and the growth process, which takes time.

Organic gardening requires this same patient observation—noticing which areas of your garden receive more sunlight, which plants thrive together, how weather affects growth, and how soil changes over seasons. Unlike industrial agriculture's "quick fix" approach, organic methods take time but produce healthier, more sustainable results.

Activity Box: Soil Testing Adventure

Discover what kind of "soil" you have in different areas around your home!

You'll need:

- Several clear glass jars with lids

- Soil samples from different locations (garden, yard, near trees, etc.)
- Water
- Small notebook and pencil

Step 1: Fill each jar about 1/3 full with different soil samples, labeling where each came from.

Step 2: Add water until jars are about 2/3 full, then tighten lids and shake vigorously.

Step 3: Set jars somewhere they won't be disturbed and observe what happens over 24 hours.

Step 4: Record your observations in your notebook: Which soil settled into clear layers? Which remained muddy? Which had material floating on top?

Healthier soils typically show distinct layers of sand (bottom), silt (middle), and clay (top), with organic matter floating. This simple test gives you clues about your soil's composition, just like the Sower in Jesus' parable needed to understand different soil types!

Creating Good Soil: Biblical Composting

Throughout Scripture, we find the principle that death leads to new life—a core concept in both our faith and in organic gardening! Jesus taught:

"Verily, verily, I say unto you, Except a corn of wheat fall into the ground and die, it abideth alone: but if it die, it bringeth forth much fruit." (John 12:24)

This spiritual principle is directly paralleled in composting, the process of transforming "dead" organic materials like food scraps, yard waste, and fallen leaves into rich, living soil. Composting is like witnessing resurrection on a small scale!

In biblical times, farmers understood this concept well. They practiced methods we might now call "sheet composting"—allowing plant materials to decompose directly on fields—and used animal manure to enrich soil fertility. These ancient techniques align perfectly with modern organic gardening practices.

Here's how to start a simple compost system:

The Compost Recipe

A good compost pile needs four ingredients:

1. **Browns**: Carbon-rich materials like fallen leaves, straw, or shredded paper (think of these as providing structure and energy)

2. **Greens**: Nitrogen-rich materials like vegetable scraps, coffee grounds, or fresh grass clippings (these provide protein for microorganisms)

3. **Water**: Just enough moisture to feel like a wrung-out sponge

4. **Air**: Oxygen for the beneficial microorganisms

Mix roughly three parts brown to one part green, keep slightly moist, and turn occasionally to add air. Over time, these materials will transform into dark, sweet-smelling compost that gardeners often call "black gold"!

Eleven-year-old Sophia started composting after learning about it at school: "At first, my parents weren't sure about keeping food scraps—they thought it might smell bad. But we found this cool countertop compost bin with a charcoal filter that prevents odors. Now, we collect coffee grounds, apple cores, and vegetable peels and take them to our backyard compost bin. Seeing banana peels and eggshells turn into rich soil for our garden is amazing. It feels like we're participating in God's recycling system!"

Harvesting Heaven's Energy: Solar Power and Biblical Wisdom

Throughout Scripture, the sun appears as a powerful symbol of God's faithfulness, provision, and light-giving presence:

"For the LORD God is a sun and shield: the LORD will give grace and glory..." (Psalm 84:11)

"From the rising of the sun unto the going down of the same the LORD's name is to be praised." (Psalm 113:3)

The sun isn't just a spiritual metaphor—it's also the ultimate source of nearly all energy on Earth! Fossil fuels like coal and oil are actually ancient sunlight, stored in plant and animal remains over millions of years. But instead of using these limited, polluting resources, Solarpunk communities take inspiration from biblical wisdom by harvesting current sunlight directly.

Solar Power Basics

Solar energy systems capture sunlight and convert it to electricity or heat through several methods:

- **Photovoltaic (PV) Panels**: These convert sunlight directly into electricity through silicon cells. You might see these shiny blue-black panels on rooftops or in solar farms.
- **Solar Thermal Systems**: These use sunlight to heat water or air for homes, reducing the need for gas or electric heating.
- **Passive Solar Design**: This involves designing buildings to naturally capture sunlight for heating in winter while blocking it in summer, reducing energy needs year-round.

Pastor Garcia's church installed solar panels as part of their creation care ministry: "Our congregation realized that harnessing the sun's energy aligns perfectly with biblical stewardship. The initial investment wasn't small, but now our electric bills are nearly zero, and we're preventing thousands of pounds of carbon emissions yearly. We see it as a practical way to honor God's command to care for creation while being wise stewards of our financial resources, too."

DIY Solar Projects for Young Stewards

You don't need a full roof of expensive panels to start exploring solar power! Here are some simple projects to try (with adult help when needed):

1. Solar Oven: Make a simple solar cooker using a pizza box, aluminum foil, plastic wrap, and black paper. On sunny days, you can harness the sun's heat to warm snacks, melt chocolate for s'mores, or even cook simple foods!

2. Solar Water Heater: Create a mini solar water heater by painting a glass jar black and filling it with water. Place it in direct sunlight and observe how the water temperature changes throughout the day.

3. Solar-Powered Art: Purchase an inexpensive small solar panel and connect it to different small motors or LED lights to create sun-powered artistic creations that spin, light up, or move when placed in sunlight.

Thirteen-year-old James created a solar demonstration for his science fair: "I built different solar projects to show how the same sunlight can be used in different ways. My favorite was a solar fountain where the sun powered a small pump that created a mini waterfall in a bucket. It helped people understand that solar energy isn't just about electricity—it can do mechanical work too!"

Biblical Wisdom for Energy Usage

Beyond harvesting solar power, Scripture offers wisdom about our energy consumption patterns:

The Principle of "Enough"

The Bible repeatedly teaches contentment with sufficiency rather than endless accumulation:

"And having food and raiment let us be therewith content." (1 Timothy 6:8)

This principle applies perfectly to energy use. Instead of constantly increasing our energy consumption, biblical wisdom suggests finding our "enough" level and being content with sufficient energy for our needs.

The Principle of Sabbath Rest

God's commandment for Sabbath rest applies not just to people but to all creation:

"Six days thou shalt do thy work, and on the seventh day thou shalt rest: that thine ox and thine ass may rest, and the son of thy handmaid, and the stranger, may be refreshed." (Exodus 23:12)

This principle suggests that constant production and consumption aren't God's design—even our energy systems benefit from periods of reduced demand and rest. Many Solarpunk communities practice "energy Sabbaths," where they minimize power use for certain periods, relying more on natural light and human-powered activities.

The Principle of Wise Planning

Jesus taught the importance of counting the cost and planning wisely:

"For which of you, intending to build a tower, sitteth not down first, and counteth the cost, whether he have sufficient to finish it?" (Luke 14:28)

This wisdom applies directly to energy systems, where thoughtful design and forward planning lead to more efficient, sustainable solutions than hasty, short-term thinking.

Project Box: Home Energy Audit

Become an energy detective in your own home with this fun investigation!

You'll need:
- Notebook and pencil
- Optional: simple thermometer

Step 1: List all the ways your home uses energy (lights, heating/cooling, appliances, etc.).

Step 2: Record when these energy users are active for one day, especially noting any that run when not needed.

Step 3: Find three opportunities to save energy, such as:
- Closing curtains on hot days to keep rooms cooler
- Unplugging "vampire" devices that use power even when turned off
- Using cold water for laundry when possible
- Adjusting thermostat settings by 1-2 degrees

Step 4: Track your impact by comparing utility bills before and after making these changes!

Self-Sufficiency and Mutual Aid: The Biblical Balance

One of the most beautiful aspects of biblical wisdom is how it balances personal responsibility with community care. Scripture never presents these as opposing values—instead, it shows how they complement each other perfectly in God's design.

The apostle Paul captured this balance in his letters:

"For even when we were with you, this we commanded you, that if any would not work, neither should he eat." (2 Thessalonians 3:10)

This teaches the importance of productive self-sufficiency. Yet Paul also wrote:

"Bear ye one another's burdens, and so fulfill the law of Christ." (Galatians 6:2)

This emphasizes our responsibility to help each other. Together, these verses outline a beautiful pattern where everyone contributes what they can while supporting others when needed.

Growing Toward Self-Sufficiency

Self-sufficiency doesn't mean isolating yourself from others—it means developing skills and systems that reduce dependence on fragile supply chains and wasteful practices. Biblical examples include:

- Joseph preparing for famine by storing grain during abundant years (Genesis 41)
- The virtuous woman providing food and clothing for her household (Proverbs 31)
- Paul working as a tentmaker to support himself while spreading the Gospel (Acts 18:3)

Modern applications might include:

- Growing some of your own food
- Learning basic repair skills instead of always replacing broken items
- Developing emergency preparedness for your family
- Creating home systems that require fewer external inputs (like rainwater harvesting)

Fourteen-year-old Anna's family has been working toward greater self-sufficiency: "We started with a small vegetable garden, then added rain barrels and a simple solar phone charger. Each year, we learn new skills—this year, my brother and I learned how to preserve vegetables through canning and fermentation. We're nowhere near completely self-sufficient, but each step makes us more resilient and connects us more directly to God's provision."

Strengthening Mutual Aid Networks

While growing in self-sufficiency, biblical wisdom also calls us to strengthen community bonds and share resources:

- The early Christians shared possessions so none would be in need (Acts 4:32-35)
- Old Testament law provided for gleaning to feed the poor (Leviticus 19:9-10)
- Paul organized collections from abundant regions to help those experiencing famine (2 Corinthians 8:1-15)

Modern Solarpunk communities practice mutual aid through:

- Tool libraries where expensive equipment is shared rather than duplicated
- Community gardens where everyone contributes and everyone benefits
- Skill-sharing workshops where knowledge spreads freely

- Time banking systems where service hours are exchanged equally

Pastor Williams explains how his congregation balances these principles: "We encourage families to develop resilience through gardening, emergency preparation, and practical skills. But we also organize community resource-sharing and skill exchanges. During a recent blizzard that caused power outages, some families had wood stoves that became warming centers for neighbors, while others had extra food supplies they shared. Some members had medical or repair skills that proved invaluable. It wasn't about complete individual self-sufficiency—it was about a community where everyone brings their gifts and resources to the table."

Solarpunk Stories: Biblical Wisdom in Action

Throughout this book, we've explored how Solarpunk communities reimagine sustainable living. Here are a few examples of communities applying biblical wisdom to create more resilient, sustainable ways of life:

The New Eden Cooperative in Oregon

Five Christian families purchased adjacent properties and created an informal cooperative based on biblical principles. Each family maintains their own home and garden, practicing a level of self-sufficiency, but they also share larger resources:

- A community orchard with various fruit and nut trees
- A barn housing shared equipment like a tractor and wood splitter
- A large greenhouse where seedlings are started each spring
- A community wood-fired oven for bread baking

"We're not trying to create a commune where everything is owned collectively," explains co-founder Sarah Chen. "Instead, we're applying the biblical model where families have their own inheritance and responsibility but also participate in community sharing and support. It's like the early church in Acts—they didn't stop owning personal possessions, but they held them with open hands, ready to share when others had needs."

The Resurrection Garden Project in Detroit

In a neighborhood once filled with abandoned lots, a coalition of churches transformed vacant spaces into productive gardens following biblical wisdom:

• They improved the soil through composting (creating "good ground" as in the Parable of the Sower)

• They installed rainwater harvesting systems (practicing wise stewardship of resources)

• They created a seed library where successful varieties are saved and shared (multiplying God's provision)

• They established a weekly market where excess produce is sold affordably (balancing fair compensation with generosity)

Twelve-year-old Marcus volunteers there every Saturday: "I've learned so much about plants, insects, and soil—but also about community. My favorite part is our harvest celebrations where everyone brings dishes made from garden ingredients to share. People from all different backgrounds come together, and it feels like a little taste of heaven."

The Living Light Village in New Zealand

This intentional community incorporated biblical principles into their built environment:

- Homes are constructed using natural, local materials like earth, stone, and timber (practicing good stewardship of resources)
- The village layout places community spaces in the center with homes around the perimeter (reflecting biblical community design where relationships are central)
- Each home has solar panels that connect to a microgrid, allowing energy sharing (balancing self-sufficiency with mutual aid)
- Community governance follows biblical conflict resolution patterns, emphasizing direct communication, listening, and reconciliation

"We're not trying to recreate the first-century church exactly," explains elder Ruth Martinez. "Rather, we're applying timeless biblical principles to modern challenges. Scripture provides a framework for relationships, resource-sharing, conflict resolution, and creation care that works just as well today as it did thousands of years ago."

Practical Steps: Starting Your Journey

Ready to apply biblical wisdom to create a more sustainable life? Here are some practical starting points for different age groups:

For Kids

1. **Start a Container Garden**: Even a few pots on a windowsill can teach important lessons about soil, seeds, and God's growing process. Try easy plants like lettuce, radishes, or herbs.

2. **Create a Solar Still**: With adult help, make a simple solar still that purifies water using sunlight. This demonstrates both science principles and God's design for the water cycle.

3. **Keep a Resource Journal**: For one week, track how you use energy, water, and food. Notice where resources might be wasted and brainstorm creative solutions.

4. **Learn One Practical Skill**: Choose a useful skill to learn, such as basic sewing, cooking a simple meal, or making homemade gifts. Being able

to make and repair things is an important part of sustainable living.

Ten-year-old Lily started with container gardening: "Mom helped me plant cherry tomatoes and basil in pots on our apartment balcony. Taking care of them taught me patience—they didn't grow overnight! When we finally got to eat our first tiny tomatoes, they tasted better than any from the store. It made me appreciate farmers and God's amazing design for plants."

For Families

1. **Establish a Family Sustainability Goal**: Choose one area to focus on together, like reducing food waste, cutting energy use, or learning to grow some of your own food.

2. **Create Regular Skill-Sharing Times**: Set aside time each month for family members to teach each other practical skills—children often have technological knowledge to share, while adults might teach traditional skills.

3. **Connect with Like-Minded Families**: Find other families interested in sustainable living and

biblical stewardship. Share resources, skills, and encouragement.

4. **Practice Hospitality and Sharing**: Look for opportunities to share tools, garden harvests, or skills with neighbors. This builds community resilience while demonstrating Christian generosity.

For Communities

1. **Start a Church Resource Library**: Collect rarely-used items that members can borrow instead of each family purchasing their own—camping gear, specialized kitchen equipment, tools, etc.

2. **Organize Seasonal Skill Workshops**: Host regular gatherings where people can learn practical skills like food preservation, basic repairs, or gardening techniques.

3. **Create a Community Garden on Church Property**: Transform underutilized lawn areas into productive garden spaces that can feed both congregation members and neighbors in need.

4. **Establish an Emergency Resilience Plan**: Develop systems for how your community will

respond to disruptions like power outages, severe weather, or other challenges, emphasizing mutual aid and resource sharing.

Project Box: Start Your "Good Ground" Container Garden

Create your first garden in a container to experience the Parable of the Sower firsthand!

You'll need:

- A container with drainage holes (a 5-gallon bucket works well)
- Potting soil mixed with compost
- Seeds for quick-growing plants (lettuce, radishes, or herbs)
- A sunny spot (windowsill, balcony, or yard)
- Watering can or repurposed spray bottle

Step 1: Prepare your "good ground" by filling the container with moistened potting soil mixed with compost.

Step 2: Plant seeds according to package directions (usually 1/4" to 1/2" deep).

Step 3: Water gently and place in a sunny location.

Step 4: Keep soil moist but not soggy as seeds germinate and grow.

Step 5: Observe and journal about your plants' growth, connecting it to the Parable of the Sower.

This simple project connects you directly to Jesus' teaching while providing fresh food and valuable gardening experience!

Looking Ahead

In our next chapter, we'll explore how technology can honor God's design and promote human flourishing rather than exploitation. We'll discover how biblical wisdom about craftsmanship, stewardship, and relationships provides guidance for evaluating and using technology wisely in a Solarpunk world.

For now, remember that Jesus' Parable of the Sower invites us to be both good soil—receiving God's Word with open hearts—and wise Sowers—spreading seeds of sustainable living in our families and communities. By combining ancient biblical wisdom with thoughtful, modern practices, we participate in God's ongoing work of renewal and restoration.

As you apply these principles in your daily life, you'll discover what generations of faithful stewards have found: that God's ways aren't just more sustainable—they're more satisfying, connecting us more deeply to our Creator, to each other, and to the wonderful world He has made.

Family Discussion Questions:

1. In the Parable of the Sower, what kind of "soil" do you think our family provides for new ideas about sustainability and creation care?

2. What's one area where our family could grow more of our own food or produce more of what we need?

3. How might our family better balance self-sufficiency with sharing and supporting others?

4. What skills do we already have that could contribute to a more sustainable community? What new skills would we like to learn?

Teacher's Corner: This chapter integrates biblical narrative with practical sustainability concepts, making complex ideas accessible to young learners while providing substantial content for adults. The Parable of the Sower serves as a perfect framework for introducing organic gardening principles, creating an intuitive connection between spiritual truth and creation care.

For classroom application, consider establishing a small container garden where students can directly experience the concepts discussed. The hands-on projects throughout the chapter—particularly the soil testing activity and container gardening—offer excellent opportunities for experiential learning across science, mathematics, and biblical studies curriculum areas.

The balance between self-sufficiency and mutual aid provides rich material for character education discussions about responsibility, generosity, and community. Consider supplementing this chapter with service-learning projects that allow students to practice developing their own skills and sharing resources with others. This would reinforce the biblical balance emphasized throughout the text.

Chapter 15:

Technology in Harmony with God's Design

Nature's Blueprints: God's Genius All Around Us

Have you ever watched a spider weave its web, glistening with morning dew, like tiny diamonds strung on silver threads? Or marveled at how a maple seed twirls through the air like a miniature helicopter? Perhaps you've wondered at the perfect hexagons in a honeycomb or how a kingfisher can dive into water without splashing?

Creation is filled with extraordinary designs that human engineers and inventors can only dream of matching! But here's something wonderful—God invites us to learn from these designs. In the Book of Job, we find this fascinating instruction:

"But ask now the beasts, and they shall teach thee; and the fowls of the air, and they shall tell thee: Or speak to the earth, and it shall teach thee:

and the fishes of the sea shall declare unto thee. Who knoweth not in all these that the hand of the LORD hath wrought this?" (Job 12:7-10)

This passage suggests something profound—that we can discover God's wisdom by studying the natural world! The creatures and plants around us aren't just pretty decorations on our planet. They're living examples of brilliant engineering, sustainable systems, and elegant solutions to complex problems. Each one bears the fingerprints of our Creator's genius.

Leonardo da Vinci was a Renaissance genius renowned for his work as an artist, scientist, and inventor. He was deeply inspired by nature and often used biomimicry—drawing ideas from the natural world—in his inventions and studies. For example, he closely studied birds to understand flight, which influenced his designs for flying machines like the ornithopter. Leonardo also examined the anatomy of plants and animals, incorporating their efficient forms and functions into his engineering ideas. His ability to merge art, science, and nature has left a lasting impact on innovation and creativity.

In this chapter, we'll explore how technology can work in harmony with God's design rather than against it. We'll discover the exciting field of biomimicry, where human innovation learns from nature's time-tested patterns. We'll consider how Christians should approach technology with both excitement and wisdom. We'll imagine how future technologies might help us become better stewards of God's creation, creating a world where human invention complements divine design!

Biomimicry: Learning from God's Living Library

Imagine having access to a design library containing over 3.8 billion years of research and development—with every solution tested and proven to work within Earth's systems. That's exactly what we have in the natural world around us! Biomimicry is the practice of learning from and then emulating nature's forms, processes, and ecosystems to create more sustainable technologies and designs.

Dr. Rachel Chen, a Christian biomimicry researcher, explains: "When we study how God designed a butterfly's wing, a prairie ecosystem, or a humpback whale's flipper, we're not just gathering scientific data. We're actually uncovering divine wisdom embedded in creation. It's like God left us an instruction manual written in the language of nature, waiting for us to read it with humble, curious hearts."

Let's explore some amazing examples of how human innovation is learning from God's designs:

Flying Like Birds and Insects

For thousands of years, humans watched birds soar through the sky and dreamed of joining them. Early attempts at flight often failed because inventors tried to copy the appearance of wings without understanding the principles behind them.

However, when the Wright brothers carefully studied how birds adjust the shape of their wings to maintain balance and control, they discovered key insights that helped them create the first successful airplane. Today's aerospace engineers continue to learn from God's flying designs:

- **Winglets** on modern airplanes were inspired by the upturned wingtips of eagles and other soaring birds, reducing fuel consumption by 5-7%
- **Quieter turbine blades** modeled after the serrated edges of owl feathers reduce noise pollution
- **Dragonfly-inspired wind turbines** that flutter in gentle breezes can generate electricity at lower wind speeds than traditional designs.

Fourteen-year-old Mateo built a science fair project based on biomimicry: "I was fascinated by how dragonflies can hover and even fly backward. I studied slow-motion videos of their wings and created a simple mechanical model that mimics their flight pattern. It helped me understand that God's designs often use motion and flexibility in ways that our rigid human machines don't. My project won first place, but more importantly, it gave me a chance to show how science can point to God's amazing creativity."

Building Like Plants and Animals

The structures that plants and animals create—from beehives to bamboo stalks—showcase incredible engineering that human architects now study:

- **The Eastgate Centre** in Zimbabwe uses no conventional air conditioning yet stays cool based on principles from African termite mounds
- **Lotus-inspired self-cleaning paints**, based on the microscopic surface pattern of lotus leaves, repel dirt and reduce the need for chemical cleaners.
- **Spider silk-inspired materials** that are stronger than steel yet incredibly lightweight and flexible
- **Velcro** was invented after a Swiss engineer examined how burrs stuck to his dog's fur under a microscope.

Twelve-year-old Sophia and her dad built a "living roof" for their garden shed: "We researched how plants like sedum naturally protect mountainsides from erosion and water damage. Then, we designed our shed roof to be covered with these same plants. Now, our shed stays cooler in summer and warmer in winter, plus it absorbs rainwater that would otherwise flood our yard. The birds and butterflies love it, too! It makes me think about how God's designs solve multiple problems at once."

Healing Like Nature

Some of the most exciting biomimicry applications are happening in medicine, where scientists are discovering how God's healing designs can inspire better treatments:

- **Gecko-inspired bandages** that stick securely yet remove painlessly, based on the microscopic structures on gecko feet
- **Sharkskin-patterned surfaces** that prevent bacterial growth without antibiotics
- **Mussel-inspired surgical glues** that work even in wet environments
- **Forest-inspired air filtration** removes pollutants using principles from how forests clean air

Pastor Williams, who serves as a hospital chaplain, sees profound connections between these innovations and biblical principles: "When Jesus healed people, He often used physical elements like mud, water, or touch—working with created materials, not against them. Today's biomimetic medicine follows a similar pattern, working with the body's natural processes rather than overriding them. This approach shows respect for God's original design while still addressing the problems that entered the world through sin."

Activity Box: Biomimicry Explorer

Become a biomimicry detective by investigating how God's designs could solve human problems!

You'll need:

- Magnifying glass (optional)
- Notebook and colored pencils
- Access to a natural area (yard, park, or even a houseplant!)

Step 1: Choose something in nature to observe closely—a flower, insect, tree, or animal.

Step 2: Draw what you see, noting interesting features and patterns.

Step 3: Ask these biomimicry questions:

- How does it move/grow/protect itself?
- How does it use water/energy efficiently?
- How does it handle extreme conditions?

- How does it work together with other living things?

Step 4: Brainstorm how these solutions might inspire human inventions!

Technology with Purpose: A Christian Perspective

Throughout history, Christians have responded differently to technology—some embracing new inventions enthusiastically, others cautiously approaching them. The Bible doesn't directly address modern technology (no verses about smartphones or solar panels!), but it does provide wisdom principles that can guide our approach.

Technology as Stewardship

From the very beginning, humans were called to be stewards of God's creation:

"And the LORD God took the man, and put him into the garden of Eden to dress it and to keep it." (Genesis 2:15)

This means that developing tools and technologies can fulfill our calling if they help us better care for the earth and serve others. Technologies that heal, restore, connect people meaningfully, or reduce waste can be seen as expressions of good stewardship.

Thirteen-year-old Emma's church youth group created a community repair café: "Once a month, we collect broken items from our neighborhood and try to fix them instead of having people throw them away. Adults with repair skills volunteer to teach us how to fix toasters, mend clothes, and repair bicycles. We've kept hundreds of items out of landfills! It's made me realize that sometimes the most earth-friendly technology isn't the newest gadget—it's the knowledge of how to repair what we already have."

Technology with Limits

While technology can be a blessing, Scripture also suggests appropriate limits. The story of the Tower of Babel (Genesis 11:1-9) warns about technology driven by pride and the desire to "make a name for ourselves" rather than honoring God.

Wisdom for evaluating technology might include questions like:

- Does this technology strengthen or weaken human relationships?

- Does it respect the natural limits and cycles that God designed?
- Does it concentrate power or distribute it more justly?
- Does it promote contentment or feed dissatisfaction and endless consumption?
- Can it be accessed by all people or only the privileged few?

These questions come from biblical values of community, stewardship, justice, contentment, and care for the vulnerable.

Pastor Garcia explains: "Technology itself isn't good or bad—it's the purpose and values behind it that matter. A smartphone can connect families across continents or isolate people sitting in the same room. Solar panels can provide affordable electricity to remote villages or become status symbols only the wealthy can afford. As Christians, we're called to develop and use technology in ways that reflect Christ's love and care for all people and all creation."

Solarpunk Technologies: Innovation Guided by Values

Throughout this book, we've explored the Solarpunk vision of sustainable, beautiful communities. Solarpunk approaches technology with specific values that align well with Christian stewardship:

Appropriate Scale

Solarpunk favors human-scaled technologies that can be understood, maintained, and controlled by the communities that use them—rather than massive, complex systems that create dependence on distant experts.

Open-Source Sharing

Knowledge and designs are freely shared rather than locked behind patents and proprietary secrets. This reflects the Christian value of generosity and allows good solutions to spread where they're needed most.

Repairability and Longevity

Products are designed to be easily repaired, upgraded, and eventually recycled—reflecting the biblical principle that resources are precious gifts to be used wisely, not disposable commodities.

Beauty and Function Together

Solarpunk technologies are designed with aesthetic beauty as well as functionality, recognizing that humans need beauty for their spiritual and emotional well-being. God created not only functional ecosystems but also stunning sunsets and colorful flowers that delight our senses.

Eleven-year-old Jayden participated in a Solarpunk design workshop at his church: "We were challenged to redesign everyday objects based on Solarpunk values. I redesigned a toaster with clear sides so you could see your bread toasting (no more burnt toast!), parts that could be easily replaced when worn out, and a beautiful wooden exterior made from scrap wood. Our teacher pointed out that God pays attention to both beauty and function in creation, so we should too!"

Emerging Technologies: Wisdom for the Path Ahead

As we look to the future, several promising technologies might help us better care for each other and for God's creation. While we can't predict exactly how these will develop, we can approach them with both excitement about their potential and wisdom about their proper use.

Clean Energy Innovations

Beyond the solar panels we discussed in earlier chapters, researchers are developing exciting new ways to capture and use renewable energy:

- **Transparent solar windows** that generate electricity while letting light through
- **Bladeless wind turbines** that are safer for birds and create less noise
- **Ocean wave and tidal generators** that harness the power of moving water
- **Bioreactors** that produce energy from algae while capturing carbon dioxide

These technologies could help us transition away from fossil fuels, which damage God's creation, while ensuring everyone has access to clean, affordable energy.

Regenerative Technologies

Some of the most exciting innovations focus not just on reducing harm to creation but actually helping heal damaged ecosystems:

- **Myco-materials** made from fungal networks that can replace plastics for packaging and building materials
- **Bioluminescent plants** are being developed to provide gentle lighting without electricity
- **Artificial photosynthesis** systems that mimic how plants convert sunlight to energy while removing carbon from the atmosphere
- **3D ocean reef printing** that creates new habitats for marine life in damaged areas

Fourteen-year-old Leila volunteers with a coastal restoration project: "We're using these amazing concrete structures designed to mimic natural reef formations. They're 3D printed with tiny crevices and holes exactly like natural reefs, so baby fish and coral can make homes there. It's incredible to think that human technology can actually help heal some of the damage we've caused to God's oceans!"

The Promise of "Free Energy"

Some visionaries speak of developing "free energy" technologies that could provide abundant power with minimal environmental impact. While many of these concepts remain unproven or theoretical, they remind us that God's creation contains possibilities we haven't fully discovered yet.

Nikola Tesla, whom we learned about in Chapter 3, believed that free energy was possible by tapping into the Earth's own electromagnetic fields. While his most ambitious visions weren't fully realized in his lifetime, his work reminds us to remain open to unexpected breakthroughs.

Mrs. Abernathy, a Christian science teacher, offers this perspective: "The concept of 'free energy' reminds me of God's abundant provision in Scripture—manna in the wilderness, loaves and fishes multiplied, water from rocks. While we should be cautious about unrealistic claims, we should also remember that our Creator is a God of abundance, not scarcity. The sun sends more energy to Earth in an hour than humanity uses in a year! The question isn't whether God has provided enough resources, but whether we'll develop the wisdom and cooperation to access and share them justly."

Digital Technology: Finding Balance

No discussion of modern technology would be complete without addressing digital tools like computers, smartphones, and the Internet. These powerful technologies connect us globally and give us access to unprecedented information—but they also present unique challenges.

Digital Wisdom from Scripture

While the Bible doesn't specifically mention digital technology, numerous passages offer relevant wisdom:

- **On information overload**: *"And further, by these, my son, be admonished: of making many books there is no end; and much study is a weariness of the flesh."* (Ecclesiastes 12:12) This ancient observation about books reminds us that even good information should have limits!

- **On genuine connection**: *"And be ye kind one to another, tenderhearted, forgiving one another, even as God for Christ's sake hath forgiven you."* (Ephesians 4:32) Online interactions should reflect these same values of kindness and tenderness.

- **On the power of words**: *"Death and life are in the power of the tongue: and they that love it shall eat the fruit thereof."* (Proverbs 18:21). This applies to our digital communications as well, reminding us that our online words impact real people.

Pastor Williams counsels families on balanced technology use: "Digital tools are just that—tools. Like any tool, from a hammer to a cooking pot, they can be used well or poorly. The key question isn't whether these tools exist but whether they serve God's purposes in our lives. Are they helping us love God and love others better? Or are they becoming idols that demand our constant attention and pull us away from our most important relationships?"

Solarpunk Digital Approaches

Solarpunk communities are exploring thoughtful approaches to digital technology:

- **Community-owned internet infrastructure** that provides equitable access while giving users control over their data and privacy

- **Digital sabbaths** where individuals or entire communities regularly disconnect from screens to reconnect with nature and each other
- **Repair cafés** that teach people how to fix and extend the life of electronic devices
- **Educational technology is designed for collaboration** rather than isolation

Project Box: Digital Detox Challenge

Try this experiment to become more aware of your relationship with technology!

Step 1: Keep a technology log for three days, recording every time you use digital devices and for what purpose.

Step 2: Reflect on your log using these questions:

- Which digital activities brought genuine value to your life?
- Which ones just filled time or became distractions?
- How did different types of technology use affect your mood and energy?

Step 3: Design a personal "technology sabbath"—a period of 4-24 hours when you'll disconnect from screens.

Step 4: Prepare for your technology sabbath by planning alternative activities (outdoor exploration, art projects, reading, face-to-face conversations).

Step 5: After your technology break, journal about what you noticed, learned, or rediscovered!

Christian Responsibility in a Technological Age

As followers of Christ in this age of rapidly advancing technology, we have special opportunities and responsibilities:

Developing Technologies with Kingdom Values

Christians in scientific and technical fields have opportunities to ensure that new technologies reflect godly values:

- **Justice and accessibility**: Ensuring innovations help all people, not just the wealthy or privileged

- **Care for creation**: Designing with full lifecycle awareness from production to eventual recycling
- **Truthfulness**: Resisting exaggerated claims and acknowledging both benefits and limitations
- **Human dignity**: Ensuring technology serves human flourishing rather than reducing people to data points or consumers

Dr. James Martinez, a Christian bioethicist, explains: "Technology tends to develop in the direction of whatever values drive it. If profit is the only consideration, technology will maximize profit—sometimes at the expense of people or creation. If military advantage is the goal, technology will develop toward weapons and control. But when Christians participate in technological development with kingdom values, we can help steer innovation toward healing, connection, sustainability, and justice."

Advocating for Ethical Guidelines

As technologies like artificial intelligence, genetic engineering, and mass surveillance develop, Christians can advocate for ethical guidelines that protect human dignity, personal freedom, and care for creation. This advocacy might happen in professional organizations, government policy discussions, or community conversations.

Teaching Digital Wisdom

Parents, teachers, and church leaders have vital roles in helping young people develop digital wisdom—not just technical skills but discernment about how, when, and why to use digital tools. This includes modeling balanced technology use ourselves!

Thirteen-year-old Marcus shares: "My youth pastor noticed how distracted everyone was during Bible study because of phones. Instead of just banning them, he helped us create our own 'digital covenant' with guidelines we all agreed to. We decided to stack phones in the center of the table during meetings, and we held each other accountable in a positive way. What's cool is that we're learning to manage our own technology use rather than just having adults make rules for us."

Looking Ahead

In our next chapter, we'll explore how facing environmental challenges requires courage and faith similar to what David needed when confronting Goliath. We'll discover biblical principles for approaching seemingly insurmountable problems with confidence in God's power and presence.

For now, remember that technology isn't good or evil—it's a tool that can be used to honor or dishonor God's design. By learning from nature's wisdom through biomimicry, approaching innovation with biblical values, and maintaining healthy boundaries around technology use, we can help create a world where human ingenuity complements divine design rather than competing with it.

As you encounter various technologies throughout your day, ask yourself, "How could this tool help me better love God, care for His creation, and serve others?" This simple question can transform how you view and use everything from a pencil to a smartphone to the most cutting-edge innovations of our time.

Family Discussion Questions:

1. What's something in nature that you think could inspire a helpful human invention?

2. How do digital devices affect our family relationships—in both positive and challenging ways?

3. If Jesus were here physically today, how do you think He might use or approach modern technology?

4. How could our family use technology more intentionally to strengthen our relationships or better care for creation?

Teacher's Corner: This chapter provides a balanced framework for discussing technology from a Christian perspective—neither uncritically embracing every innovation nor fearfully rejecting technological progress. For classroom application, the biomimicry activity offers an excellent interdisciplinary project connecting biology, engineering, art, and theology. Consider expanding this into a longer-term design challenge where students identify problems in their school or community and develop nature-inspired solutions.

The digital technology section addresses one of the most pressing challenges for today's families and educators. Consider using the Digital Detox Challenge as a whole-class experiment. This would allow students to compare experiences and develop their own thoughtful approach to technology use. This would build media literacy and self-regulation skills while prompting deeper reflection on values and priorities.

This chapter offers opportunities for Christian education settings to discuss how technological development can be a spiritual vocation—one way of participating in God's ongoing creative and restorative work in the world. Students who excel in STEM subjects can be encouraged to see these talents as potential gifts for kingdom service, while all students can develop discernment about responsible technology use.

Chapter 16:

Overcoming Giants: Facing Climate and Social Challenges

The Boy Who Faced a Giant

Imagine standing in a dusty valley, the hot sun beating down on your shoulders. Across the field stands a warrior so enormous that he makes grown men tremble with fear. He's over nine feet tall, covered in heavy bronze armor, and carrying weapons that look like they could flatten a small house! For forty days, this terrifying giant has been taunting your people, challenging anyone to fight him—but no one has been brave enough to step forward.

This was the scene that young David faced in one of the Bible's most famous stories:

"And there went out a champion out of the camp of the Philistines, named Goliath, of Gath, whose height was six cubits and a span... And he stood and cried unto the armies of Israel, and said

unto them, Why are ye come out to set your battle in array? am not I a Philistine, and ye servants to Saul? choose you a man for you, and let him come down to me." (1 Samuel 17:4, 8)

Day after day, Goliath's booming voice had struck fear into the hearts of Israel's army. Even King Saul, who stood head and shoulders above most Israelites, hid in his tent rather than face this formidable enemy.

But then something unexpected happened. A young shepherd boy named David arrived at the camp, bringing food for his older brothers, who were soldiers. When David heard Goliath's taunts and saw everyone's fear, he was puzzled. Where others saw an unbeatable enemy, David saw something different—a challenge that required courage, wisdom, and, most importantly, faith in God.

"And David said to Saul, Let no man's heart fail because of him; thy servant will go and fight with this Philistine... The LORD that delivered me out of the paw of the lion, and out of the paw of the bear,

he will deliver me out of the hand of this Philistine." (1 Samuel 17:32, 37)

You probably know how the story ends. David faced Goliath with just a sling and five smooth stones. He launched a stone with perfect accuracy using the skills he had developed while watching his father's sheep. It struck Goliath in the forehead, and the mighty giant fell. David's courage, practical skills, and unwavering faith had won an impossible victory!

This ancient story contains powerful wisdom for us today as we face our own seemingly insurmountable challenges. In this chapter, we'll explore how the lessons from David and Goliath can help us address modern "giants" like climate change and social inequality. We'll discover how to balance scientific understanding with faithful action and how to respectfully engage with those who might be skeptical about these challenges.

Modern Goliaths: Challenges That Seem Too Big

Today, we face challenges that can feel as intimidating as Goliath appeared to Israel's army.

These modern "giants" are different from a nine-foot warrior with a spear, but they can still make us feel small, scared, and powerless:

The Climate Change Giant

Earth's climate is changing faster than at any time in human history. Rising temperatures are causing more extreme weather events, such as powerful hurricanes, devastating wildfires, prolonged droughts, and destructive floods. Ice caps are melting, raising sea levels and threatening coastal communities. Plants and animals are struggling to adapt, and some species face extinction.

This challenge can feel overwhelming because:

- It affects the entire planet
- It involves complex scientific processes
- It requires cooperation between nations
- The consequences unfold gradually over time
- Addressing it means changing how we produce energy, grow food, and build communities

Thirteen-year-old Miguel shares: "After Hurricane Maria destroyed my grandmother's home in Puerto Rico, climate change stopped being just something we talked about in science class—it became personal. When I learned that warmer oceans could strengthen hurricanes, I felt scared but determined to do something about it."

The Inequality Giant

Resources and opportunities aren't distributed evenly worldwide. Many communities lack access to clean water, nutritious food, quality education, safe housing, and healthcare. The communities with the fewest resources are often the most vulnerable to environmental problems.

This challenge can feel intimidating because:

- The gaps between the wealthy and the poor have deep historical roots
- Economic systems can seem too complex to change
- Privilege can be invisible to those who have it
- Addressing inequality requires both personal and systemic changes
- Solutions must respect human dignity and promote justice, not just charity

Twelve-year-old Sophia observed: "In my city, you can literally see the inequality by driving ten minutes in different directions. Some neighborhoods have beautiful parks, grocery stores with fresh food, and good schools. Other areas have vacant lots, only fast food, and schools without enough resources. It doesn't seem fair, but it's hard to know where to even start fixing something so big."

The Polarization Giant

In many communities, people have become divided into opposing groups that struggle to communicate respectfully or work together. Social media and news sources often amplify disagreements rather than help people find common ground. This division makes it harder to address other challenges that require cooperation.

This challenge feels especially difficult because:

• It can damage friendships and even family relationships

• Strong emotions make calm discussions difficult

• Complex issues get reduced to simplified "for" or "against" positions

- Finding solutions requires listening to different perspectives
- Social media algorithms often show us only viewpoints we already agree with

Just like the Israelite soldiers who stood paralyzed by fear as Goliath taunted them, we might feel tempted to hide from these modern giants. We might think, "These problems are too big for someone like me to solve," or "Nothing I do will really make a difference." But David's story reminds us that even the most intimidating challenges can be overcome with courage, practical skills, and faith.

David's Toolkit: Lessons for Facing Modern Giants

When we look closer at how David approached his seemingly impossible challenge, we find valuable wisdom for addressing our own giant problems:

1. David Refused to Be Paralyzed by Fear

While others focused on Goliath's terrifying size and strength, David focused on God's power and faithfulness. He remembered how God had helped him protect his sheep from lions and bears, giving him the confidence to face this new challenge.

Today, instead of being overwhelmed by the scope of climate change or inequality, we can focus on specific actions within our reach. Each step forward, however small, is progress. We can also draw confidence from past successes—both our own experiences and the many examples of communities that have already made positive changes.

Fourteen-year-old Aiden found this approach helpful: "When our science teacher first explained the climate crisis, I felt hopeless—like the problem was too massive for anything I did to matter. But then, our class visited a community solar project that powers 200 homes with clean energy. Seeing real people creating real solutions helped me move from fear to action. Now, our youth group is working on a similar project for our church building."

2. David Used the Skills He Already Had

King Saul offered David heavy armor and weapons, but David knew he couldn't move effectively in unfamiliar gear. Instead, he used the sling he had practiced with for years while protecting his father's sheep.

Today, we don't all need to become climate scientists or policy experts to make a difference. Each of us has existing skills, talents, and interests that can be directed toward solutions:

- Artists can create works that help people emotionally connect with environmental issues
- Writers can share stories that inspire action
- Engineers can design more sustainable systems
- Teachers can educate the next generation
- Builders can construct more efficient homes
- Gardeners can grow food locally
- Organizers can bring communities together

Eleven-year-old Maya discovered this principle through her school's environmental club: "I love art and design, so I created colorful signs for our recycling bins that actually show what goes where. Contamination in our recycling dropped by 60%! Then, I designed a mural for our school garden that teaches about native plants. I realized I don't have to become a different person to help—I can use what I already love doing."

3. David Chose the Right "Stones"

From the streambed, David carefully selected five smooth stones for his sling—not random rocks, but projectiles perfectly suited for his purpose. He was thoughtful and strategic in his preparation.

Today, we must also choose our "stones" carefully, selecting the most effective approaches to addressing complex challenges. This requires understanding the science behind climate change, the systems that create inequality, and the evidence for what solutions actually work.

Pastor Williams explains: "Faith doesn't mean ignoring facts or evidence. David didn't just pray about Goliath—he also selected proper stones and used his well-practiced sling technique! Similarly, our faith should motivate us to understand the science of climate change and the root causes of inequality so we can address them effectively. God gave us both faith and intellect, and He expects us to use both."

4. David Acted with Courage and Conviction

Once David decided to face Goliath, he moved forward confidently. He didn't wait for someone else to solve the problem or pretend the threat wasn't real. He took responsibility and acted with conviction.

For us today, Climate change and inequality won't be solved by people waiting for others to take the first step. These challenges require courage—the willingness to change habits, speak up for better policies, and sometimes make choices that others might not understand.

Thirteen-year-old Leila's family demonstrated this courage: "We decided to become a one-car family, even though everyone else in our neighborhood has at least two. It was hard at first—we had to plan our schedules more carefully and sometimes use bikes or public transportation. Some neighbors thought we were weird or couldn't afford another car. But it's gotten easier. We're healthier from more walking and biking, and we've shown our community that it's possible to live differently."

Activity Box: Your Five Stones

Just as David carefully chose five smooth stones for his confrontation with Goliath, you can select five specific actions to address today's challenges!

You'll need:

- Five small, smooth stones (from a garden or craft store)
- Paint or permanent markers
- A small bowl or container

Step 1: Research and brainstorm actions you could take to address climate change, inequality, or other challenges your community faces.

Step 2: Select five specific, achievable actions that match your skills and resources.

Step 3: Write one action on each stone using a permanent marker or paint.

Step 4: Place your stones in a small bowl where you'll see them regularly.

Step 5: As you complete each action, turn that stone over or move it to a different container to track your progress.

Examples of "stones" might include starting a vegetable garden, reducing single-use plastics in your home, learning about environmental justice, writing to a local official about a community need, or organizing a neighborhood clean-up event.

Faith and Science: Partners in Problem-Solving

When facing today's giant challenges, we sometimes hear that faith and science are opponents—that we must choose one or the other. However, David's approach shows us a better way: combining practical knowledge with deep faith. He understood the physics of slings and carefully selected aerodynamic stones (the science) while also trusting wholly in God's power and purpose (the faith).

How Faith Supports Scientific Progress

Far from opposing science, biblical faith actually provides a strong foundation for scientific inquiry and environmental care:

1. **Faith gives us a "why" for scientific work.** When we understand Earth as God's beloved creation—not just random matter—we have a

profound motivation to study and protect it. As Psalm 24:1 reminds us, "*The earth is the LORD's, and the fulness thereof; the world, and they that dwell therein.*"

2. **Faith provides ethical guidance for using scientific knowledge.** The biblical commands to love our neighbors and care for the vulnerable help us evaluate whether technological solutions promote justice or merely benefit the privileged few.

3. **Faith offers hope when challenges seem overwhelming.** Climate science can tell us what's happening to our planet, but faith reminds us that God is still at work and invites us to participate in restoration and renewal.

4. **Faith communities provide networks for collective action.** Churches and other faith communities bring people together across differences, creating powerful networks for environmental and social action.

Dr. Katherine Hayhoe, a climate scientist and Christian, explains: "Science tells us what is happening to our world and why. Our faith tells us why it matters and what we should do about it. We need both."

How Science Strengthens Faithful Action

While faith provides purpose and hope, science gives us crucial tools for effective stewardship:

1. **Science helps us understand complex systems.** Climate science reveals how carbon dioxide traps heat in the atmosphere, how ocean acidification affects marine ecosystems, and how weather patterns shift as temperatures rise—knowledge we need for effective solutions.

2. **Science measures the impact of different approaches.** Research shows which farming methods best protect soil health, which energy technologies deliver the most benefits with the least harm, and which policy approaches effectively reduce inequality.

3. **Science enables innovation.** Scientific progress gives us solar panels that generate clean energy, efficient building techniques that reduce resource use, and communication technologies that connect global communities.

Mrs. Chen, who teaches science at a Christian school, shares: "I tell my students that studying science is one way we can love God with all our minds, as Jesus commanded. When we understand how Earth's systems work, we become better caretakers of God's creation and better neighbors to vulnerable communities."

Project Box: Faith and Science Journal

Create a special journal that combines your observations of God's creation with scientific facts and spiritual reflections.

Each week, choose something in nature to observe closely (a plant, animal, weather pattern, or geological feature). In your journal, create three sections for each observation:

1. "I Notice" (Scientific Observation): Record detailed observations and measurements. Research scientific facts about what you're studying.

2. "I Wonder" (Questions): Write questions that arise from your observations—both scientific questions and bigger philosophical or theological ones.

3. "I Reflect" (Spiritual Connections): Consider how what you've observed connects to your faith. Does it remind you of a Bible verse? Does it reveal something about God's character?

Over time, this practice helps integrate scientific understanding with spiritual growth, developing both your mind and your heart.

Meeting Skepticism with Grace and Wisdom

As you learn about environmental challenges and get involved in solutions, you'll likely encounter people who are skeptical—about climate science, about the severity of inequality, or about proposed solutions. Some skeptics may even be family members or friends from your church or school.

How can we engage respectfully with those who see these issues differently? Once again, Scripture offers wisdom:

"But sanctify the Lord God in your hearts: and be ready always to give an answer to every man that asketh you a reason of the hope that is in you with meekness and fear." (1 Peter 3:15)

This verse reminds us to explain our convictions with both clarity ("give an answer") and respect ("with meekness and fear"). Here are practical ways to apply this guidance:

Listen First to Understand Concerns

Different types of skepticism have different roots. Some people worry about the economic costs of environmental policies. Others have received conflicting information and aren't sure what to believe. Some fear that proposed solutions might threaten values they hold dear, like individual freedom or traditional ways of life.

By listening carefully before responding, you can show respect and gain insight into what is really behind someone's objections.

Fourteen-year-old James found this approach helpful: "My grandfather used to dismiss climate change whenever I mentioned it. Instead of arguing, I asked questions about his life growing up on a farm. He shared amazing knowledge about weather patterns and how farming practices have changed. Now we talk about how some new sustainable farming methods actually restore traditional practices he values. We still don't agree on everything, but we can have real conversations."

Find Common Ground

Most people, regardless of their views on climate science, value clean air and water, healthy children, strong communities, and responsible use of resources. Starting conversations around these shared values creates a foundation for discussing more contentious issues.

Pastor Garcia uses this approach in his diverse congregation: "We have members across the political spectrum who disagree about climate policy. But everyone agrees that our church should be good stewards of our resources. We started with simple projects everyone supported—fixing water leaks, improving insulation, and planting trees on our property. These practical steps built relationships and trust, allowing us to tackle more complex environmental projects together."

Share Stories, Not Just Statistics

While scientific data matters, personal stories often connect more deeply with people's hearts.

Share specific examples of communities affected by environmental changes or successful projects that have made a positive difference.

Twelve-year-old Mia found that photos were more powerful than words: "When people questioned why I was concerned about plastic pollution, I showed them pictures I'd taken of birds tangled in plastic at our local beach. That made the issue real in a way my words couldn't."

Respect the Journey

Remember that most people don't change their minds immediately. New ideas—especially ones with significant implications for how we live—often need time to take root. Be patient and respectful of each person's journey, just as you'd want others to respect yours.

Maintain Relationship Above "Winning"

The goal of these conversations isn't to defeat others in debate. It's to maintain relationships while working together toward truth and positive action. Sometimes, the most powerful witness is continuing to live your convictions joyfully without demanding that everyone immediately agree with you.

Solarpunk Stories: Communities Overcoming Giants

Throughout history, communities have faced seemingly insurmountable challenges and overcome them through collective action, innovative thinking, and persistent hope. Here are a few inspiring examples of modern-day "David and Goliath" stories:

The Great Green Wall of Africa

Faced with the giant threat of desertification (the spread of desert conditions into formerly fertile land), 20 African nations embarked on an ambitious project: planting a 4,800-mile "wall" of trees across the continent. This massive reforestation effort is already transforming degraded landscapes into productive, resilient ecosystems that support wildlife and human communities.

What seemed impossible for any single nation has become achievable through cooperation, indigenous knowledge, and youthful energy. Thousands of young people have joined the effort, planting millions of trees that provide food, shade, soil stabilization, and carbon capture.

The Plastic Bank: Turning Pollution into Opportunity

The overwhelming problem of ocean plastic pollution seemed too vast for any solution—until entrepreneur David Katz had an insight: what if plastic waste could become a resource for people living in poverty?

The Plastic Bank now operates in coastal communities where plastic pollution is worst, paying people to collect plastic waste and bring it to recycling centers. Collectors receive digital payments that help lift their families out of poverty, while the collected plastic is recycled into new products. This innovative approach addresses both environmental degradation and economic inequality simultaneously.

Glasgow Church Tackles Fuel Poverty

When members of a church in Glasgow, Scotland, realized that many elderly people in their neighborhood couldn't afford to heat their homes adequately in winter, they faced a complex challenge involving energy costs, poorly insulated buildings, and limited incomes.

Rather than tackling just one aspect, they developed a comprehensive approach—training church members to perform basic energy audits, partnering with contractors to improve insulation at reduced rates, creating an emergency heating fund, and advocating for better energy policies. Their persistence and creativity have helped hundreds of vulnerable residents stay warm while reducing overall energy consumption.

These examples show that just as David faced Goliath with courage and creative thinking, communities today are finding effective ways to address even the most intimidating challenges.

Your Place in the Story: Finding Your Role

As we conclude this chapter, you might wonder: "What's my place in these giant stories? How can someone my age make a meaningful difference?"

Remember that David was young too—likely a teenager—when he faced Goliath. His age didn't limit his impact; in fact, his youthful perspective allowed him to see possibilities that older, more experienced warriors missed.

Here are some ways you can find your unique role in addressing today's challenges:

Start with Your Sphere of Influence

You might not be able to affect international climate policy directly, but you can influence your home, school, church, and local community. These spaces matter—both for the concrete impact of changes you make and for their ripple effects as others see what's possible.

Thirteen-year-old Riley focused on his school: "After learning how food waste contributes to climate change, I noticed our cafeteria was throwing away tons of unopened milk cartons and whole fruit. I worked with our principal to set up sharing tables where students could leave unwanted food items for others who might want extras. We reduced our school's food waste by 40% in just two months!"

Connect with Like-Minded Friends

Just as David's victory inspired Israel's army to find their courage, your actions can inspire friends to get involved. Consider starting an environmental club, organizing a neighborhood improvement project, or simply having conversations about these issues with peers.

Develop Your Knowledge and Skills

What subjects interest you most? Science, art, writing, public speaking, organizing people, working with your hands? Developing your God-given talents prepares you for future opportunities to make a difference.

Look for Internships and Youth Programs

Many environmental organizations, community development agencies, and houses of worship offer special programs for young people. These can provide valuable mentoring, hands-on experience, and connections with others who share your concerns.

Keep the Conversation Going

Perhaps the most important thing you can do right now is simply keep environmental and social justice issues part of the conversation—in your family, school, church, and friend groups. By raising awareness respectfully and consistently, you help ensure these critical issues aren't forgotten or ignored.

Looking Ahead

In our next chapter, we'll explore how to maintain courage and hope during challenging times. We'll discover biblical principles for perseverance and practical approaches to preventing burnout while working for positive change.

For now, remember that when David faced Goliath, he didn't see just a fearsome enemy—he saw an opportunity to demonstrate God's power and provision. In the same way, today's environmental and social challenges, while daunting, also present opportunities for us to show God's love for creation and all people through creative, courageous action.

As you consider the "giants" facing our world, don't be intimidated by their size. Instead, gather your five smooth stones—the specific actions you can take with the skills, resources, and relationships God has given you. Step forward with scientific understanding and faithful confidence, knowing that the God who stood with David stands with you as you work for a more just, sustainable world.

Family Discussion Questions:

1. What "giant" problem in our world or community concerns you most? What makes it seem intimidating or difficult to solve?

2. What skills, interests, or resources does our family have that could contribute to addressing environmental or social challenges?

3. How have you seen faith and scientific understanding work together to solve problems?

4. When have you encountered skepticism about environmental issues? How did you respond, and what might you do differently next time?

Teacher's Corner: This chapter addresses the cognitive, emotional, and spiritual dimensions of addressing complex global challenges. For classroom application, consider adapting the Five Stones activity into a collaborative project in which students identify community-level environmental or social justice issues and develop concrete action plans. This builds agency and hope while providing practical experience in civic engagement.

The Faith and Science Journal offers an excellent ongoing assignment that integrates scientific observation with ethical and theological reflection. This approach supports the development of both critical thinking skills and spiritual formation, helping students see that these dimensions of learning complement rather than compete with each other.

The principles in the "Meeting Skepticism with Grace and Wisdom" section provide helpful guidelines for fostering respectful dialogue when discussing climate change or other potentially controversial topics. Consider establishing classroom norms based on these principles before engaging in discussions where students may hold differing viewpoints.

Chapter 17:

Be Strong and Courageous: Trusting God in a Changing World

The Promise That Changes Everything

Imagine standing at the edge of a rushing river. On the other side lies a land you've heard about your whole life—a place of promise and possibility. But between you and that future stands swirling water, unknown dangers, and the enormous responsibility of leading an entire nation forward. How would you feel? Excited? Terrified? Probably both at once!

This was precisely the situation Joshua faced after Moses died. The Israelites had wandered in the wilderness for forty years, and now it was finally time to enter the Promised Land. But Moses—their trusted leader for as long as most could remember—was gone. Joshua had to step up and lead God's people into an uncertain future.

At this pivotal moment, God spoke words to Joshua that still echo through the centuries, bringing courage to hearts in challenging times:

"Have not I commanded thee? Be strong and of a good courage; be not afraid, neither be thou dismayed: for the LORD thy God is with thee whithersoever thou goest." (Joshua 1:9)

What wonderful encouragement! God didn't promise Joshua that the journey would be easy or that challenges wouldn't come. Instead, He promised something far more powerful—His presence every step of the way. With God beside him, Joshua could face whatever lay ahead with strength and courage.

In our world today, we stand at our own kind of river's edge. Changes in climate, technology, society, and economies create uncertainty about what the future holds. Like Joshua, we might feel both excitement about new possibilities and anxiety about potential challenges. And like Joshua, we need courage to move forward—not with reckless confidence that everything will work out exactly as we wish, but with faithful trust that God walks with us through whatever comes.

Brave Hearts in Changing Times

What does courage look like in a world experiencing environmental and social changes? It's not the absence of fear but rather moving forward despite our fears, trusting God while taking responsible action.

Courage to Face Reality

The first kind of courage we need is the bravery to face our situation honestly. The Israelites couldn't enter the Promised Land until they acknowledged that they were still in the wilderness. Similarly, we can't address climate change or social challenges until we acknowledge they exist.

Fourteen-year-old Sophia experienced this after wildfires threatened her community: "For years, climate change was just something in science books. But when we had to evacuate our home with smoke filling the sky, it became real. At first, I just wanted to pretend everything was normal, but my youth pastor helped me see that having the courage to face reality is the first step toward making things better."

This doesn't mean dwelling on worst-case scenarios that paralyze us with fear. Instead, it means honestly assessing our situation so we can respond wisely. As Proverbs 27:12 tells us, "*A prudent person foresees danger and takes precautions. The simpleton goes blindly on and suffers the consequences*" (NLT).

Courage to Imagine Better Futures

The second type of courage is the boldness to envision and work toward positive possibilities even when current trends seem discouraging. The Israelites needed to believe that the Promised Land was actually worth the journey and the challenges of settling in a new place.

This imaginative courage is where Solarpunk visions shine! Rather than getting stuck in either denial ("nothing needs to change") or despair ("nothing can change"), Solarpunk communities creatively design flourishing futures that work with nature rather than against it.

Twelve-year-old Aiden discovered this courage through art: "Our science teacher showed us projections about rising sea levels that could affect our coastal town. It was scary. But then, our art teacher had us design floating neighborhoods and cities built on stilts with gardens everywhere. Making these models helped me see that humans are really creative problem-solvers. We can adapt to changes if we use our imaginations and work together."

Courage to Take Imperfect Action

The third kind of courage is the courage to take action even when we don't have perfect solutions or guaranteed outcomes. Joshua didn't know exactly what challenges awaited him in Canaan, but he still had to lead the people forward.

Pastor Garcia explains: "Sometimes we get paralyzed waiting for perfect solutions to climate change or social problems. But God rarely gives us complete blueprints—He gives us principles, wisdom, community, and His presence. Then He expects us to step out in faith, trying our best with what we know now, learning and adjusting as we go."

Thirteen-year-old Marco found this courage when starting an anti-waste initiative at his school: "I was nervous about proposing a composting program because I wasn't an expert and wasn't sure if it would work. My dad reminded me that courage isn't about knowing all the answers—it's about being willing to try, learn, and keep going even when things get complicated. Our program isn't perfect, but we've already diverted tons of food waste from landfills!"

Activity Box: Courage Stones

Create tangible reminders of God's promise to be with you in challenging times!

You'll need:

- Several smooth stones (from your garden or a craft store)
- Acrylic paint or permanent markers
- Clear sealer (optional)

Step 1: Clean your stones and let them dry completely.

Step 2: On each stone, write a Bible verse or phrase about courage, such as:

- "*Be strong and courageous*" (Joshua 1:9)
- "*God is with me*" (Isaiah 41:10)
- "*I can do all things through Christ*" (Philippians 4:13)

Step 3: Decorate your stones with symbols of strength, hope, or God's creation.

Step 4: If available, seal your stones with a clear sealer to protect the designs.

Step 5: Place your courage stones where you'll see them regularly—in your pocket, desk, or garden—as reminders that God is with you as you face challenges.

Solarpunk Resilience: Bending Without Breaking

One of the most exciting aspects of Solarpunk communities is their focus on resilience—the ability to adapt to changes and recover from difficulties while maintaining core values and functions. Instead of rigid systems that either resist all change (until they catastrophically fail) or collapse under pressure, resilient systems can bend without breaking.

Nature beautifully demonstrates this principle. Consider how bamboo responds during intense storms—it flexes with the wind rather than standing rigid like an oak tree. This flexibility makes bamboo one of the most resilient plants on Earth! Similarly, resilient communities develop systems that can adapt to changing conditions while preserving what matters most.

Physical Resilience

Resilient Solarpunk communities design infrastructure with both present needs and future changes in mind:

- **Flexible Energy Systems**: Instead of depending entirely on one massive power plant, resilient communities create networks of diverse energy sources—solar panels on rooftops, small wind turbines, micro-hydro in streams, and battery storage. If one system fails, others continue providing power.

- **Adaptive Architecture**: Buildings are designed to work with changing conditions—

elevated foundations in flood-prone areas, passive cooling systems for hotter temperatures, rainwater collection systems for drier periods, and modular designs that can be modified as needs change.

- **Redundant Food Systems**: Rather than relying on just one food source, resilient communities grow food in multiple ways—community gardens, urban farms, food forests, balcony containers, vertical growing systems, and partnerships with nearby rural farmers.

Eleven-year-old Maya's coastal town is developing this kind of resilience: "After two major hurricanes, our town council worked with architects to redesign our community center. The new building is circular to better allow the wind to flow around it. It has solar panels with battery backup, raised electrical systems, an advanced rainwater collection system, and a commercial kitchen that can feed the whole community during emergencies. It's also beautiful, with huge windows that can be shuttered during storms and a living roof covered with native plants. Now it's not just a meeting place—it's our community's safety hub for whatever weather comes our way."

Social Resilience

Physical infrastructure isn't the only thing that needs resilience. Communities also need social systems that can adapt to changes while maintaining strong relationships and care for all members:

- **Mutual Aid Networks**: Formal and informal systems for neighbors to help each other during challenges—from childcare cooperatives to tool-sharing libraries to emergency response teams.
- **Intergenerational Connections**: Communities that bring together people of all ages share both the wisdom of experience and the energy of youth, creating stronger collective problem-solving abilities.
- **Diverse Skills**: Resilient communities value many different types of knowledge—from traditional crafts to technical expertise to social organizing—creating a rich skillset for addressing various challenges.

- **Conflict Resolution Practices**: Healthy communities develop ways to respectfully resolve disagreements, allowing them to stay unified even during stressful times.

Pastor Williams saw this social resilience in action: "During a weeklong power outage after a severe ice storm, our church became a community hub. People with medical needs stayed in our building, which had generator power. Those with wood stoves opened their homes for neighbors to warm up and cook meals. Teenagers organized a system to check on elderly residents. What amazed me was how quickly people self-organized—because we'd already built relationships during normal times, we had the social foundation to respond effectively during crisis."

Spiritual Resilience

For Christians, resilience must also include spiritual dimensions—the ability to maintain faith, hope, and love even during difficult transitions. Spiritual resilience doesn't mean denying challenges or pretending everything is fine.

Instead, it means honestly facing difficulties while trusting God's presence and purposes.

Fourteen-year-old Leila discovered this during her family's difficult move from Texas to Minnesota: "When my dad lost his job in the oil industry and found new work in renewable energy, we had to move across the country. I was so angry about leaving my friends and everything familiar. My youth pastor encouraged me to read the book of Joshua and notice how God was present with the Israelites during their big transition. I started journaling about where I saw God in our family's journey. Some days I still feel sad about what we left behind, but I'm also discovering how God is with us in our new home and new future."

Project Box: Resilience Garden

Create a mini garden that demonstrates resilience principles!

You'll need:
- A container or small garden plot
- Soil and compost
- Several types of plant seeds or seedlings

- Mulch material (straw, wood chips, or dried leaves)
- Watering can

Step 1: Choose a diverse selection of plants that support each other. Good combinations include:

- Tomatoes + Basil + Marigolds (marigolds repel pests, basil improves tomato flavor)
- Beans + Corn + Squash (the "Three Sisters" - beans fix nitrogen, corn provides support, squash shades soil)
- Lettuce + Radishes + Carrots (using vertical space efficiently)

Step 2: Plant according to each plant's needs, grouping them so they help each other.

Step 3: Add mulch to conserve water and suppress weeds.

Step 4: Maintain your garden and observe how diversity creates strength!

As your garden grows, notice how plants growing in a community are more resilient than those growing alone—just like human communities!

Faith That Empowers Action

Some people mistakenly think that faith means passively waiting for God to solve all problems. But throughout Scripture, we see that authentic faith actually empowers bold action! Noah built an ark, Moses confronted Pharaoh, Esther approached the king at great personal risk, and the early Christians reorganized their community to care for those in need.

Faith doesn't replace human responsibility—it provides the foundation, motivation, and courage for responsible action. Let's explore how faith enables and shapes our response to environmental and social challenges:

Faith Gives Us Purpose Beyond Fear

When we trust God's purposes and presence, we can move beyond both denial and despair. Instead of being paralyzed by fear or overwhelmed by the scope of problems, faith helps us act from a place of hope and conviction.

Mrs. Chen, a Christian science teacher, explains it this way: "Climate science tells us what is happening to our planet, but faith tells us why it matters and how to respond. Because we believe Earth is God's beloved creation—not just random matter—we have the profound motivation to protect it. Because we trust God is still working in our world, we can take action without being crushed by the weight of saving everything ourselves."

Faith Provides Ethical Guidance

Faith offers crucial ethical guidance as we develop new technologies and social systems to address environmental challenges. Biblical principles about justice, care for the vulnerable, truthfulness, and stewardship help us evaluate which solutions genuinely reflect God's character and purposes.

For example, when a coastal community faces rising sea levels, faith might guide them to ensure that both wealthy beachfront property owners and low-income residents have a voice in planning adaptations. Faith reminds us to consider the impacts on workers whose livelihoods may be affected when designing new energy systems.

Faith Fosters Community and Cooperation

The enormous challenges we face cannot be solved by individuals acting alone—they require community effort and cooperation across differences. Faith communities already bring together people of various ages, backgrounds, and perspectives around shared values and practices. This makes them powerful potential centers for collaborative action.

Twelve-year-old Miguel witnessed this at his church: "When our pastor preached about creation care, he invited everyone to contribute ideas for our church's environmental stewardship plan. I was amazed how people with different political views all found ways to work together—the businessman who cared about efficient resource use, the artist who wanted to celebrate creation's beauty, the grandmother concerned about her grandchildren's future, and kids like me full of energy and ideas. We didn't agree on everything, but we found enough common ground to start making real changes."

Faith Sustains Us for the Long Journey

Addressing complex challenges like climate change requires sustained effort over many years—not just short bursts of enthusiasm. Faith provides the spiritual resources for this long journey: regular practices of worship, prayer, Scripture study, and Sabbath rest that renew our energy and perspective.

Pastor Garcia shares: "I remind our congregation that care for creation isn't a sprint—it's more like the Israelites' 40-year journey through the wilderness. We need daily manna—God's provision of strength, wisdom, and community. We need Sabbath rhythms of rest and renewal. We need to celebrate small victories along the way. Most importantly, we need the constant reminder that God walks with us, even when the journey feels long and the destination seems far away."

Solarpunk Stories: Faith in Action

Around the world, people of faith combine spiritual courage with practical action to create more resilient, sustainable communities. Here are a few inspiring examples:

The Resurrection Gardens of Detroit

After decades of economic decline left many Detroit neighborhoods with abandoned lots and limited access to fresh food, a coalition of churches developed "Resurrection Gardens"—community gardens on vacant land that produce fresh vegetables while bringing neighbors together.

Deacon Washington explains the project's name: "Just as Christ transforms death into new life, these gardens transform abandoned spaces into places of abundance and hope. Working the soil connects us with God's creation while growing food connects us with God's provision. And doing it together as a community connects us with God's love flowing through neighbors who might otherwise remain strangers."

Now, dozens of church-supported gardens across the city produce tons of fresh produce each year while also providing youth mentoring, job training, and neighborhood beautification.

The New Eden Energy Cooperative

In rural North Carolina, a group of churches formed a cooperative to help members transition to renewable energy. The cooperative purchases solar equipment in bulk to reduce costs, organizes volunteer installation days where members help each other, and provides no-interest loans for families who couldn't otherwise afford the upfront investment.

"We named it 'New Eden' because we're trying to restore the right relationship with God's creation," explains founder Sarah Chen. "But it's not just about solar panels—it's about building a community that reflects God's love and justice. That's why we ensure that at least half of all systems go to lower-income families. Energy bills can be a crushing burden for people on fixed incomes, so this technology brings both environmental and economic benefits."

The Reconciliation Bridge Project

In a small town divided by a physical river and longstanding social tensions, churches on both sides initiated a project to build a footbridge connecting two neighborhoods—one predominantly white and affluent and the other historically Black with fewer resources.

The physical bridge became a catalyst for more profound reconciliation work. As Pastor James explains, "Building the bridge required cooperation, and that cooperation opened doorways for honest conversations about historical inequities and current needs. Now, the physical connection has led to shared community gardens on both sides, a tool-sharing program, emergency response teams that serve both neighborhoods and a youth program where teens work together on climate adaptation projects."

These examples show how faith motivates and provides a framework for addressing complex challenges through community action. Each project reflects biblical values of stewardship, justice, and love of neighbor while creating practical solutions to local needs.

Starting Where You Are: Faithful Next Steps

You might wonder, "What can I do right now to make a difference?" The good news is that you don't need to move to a perfect Solarpunk community or solve all environmental challenges at once. You can start right where you are with the resources and relationships God has already given you.

Here are some age-appropriate ways young people can combine faith and action:

For Younger Children (Ages 8-11)

1. **Creation Care Prayer Walks**: Take regular walks with a parent or trusted adult, noticing and giving thanks for the natural world while praying for wisdom to care for it better.

2. **Resourceful Crafting**: Learn to make useful items from materials that would otherwise be discarded—bird feeders from plastic bottles, garden containers from food packaging, or art from natural materials.

3. **Garden Helpers**: Join family or community garden projects and learn how growing food

connects us to God's provision while reducing the transportation impacts of store-bought produce.

4. **Energy Detectives**: Work with parents to identify ways your household could save energy, such as opening curtains for natural light, turning off unused electronics, and adjusting thermostat settings slightly.

For Older Children and Teens (Ages 12-15)

1. **Faith-Based Environmental Clubs**: Start or join a group at your school or church focused on creation care projects like campus cleanups, recycling initiatives, or habitat restoration.

2. **Skill Development**: Learn practical skills that contribute to resilience—basic cooking, simple repairs, gardening, first aid, or natural crafts—and find opportunities to share these skills with others.

3. **Intergenerational Interviews**: Record conversations with grandparents or elderly church members about how they lived sustainably in earlier times (often out of necessity), preserving valuable knowledge about repairing, reusing, gardening, preserving food, etc.

4. **Community Needs Assessment**: Work with adult mentors to identify environmental or social needs in your community that align with your interests and skills, then develop manageable projects to address them.

Thirteen-year-old Zoe found her own way to make a difference: "I've always loved art and design, so when I learned about fast fashion's environmental impact, I started a 'Repurposed Fashion' club at my school. We transform secondhand clothes into new styles instead of buying new things all the time. Last month, we held a fashion show to raise money for clean water projects. It combines things I care about—creativity, environmental protection, and helping others—in a way that feels both fun and meaningful."

Walking Forward with Courage

As we conclude this chapter, let's return to God's powerful words to Joshua: "Be strong and of a good courage; be not afraid, neither be thou dismayed: for the LORD thy God is with thee whithersoever thou goest."

This promise remains true today. We face significant challenges, from climate change to social division to economic uncertainty. The path forward isn't always clear, and perfect solutions rarely exist. But we don't walk this path alone. God's presence goes with us, providing wisdom, community, and strength for the journey.

Having courage doesn't mean we'll never feel afraid. Joshua probably felt plenty of fear as he led Israel toward the Jordan River! Instead, courage means moving forward despite our fears, trusting God's presence and purposes even when we can't see the entire path ahead.

As you face changes in your world—whether environmental shifts, social transformations, or personal transitions—remember that you're part of a long line of faithful people who stepped forward with courage. Noah built an ark when rain was just a concept. Abraham left home for an unknown destination. Esther approached the king without a guarantee of safety. The disciples left their fishing nets for an uncertain future.

In each case, faith didn't eliminate challenges or guarantee specific outcomes. Instead, it provided the courage to take the next steps, trusting God's presence and purposes even in uncertain times.

Pastor Williams offers this encouragement: "When we face climate change or any other significant challenge, we don't need to have all the answers or a perfect plan. We simply need enough faith for the next faithful step. God doesn't usually give us a complete blueprint for the future. Instead, He gives us principles, wisdom, community, and His presence. Then He invites us to walk forward with courage, adapting and learning as we go."

As you conclude this chapter, take a moment to reflect on your own next steps. What challenges in your world feel most intimidating? Where might God be inviting you to move forward with courage? How could your unique gifts and interests contribute to creating more resilient, sustainable communities?

Whatever your answers, remember that you don't walk alone. God goes with you. Communities of faith and purpose surround you. And countless others—known and unknown, past and present—walk the same path of courage, creating ripples of positive change that extend far beyond what any individual could accomplish alone.

Family Discussion Questions:

1. When have you needed courage to face a challenging situation? What helped you find that courage?

2. What changes in our world feel most concerning to you? What possibilities in those changes might actually be exciting?

3. Where do you see resilience in nature around us? What could we learn from these examples?

4. What's one specific step our family could take to become more resilient or to help our community adapt positively to changes?

Teacher's Corner: This chapter addresses the emotional and spiritual dimensions of environmental engagement—particularly the interplay between legitimate concern about serious challenges and the hope necessary for constructive action. The Resilience Garden project offers an excellent hands-on metaphor for classroom application that connects ecological principles with community resilience.

Consider supplementing this chapter with age-appropriate mindfulness or emotional regulation exercises that help students process eco-anxiety in healthy ways. The Courage Stones activity provides one such tool, creating tangible reminders of spiritual resources available during challenging times.

The emphasis on "next faithful steps" rather than perfect solutions offers a developmentally appropriate framework for environmental engagement—encouraging meaningful action without placing the entire burden of global issues on young shoulders. This approach helps prevent both the paralysis that can come from overwhelming information and the potential cynicism when grand solutions prove elusive.

Chapter 18:

The Garden of Humanity: Celebrating God's Diverse Creation

A World of Wonderful Differences

Have you ever wandered through a garden blooming with dozens of different flowers? Perhaps you've noticed how some blossoms reach tall toward the sky while others spread low along the ground. Some flowers might dazzle with brilliant reds and oranges, while others charm with delicate purples or pristine whites. Some bloom in spring, others in summer, and others save their beauty for autumn.

Imagine someone saying, "I think gardens should only have red roses and nothing else." Wouldn't that seem strange? The garden would still be beautiful—roses are lovely, after all—but it would be missing so much! The cheerful faces of daisies, the proud stand of sunflowers, the gentle nod of bluebells, and the sweet perfume of lilacs would all be absent. The garden would be simpler, yes, but also so much poorer without its wonderful variety.

When God created our world, He clearly loved variety! The Bible tells us:

"And God said, Let the earth bring forth grass, the herb yielding seed, and the fruit tree yielding fruit after his kind, whose seed is in itself, upon the earth: and it was so. And the earth brought forth grass, and herb yielding seed after his kind, and the tree yielding fruit, whose seed was in itself, after his kind: and God saw that it was good." (Genesis 1:11-12)

Did you notice that phrase "after his kind"? God didn't just create one type of plant—He created thousands upon thousands of different kinds! Scientists estimate there are about 390,000 different species of plants on Earth, from tiny mosses to towering sequoia trees. And this incredible variety wasn't an accident or afterthought. The Bible tells us that God looked at all this diversity and "saw that it was good."

In this chapter, we'll discover how God's love of diversity extends beyond plants to people as well. We'll explore how the differences between cultures, abilities, perspectives, and gifts make our human community stronger and more beautiful—just like biodiversity strengthens ecosystems. And we'll learn how Solarpunk communities celebrate both natural and human diversity as essential parts of a flourishing world.

Wonderfully Made: Each Person a Masterpiece

Let's start with something extraordinary: YOU are a one-of-a-kind miracle! As King David wrote in Psalm 139:

"For thou hast possessed my reins: thou hast covered me in my mother's womb. I will praise thee; for I am fearfully and wonderfully made: marvellous are thy works; and that my soul knoweth right well." (Psalm 139:13-14)

The phrase "fearfully and wonderfully made" means you were created with awe-inspiring skill and attention. The Creator of galaxies and oceans crafted you with care and delight! And what's especially remarkable is that God made each person unique—with different appearances, personalities, abilities, and perspectives.

Think about your fingerprints. Out of the billions of people on Earth, no one else has fingerprints exactly like yours! Scientists tell us that even identical twins have different fingerprints. Your eye pattern, voice, and even the way you walk are uniquely yours.

But God's creativity goes far beyond physical differences. Each person has a unique combination of:

- **Talents and abilities**: Some people have amazing musical gifts, while others can solve complex math problems or tell stories that captivate listeners.
- **Personality traits**: Some are outgoing and energetic, while others are thoughtful and observant.
- **Life experiences**: Each person's journey includes different joys, challenges, and lessons that shape their understanding of the world.

- **Cultural heritage**: The languages, traditions, foods, arts, and values passed down through families and communities add rich dimensions to human experience.
- **Spiritual gifts**: The Bible teaches that God gives different gifts to different people—teaching, encouraging, serving, leading, showing mercy, and many more.

Twelve-year-old Amara discovered this truth when her family moved from Nigeria to Canada: "At first, I felt so different from everyone at my new school. I missed the foods, music, and traditions from home. But then, our class did a heritage celebration, and I shared stories and photos from Nigeria. My classmates were fascinated! I realized my different background wasn't something to hide—it was a gift I could share. And I discovered that everyone has unique stories, even people who look like they might be the same."

God didn't create this wonderful human variety by accident. Just as a master artist might use many colors to create a beautiful painting, God designed human diversity as part of His masterpiece. When we respect and celebrate our differences, we honor the creativity of our Creator!

Activity Box: Unique Fingerprint Art

Create a colorful display that celebrates how each person is uniquely designed!

You'll need:

- Washable ink pads in various colors (or washable markers)
- White paper
- Colored pencils or fine-tip markers
- Soap and water for clean-up

Step 1: Press your finger gently on an ink pad (or color the tip of your finger with a washable marker).

Step 2: Press your finger onto the paper to make a fingerprint.

Step 3: Repeat with different fingers and colors to create multiple prints.

Step 4: Use markers or colored pencils to transform your fingerprints into tiny people by adding facial features, arms, legs, hair, and clothes.

Step 5: Add speech bubbles with positive messages about diversity, such as "God made me unique!" or "Different and wonderful!"

When finished, wash your hands thoroughly. Your fingerprint people can serve as a reminder that God made each person unique and special!

Biodiversity: God's Design for Resilient Ecosystems

God's love of diversity isn't just about aesthetics but also function and resilience. Scientists have discovered that ecosystems with greater biodiversity (more different species) are generally healthier and more resilient than those with fewer species.

Think of a prairie with dozens of different plant species growing together. If a disease affects one type of grass, the other plants continue thriving. If a drought occurs, some deep-rooted plants can still access water. If insects attack certain flowers, others remain unaffected. The diversity itself creates strength!

By contrast, a cornfield with only one crop (called a monoculture) faces serious risks. The entire field could be lost if a corn disease or pest arrives. The harvest suffers dramatically if weather conditions aren't perfect for corn that year. This lack of diversity creates vulnerability.

The same principle applies to forests. A diverse forest with many types of trees, shrubs, and ground plants provides a habitat for countless creatures and can better withstand challenges like insects, diseases, or climate changes. A tree plantation with just one species of pine or eucalyptus provides far less habitat and faces greater risks from threats that target that specific tree.

Thirteen-year-old Marco observed this principle during a forest field trip: "Our science class visited two different forest areas. The first was an old-growth forest with tons of different trees, plants, and fungi. Our teacher showed us how when one old tree dies, it becomes a habitat and nutrients for hundreds of species. The second site was a tree farm with rows of identical pines. It looked neater, but our teacher explained that it needed constant human intervention to prevent diseases from wiping everything out. It made me realize that

God's diverse design is actually stronger than our human attempts to simplify everything."

Human Diversity: Strength Through Difference

Just as biodiversity strengthens ecosystems, human diversity strengthens communities. When people with different backgrounds, abilities, perspectives, and gifts come together, the community gains:

Broader Problem-Solving Abilities

People with different experiences and thinking styles approach problems differently. A challenge that stumps one person might be easily solved by someone with a different perspective. When diverse minds work together, more solutions emerge!

Fourteen-year-old Sophia experienced this during a school engineering project: "Our team was trying to design a rainwater collection system for our school garden. We kept getting stuck on how to filter the water efficiently. Then Mateo, who had recently moved from the Philippines, shared how his grandmother used layers of sand, charcoal, and gravel to purify rainwater. Combined with Jason's knowledge of local materials and my measurements, we created a system that worked perfectly. We would never have succeeded with just one person's knowledge."

Richer Cultural Expression

Music, art, literature, dance, food, and celebrations become more vibrant and interesting when diverse cultural traditions contribute. Take Musical Fusions, for example. Two different genres of music come together to create an entirely new sound. Think on how much poorer our world would be without the colorful patterns of West African textiles, the mathematical precision of Islamic geometric art, the moving spirituals born in African American communities, or the delicious spices of Indian cuisine!

Stronger Adaptability to Change

Communities with diverse skills and knowledge can better adapt to changing circumstances. During the COVID-19 pandemic, many communities discovered this truth—some people had medical knowledge, others technical skills for online connection, others gifts for checking on vulnerable neighbors, and still others talents for creating learning materials for children at home. Musicians hold impromptu concerts to lift the spirits of their neighbors.

Deeper Spiritual Understanding

Different cultural and personal perspectives help us see aspects of God's character and Scripture's teaching that we might otherwise miss. Throughout church history, Christians from various cultures have emphasized different aspects of faith—from African churches' vibrant worship and community focus to Asian traditions of meditation and respect for elders to European intellectual traditions of systematic theology.

Pastor Williams explains, "I've been blessed to serve in multicultural congregations throughout my ministry. I've discovered that no single cultural approach to faith captures everything about God. Every culture has both gifts and blind spots in how it understands Scripture. When we learn from different traditions, our understanding of God becomes fuller and richer—more three-dimensional instead of flat."

Project Box: Community Diversity Map

Create a visual representation of how diversity strengthens your community!

You'll need:
- Large poster board or paper
- Colored markers, pencils, or paints
- Optional: photos, magazine cutouts, or printed images

Step 1: In the center of your poster, draw or write the name of your community (neighborhood, school, church, town, etc.)

Step 2: Create branches extending outward from the center, each representing a different type of diversity in your community:
- Cultural backgrounds and languages
- Ages and generations
- Skills and occupations
- Interests and hobbies
- Ways of thinking and learning

Step 3: On each branch, add specific examples from your community—names of people, cultural celebrations, languages spoken, occupations represented, etc.

Step 4: Use images or drawings to make your map visually engaging.

Step 5: Add a title like "Our Community Garden of Diversity" and share it with others!

Solarpunk Celebration of Diversity

Throughout this book, we've explored how Solarpunk communities reimagine sustainable living. One of the core principles of the Solarpunk vision is celebrating biodiversity and human diversity, recognizing that these forms of diversity strengthen and enrich each other.

Biodiverse Urban Landscapes

Rather than creating sterile, uniform city spaces, Solarpunk communities incorporate wildly diverse plants and habitats even in urban settings:

- **Food forests** with multiple layers of edible plants—tall nut and fruit trees, smaller berry bushes, vines, herbs, and root vegetables—all growing together like a natural forest ecosystem

- **Native plant corridors** that provide habitat for local wildlife while reflecting regional ecological identity
- **Pollinator gardens** filled with many different flowering plants to support bees, butterflies, and other essential insects
- **Living buildings** where roofs, walls, and balconies overflow with diverse plant life, creating vertical ecosystems

Twelve-year-old Leila's neighborhood transformed in this direction: "Our town council decided to stop mowing some areas of our public parks and instead plant native wildflower meadows. Now, instead of boring grass that needs constant maintenance, we have amazing spaces full of different flowers that bloom throughout the seasons. I've counted over twenty types of butterflies where there used to be none! The best part is how different the meadows look each month as new flowers bloom and others fade. It's never the same twice."

Culturally Diverse Design and Knowledge

Solarpunk communities recognize that different cultures have developed valuable sustainability practices over centuries of living in particular environments. Rather than imposing one standardized approach, these communities:

- Incorporate traditional ecological knowledge from Indigenous and local cultures
- Adapt architectural styles from diverse regions to local conditions
- Preserve and celebrate cultural food traditions that connect people to local ecosystems
- Honor multiple languages and communication styles

The New Harmony neighborhood in Arizona demonstrates this approach: "Our community includes people from Navajo, Hispanic, Anglo, and Somali backgrounds," explains community organizer Maria Begay. "When we designed our community center and gardens, we incorporated wisdom from each tradition—Navajo knowledge about desert plants and rainwater harvesting, Hispanic expertise in adobe building techniques, Anglo engineering for solar systems, and Somali approaches to community decision-making. The result is far stronger and more beautiful than any single cultural approach could have created."

Inclusive Accessibility

Solarpunk communities recognize that human bodies and minds work in wonderfully diverse ways. Rather than designing spaces just for one "standard" type of person, they create environments that welcome people of all ages, abilities, and ways of experiencing the world:

- **Universal design** principles ensure buildings and public spaces are accessible to people with various mobility needs
- **Sensory-friendly areas** provide options for those who experience sensory processing differences
- **Intergenerational spaces** encourage meaningful connection across age groups
- **Multiple communication methods** ensure information is available in various formats—visual, auditory, tactile, and digital

Fourteen-year-old Elijah, who uses a wheelchair, appreciates this approach: "In our

Solarpunk community design class, we learned that good design means everyone can participate fully. We're creating a community garden where the paths are wide enough for wheelchairs, some planting beds are raised for people who can't bend down, and there are sensory plants for people with visual impairments to enjoy through touch and smell. There's even a quiet corner with less stimulation for people who get overwhelmed by too much noise or activity. It's not about special accommodations—it's about designing for real human diversity from the beginning."

God's Garden of Humanity

Throughout Scripture, we find garden metaphors for God's relationship with people. Eden was the first garden where humans walked with God. The Song of Solomon compares the beloved to a beautiful garden. Jesus used many agricultural parables about seeds, soils, vines, branches, and fruit to explain spiritual truths.

These garden images help us understand God's vision for human communities—not as a sterile monoculture where everyone looks, thinks, and acts the same, but as a vibrant, diverse ecosystem where each person contributes their unique gifts to the whole.

Pastor Garcia suggests: "Imagine human community as God's garden, where:
- Some people are like tall trees providing shelter and wisdom
- Others are like flowering plants bringing beauty and joy
- Some are like herbs with healing gifts for hurting hearts
- Others are like sturdy shrubs offering stability and protection
- Some are like vines that connect different parts of the community
- Others are like groundcover that creates safe spaces for vulnerable growth
- And still, others are like fungi—not always visible but creating essential connections below the surface

None is more important than the others; each contributes something essential to the garden's health. Together, they create an ecosystem far more beautiful, productive, and resilient than any single species could alone."

This metaphor helps us see human differences not as problems to be solved but as gifts to celebrate—expressions of God's creative delight that strengthen and beautify our communities.

Practical Ways to Celebrate Diversity

How can we honor both biodiversity and human diversity in our daily lives? Here are some age-appropriate ideas:

For Kids

1. **Learn about different cultures** through books, foods, music, and friendships with people from various backgrounds.

2. **Notice and appreciate the biodiversity** in your neighborhood. How many different types of trees, flowers, birds, or insects can you identify?

3. **Share your own unique gifts and culture** with others, and show interest when others share theirs with you.

4. **Stand up for inclusion** when you notice someone being left out because of differences.

Ten-year-old Maya found her own way to promote diversity: "I started a 'Cultural Recipe Exchange' at my school where kids bring recipes from their family traditions. We compile them in a class cookbook, and sometimes, we even get to cook them together! I've learned so much about my classmates through the foods they love, and it's helped us appreciate our differences."

For Families

1. **Diversify your bookshelf, music playlist, and movie collection** to include voices and perspectives from various cultures.

2. **Plant diverse gardens** that support local pollinators and reflect the native ecosystem of your region.

3. **Attend cultural festivals and events** in your community to learn about different traditions.

4. **Examine family routines and traditions** to ensure they're welcoming to family members with different needs, abilities, and preferences.

For Communities

1. **Reimagine public spaces** to incorporate both greater biodiversity and more inclusive design for human diversity.

2. **Create multilingual signage and communications** that welcome people who speak different languages.

3. **Develop decision-making processes** that ensure diverse voices are included, especially those often marginalized.

4. **Sponsor cultural exchange events** where community members can share food, music, stories, and traditions.

Activity Box: "Beautiful Differences" Nature Journal

Create a special journal celebrating the beauty of diversity in God's creation!

You'll need:

- A notebook or journal
- Colored pencils or markers
- Optional: glue stick, pressed leaves or flowers

Each week, choose a different aspect of natural diversity to observe and record:

1. Leaf shapes: Collect and trace or press leaves from different trees

2. Flower colors: Draw or describe the variety of colors in local flowers

3. Bird behaviors: Observe how different birds move, eat, and interact

4. Seed designs: Notice the fantastic variety of seed shapes and dispersal methods

5. Insect adaptations: Observe how different insects have unique features

After each nature observation, reflect on how this natural diversity might parallel human diversity. For example: "Just as different leaf shapes help trees capture sunlight differently, people's diverse thinking styles help communities solve problems from different angles."

When Differences Create Challenges

While diversity brings tremendous strength and beauty to communities, we should acknowledge that differences sometimes create challenges. People with different cultural backgrounds may misunderstand each other's intentions, and those with different thinking styles might find communication difficult. Communities with diverse perspectives sometimes struggle to reach a consensus on important decisions.

These challenges don't mean diversity is a problem—they simply reflect the learning and growth required for diverse communities to flourish together. The Bible recognizes this reality and offers wisdom for navigating differences with grace:

- **Practice humble listening**: "*Wherefore, my beloved brethren, let every man be swift to hear, slow to speak, slow to wrath*" (James 1:19).

- **Seek understanding before judgment**: "*Judge not according to the appearance, but judge righteous judgment*" (John 7:24).

- **Emphasize unity within diversity**: "*That they all may be one; as thou, Father, art in me, and I in thee, that they also may be one in us*" (John 17:21).

- **Value others above yourself**: "*Let nothing be done through strife or vainglory, but in lowliness of mind let each esteem other better than themselves*" (Philippians 2:3).

Pastor Rodriguez shares: "In our multicultural congregation, we sometimes have misunderstandings because of different cultural expectations about time, communication styles, or decision-making processes. We've learned that these moments aren't failures—they're opportunities to practice the fruits of the Spirit: patience, kindness, and gentleness. When we approach differences with curiosity instead of judgment, we often discover beautiful new insights about God and each other."

Looking Ahead

In our next chapter, we'll explore how to share the light of hope through action, examining how we can spread positive change through advocacy and example. We'll discover how small actions can create ripples of transformation far beyond what we might imagine.

For now, take some time this week to notice and celebrate the wonderful diversity God has created—both in the natural world and in the human community. Look for ways that differences strengthen and beautify your neighborhood, school, or church. And remember that you yourself are a unique creation, *"fearfully and wonderfully made,"* with specific gifts to contribute to God's diverse garden of humanity.

As you move through your days, pay special attention to people whose backgrounds, abilities, or perspectives differ from your own. What might you learn from them? How might their unique gifts complement yours? And how might your community become stronger and more beautiful by fully including everyone's contributions?

Family Discussion Questions:

1. What's something you appreciate about a person who is different from you in some way?

2. How have you seen diversity (either in nature or in human communities) create strength?

3. When have differences created challenges in our family or community? How did we address those challenges?

4. How could our family better celebrate and support diversity in our neighborhood or church?

Teacher's Corner: This chapter approaches diversity from an integrated ecological and social perspective, helping students understand the theological foundations for valuing both biodiversity and human diversity. For classroom application, consider supplementing the nature journal activity with structured observation opportunities, perhaps partnering with the science curriculum on ecosystem studies.

The community diversity mapping project offers an excellent opportunity for social studies integration. It helps students recognize and appreciate the various forms of diversity in their own communities. Consider expanding this into an interview project in which students document the stories and contributions of community members from different backgrounds.

For faith-based educational settings, this chapter offers a framework for discussing diversity that goes beyond political divisions by grounding the conversation in theological concepts of God's creative design and the inherent worth of every individual. The garden metaphor serves as an accessible entry point for younger students while still allowing for deeper discussions with older students.

Chapter 19:

Let Your Light Shine: Spreading Hope Through Action

Candles in the Darkness

Have you ever held a single candle in a dark room? It's amazing how that tiny flame pushes back the darkness, creating a circle of golden light where there was only shadow moments before. If you've ever been camping or experienced a power outage, you know how precious even a small light can be when everything else is dark.

Now imagine if someone brought a second candle and lit it from yours. Suddenly, the room is a little brighter! Then imagine a third candle joining and a fourth until a whole circle of people stand with glowing lights. What was once a dark room now dances with warm illumination—not because any single flame grew enormous, but because many small lights joined together.

This beautiful image helps us understand what Jesus meant when He said:

"Ye are the light of the world. A city that is set on an hill cannot be hid. Neither do men light a candle, and put it under a bushel, but on a candlestick; and it giveth light unto all that are in the house. Let your light so shine before men, that they may see your good works, and glorify your Father which is in heaven." (Matthew 5:14-16)

When Jesus spoke these words during His Sermon on the Mount, He was teaching His followers something remarkable—that ordinary people like us can shine with God's light in a world that sometimes feels dark or discouraging. We don't need to be perfect, or famous, or powerful. We simply need to let the light of God's love and truth shine through our daily actions and choices.

In this chapter, we'll discover how living in ways that care for God's creation can be a powerful form of witness to others. We'll meet people whose eco-conscious choices have inspired their communities to positive change. And we'll explore practical, age-appropriate ways that you can let your own light shine, spreading hope through action in your home, school, church, and neighborhood.

Your Light Matters: Small Actions with Big Impact

Sometimes, young people wonder if their actions really matter when facing big challenges like climate change or environmental degradation. "I'm just one kid," you might think. "How can anything I do make a difference?" This feeling is perfectly normal—even adults feel this way sometimes!

But Jesus' candle metaphor reminds us that small lights still matter. In fact, they matter tremendously! Consider these encouraging truths:

Small Actions Can Inspire Others

When you make creation-friendly choices—like carrying a reusable water bottle, starting a compost bin, choosing to walk or bike instead of asking for a ride, or taking time to appreciate nature—people notice. Friends, classmates, family members, and neighbors observe what you do, and your example can spark new thoughts or actions in their own lives.

Twelve-year-old Maya discovered this when she started bringing waste-free lunches to school: "At first, I was the only one using reusable containers instead of plastic bags. Some kids even teased me about it. But after a while, a few friends got curious and asked why I was doing it. I explained how to reduce plastic waste in the oceans and showed them my cool bento box with different compartments. By the end of the year, about ten kids in my class had switched to reusable containers! My small choice started a mini movement."

Your Voice Has Unique Influence

Each person has a circle of influence where their voice carries special weight. Your friends, siblings, and sometimes even your parents might listen to you in ways they wouldn't listen to others. When you speak up about issues you care about—especially with knowledge, enthusiasm, and practical suggestions rather than criticism—you can help change hearts and minds.

Fourteen-year-old Aiden influenced his entire family: "When I learned about energy waste at school, I started going around our house turning off lights and unplugging chargers when not in use. At first, my parents thought I was just being picky, but when our electricity bill went down, they got interested! I showed them what I was learning about phantom energy use, and now our whole family is more conscious about it. My dad even installed smart power strips that automatically cut power to devices not in use."

Today's Seeds Grow Tomorrow's Forests

Many of history's most important changes began with small actions that seemed insignificant at the time. The mighty oak tree grows from a tiny acorn! The creation-friendly habits and knowledge you develop now might seem small today, but they're laying the groundwork for bigger impacts in the future.

Pastor Williams shares this perspective: "I've been a pastor for thirty years, and I've watched children in our congregation grow into adults who are changing the world. The girl who organized church cleanup days is now an environmental lawyer. The boy who was always rescuing injured animals is now a wildlife veterinarian. The teenagers who started our church garden are now teaching sustainable agriculture in developing countries. Never underestimate how today's small actions shape tomorrow's world-changers."

Activity Box: Light-Spreader Journal

Start tracking how your actions create ripples of positive change!

You'll need:

- A notebook or journal
- Colored pens or pencils
- Optional: stickers or decorative elements

Create sections in your journal for recording:

1. Light Actions: Eco-friendly or creation-care choices you make

2. Ripple Effects: How others respond or what positive results you observe

3. New Ideas: Inspiration for future actions you might take

Set aside a few minutes each week to update your journal. Over time, you'll create a beautiful record of how your small lights are helping illuminate the world around you!

Living as Witnesses: Action Speaks Louder Than Words

In the early church, Christians were known for living differently from the surrounding culture. They shared possessions so no one would be in need, cared for the sick during plagues when others fled, treated slaves and women with unprecedented dignity, and demonstrated remarkable joy amid persecution. Their distinctive lifestyle prompted questions and opened doors for sharing their faith.

Today, eco-conscious living can serve a similar witnessing purpose. When we make choices that honor God's creation—using resources wisely, caring for plants and animals, reducing waste and pollution—we demonstrate important truths about God's character and purposes:

Our Actions Show That Creation Matters to God

When Christians invest time, energy, and resources in caring for the natural world, we communicate an important theological truth: God values His creation! The opening chapters of Genesis reveal that God declared the physical world "very good" even before humans were created. Jesus taught using examples from nature and emphasized God's care for even sparrows and lilies. Our creation care efforts witness to God's ongoing love for all He has made.

Our Choices Reveal Faith That Transcends Consumption

In a culture that often measures worth by possessions and encourages constant consumption of more and newer things, creation-friendly living offers a powerful counter-witness. When Christians choose sufficiency over excess, quality over quantity, sharing over hoarding, and contentment over endless acquisition, we demonstrate faith in something beyond material wealth.

Thirteen-year-old Sofia experienced this firsthand: "For my birthday, I asked for experiences instead of things—like a family camping trip and cooking lessons with my grandmother. Some of my friends thought it was weird that I didn't want 'real presents,' but it led to amazing conversations about what actually makes life good. I got to share how my faith helps me value relationships and memories more than stuff. Now a few of my friends are asking for experience gifts too!"

Our Care for Creation Demonstrates Love for Others

Climate change and environmental degradation often hurt vulnerable communities first and worst—those with fewer resources to adapt or relocate. When Christians take steps to reduce pollution, conserve resources, and advocate for environmental protection, we're demonstrating Christ's command to "love thy neighbor as thyself" in practical ways.

Pastor Garcia clarifies this connection: "In our congregation, we talk about environmental stewardship as a justice issue, not just a scientific one. When we installed solar panels on our church roof, we explained it as living out Jesus' teaching to love our neighbors—both current neighbors affected by pollution and future neighbors who will inherit the world we leave behind. This framing has helped bridge political differences in our congregation because it connects to core values we all share."

Modern Light Bearers: Stories of Hopeful Witness

Throughout the world, Christians and Solarpunk communities are finding creative ways to witness through eco-conscious living. Here are some inspiring examples that demonstrate how small lights can grow into powerful beacons of hope:

The Neighborhood Transformation Garden

In Detroit, Michigan, a church youth group started with a simple project—converting an abandoned lot into a small vegetable garden. They didn't have a master plan or large budget, just willing hands and a desire to bring beauty to a neglected space.

"At first, neighbors were skeptical," recalls youth leader Ms. Washington. "This lot had been a dumping ground for years. But when people saw our teenagers out there every Saturday, pulling weeds and hauling away trash, attitudes began to change. Neighbors started stopping by to chat, then to offer advice about what grows well in our climate, and eventually to help with the work."

Five years later, this initial garden has expanded to fifteen lots throughout the neighborhood. The project now includes:

- Vegetable gardens that supply fresh produce to local families
- A community kitchen where cooking classes teach healthy meal preparation
- A seed library preserving heirloom varieties
- Paid apprenticeships teaching gardening skills to neighborhood youth
- Weekly community meals that bring diverse neighbors together

"People often ask why we do this work," says sixteen-year-old Marcus, who joined the project as a twelve-year-old. "That's when we get to share about how God created humans to tend gardens and how Jesus taught us to love our neighbors. We don't force conversations about faith, but they happen naturally because our actions prompt questions. Last year, five families started attending our church after first connecting through the garden!"

The School That Changed a Town

At Riverside Middle School in Oregon, a seventh-grade science project about watershed pollution expanded into a community-wide environmental transformation. Teacher Mrs. Chen challenged her students to test water quality in local streams and research solutions to the contamination they found.

"We discovered that road runoff was carrying all kinds of pollutants into our waterways," explains former student Leila, now in high school. "Instead of just writing a report, we decided to actually do something about it. We designed simple rain gardens that could filter water naturally before it reached the streams."

The students created a demonstration rain garden on school property and then presented their findings to the town council with a proposal to install more rain gardens throughout the community. Their well-researched, solution-oriented approach impressed the council members, who approved funding for three initial public rain gardens.

"What happened next was amazing," recalls Mrs. Chen. "Local businesses started sponsoring more rain gardens. Homeowners began installing them in their yards. The garden club adopted the project and added native flowering plants that support pollinators. Now our town is known regionally for its beautiful rain gardens, and water quality in our streams has measurably improved."

Although the project didn't explicitly start as a faith-based witness, the Christian students involved naturally shared their motivations when asked. "When people complimented our work, it gave me chances to explain how my faith teaches me to care for God's creation," says Jamal, one of the original project members. I wasn't trying to preach at anyone—I was just honestly answering when they asked why I cared so much about this project."

The Faith Network for Earth Stewardship

In North Carolina, an interfaith coalition was formed to address environmental challenges through collaborative action. What began as a small group of faith leaders meeting monthly has grown into a network of over fifty congregations—Christian, Jewish, Muslim, Unitarian, and others—working together on practical projects:

- A solar bulk-purchasing program that has helped hundreds of families and several houses of worship install affordable solar power
- Community weatherization days where volunteers help low-income households improve energy efficiency
- A green certification program for religious buildings
- Environmental education materials designed for various faith traditions
- Advocacy for clean energy policies at the state level

"We discovered that creation care provides common ground where people with different theological perspectives can work together," explains Reverend Thompson, one of the founding members. "While we maintain our distinct faith identities, we've found that caring for the Earth gives us meaningful ways to collaborate and build relationships across traditional boundaries."

Network coordinator Sarah Chen adds: "This work has been a powerful witness both within and beyond our faith communities. Within our congregations, it demonstrates that environmental stewardship is deeply rooted in our spiritual traditions, not just a secular concern. Beyond our walls, it shows a divided world that diverse faith communities can work together constructively for the common good."

Practical Ways to Let Your Light Shine

Ready to become a more effective light-bearer in your own community? Here are age-appropriate ideas for different stages of life:

For Kids (Ages 8-13)

1. **Be a Waste Warrior**: Take responsibility for recycling in your home, learn what can and can't be recycled in your community, and gently help family members put items in the right bins. Create homemade signs with pictures to make it easier for everyone.

2. **Start a Nature Club**: Invite friends to observe and protect nature in your neighborhood.

You might monitor bird populations, pick up litter in local parks, or create wildlife-friendly spaces.

3. **Become a Resource Detective**: Learn about your home's energy and water use, then look for ways to reduce waste. Simple actions like turning off lights, taking shorter showers, or unplugging chargers can make a difference—especially when you explain to others why you're doing them!

4. **Create Eco-Art**: Use your artistic talents to create posters, comics, videos, or social media posts that share environmental care tips in fun, non-preachy ways. Let your creativity spark conversations!

Eleven-year-old Zoe found her own unique approach: "I love making friendship bracelets, so I started creating them from recycled materials like plastic bag yarn and old t-shirt strips. When friends ask about them, I explain why I'm trying to reuse materials instead of buying new stuff. Now, several of us have a weekly craft circle where we make cool things from materials that would have been thrown away."

For Families

1. **Adopt a "One In, One Out" Rule**: When bringing new items into your home, identify something you no longer need that can be donated or repurposed. This practices both simplicity and generosity.

2. **Create Family Stewardship Goals**: Together, set specific targets for reducing waste, conserving energy, or other environmental practices. Track your progress visually and celebrate milestones!

3. **Choose Experience Gifts**: For birthdays and holidays, consider giving experiences (museum trips, special outings, lessons) rather than material items. This creates precious memories while reducing consumption.

4. **Share Skills with Others**: Does your family have particular eco-friendly skills like gardening, repair abilities, or efficient cooking? Host workshops where you can share these skills with friends, neighbors, or church members.

For Schools and Churches

1. **Start a Creation Care Team**: Gather like-minded students or congregation members to identify environmental improvements for your institution. Focus on practical projects that demonstrate visible benefits.

2. **Host a Green Fair**: Organize an event where people can learn about sustainable practices, repair broken items, swap useful goods, or learn new skills. Make it festive and solution-oriented rather than doom-focused!

3. **Create Educational Materials**: Develop age-appropriate resources that connect faith teachings with environmental stewardship. Share these with other classes or congregations.

4. **Form Community Partnerships**: Connect with local environmental organizations, other faith communities, or civic groups to collaborate on projects that benefit your wider community.

Project Box: Create an "Eco-Evangelist" Kit

Prepare a toolkit that helps you share environmental care in positive, engaging ways!

You'll need:

- A container (box, bag, or basket)
- Small items demonstrating eco-friendly alternatives (reusable straw, beeswax wrap, cloth napkin, etc.)
- Cards with simple facts about environmental challenges AND solutions
- Photos or drawings showing creation beauty worth protecting
- A journal for recording questions people ask and effective responses

When conversations about environmental topics arise, your kit provides tangible examples and helpful information. Remember to focus on positive solutions rather than just problems and connect your care for creation to your faith in ways that feel natural and authentic!

Navigating Conversations with Grace and Wisdom

As you share your eco-conscious lifestyle with others, you'll inevitably encounter different responses—from enthusiastic support to genuine curiosity to skepticism or even opposition. Here are some tips for navigating these conversations with both grace and effectiveness:

Lead With Actions, Follow With Words

The most powerful witness often comes when others notice your actions and ask about them. Instead of leading with lectures or criticism of others' choices, focus on living your values consistently. When people express curiosity about why you bring your own bags, choose different transportation, or abstain from certain products, these questions open natural doorways for sharing your motivations.

Fourteen-year-old Marcus discovered this principle through trial and error: "When I first learned about plastic pollution, I went around pointing out everything everyone was doing wrong. I just made people defensive and annoyed. My youth pastor suggested I try modeling alternatives instead of criticizing. When I switched to just using my own reusable items without comment, people actually got curious and started asking questions. Those conversations were way more productive!"

Connect Environmental Care to Core Values

When explaining your eco-conscious choices, try connecting them to widely shared values rather than specialized knowledge or controversial topics. Most people—regardless of their views on climate science or politics—value clean air and water, healthy children, thriving communities, and responsible use of resources.

Pastor Williams uses this approach in his diverse congregation: "Rather than debating climate change, we talk about being good neighbors by reducing pollution, being good stewards of what God has given us, and leaving a healthy world for our grandchildren. These values-based frames help us find common ground even with people who might approach environmental issues from different perspectives."

Offer Invitations, Not Obligations

The most effective eco-evangelists don't pressure others to make immediate, dramatic changes. Instead, they invite people to join specific, manageable actions that provide positive experiences.

Thirteen-year-old Sofia shares: "Instead of telling my friends they should stop using plastic water bottles, I invited them to join me in decorating reusable bottles with cool stickers and designs. We made it a fun craft project, and now several friends have awesome personalized bottles they actually want to use. It worked better than lectures ever would have!"

Balance, Honesty, and Hope

When discussing environmental challenges, it's important to be truthful about the seriousness of issues like climate change, biodiversity loss, or pollution. However, effective witnesses balance this honesty with genuine hope and emphasis on positive solutions.

Youth leader Mr. Garcia explains this balance: "We don't sugar-coat environmental problems when working with young people—they deserve the truth. But we always pair honest assessments with hopeful examples of solutions already working in communities around the world. This approach respects their intelligence while protecting them from despair or cynicism."

The Power of Story: Sharing Your Journey

One of the most effective ways to share your creation care values is through personal stories rather than abstract arguments. People connect with authentic accounts of your experiences, challenges, learnings, and motivations.

Consider preparing brief, engaging stories about:

• What first sparked your interest in caring for creation

• A moment when you felt especially connected to nature

• How your faith inspires your environmental choices

• A small success you've experienced in changing habits

• What you've learned through mistakes or challenges

Twelve-year-old Aiden from California discovered the power of story during a school presentation: "I was nervous about speaking to my class about ocean conservation because some kids think caring about the environment isn't cool. Instead of giving a bunch of facts, I shared about finding a seal tangled in plastic at our local beach and how helping with the rescue changed how I saw the problem. The story grabbed everyone's attention in a way statistics never would have, and several classmates asked how they could help with beach cleanups."

Personal stories are powerful because they:

- Create emotional connection rather than intellectual arguments
- Invite others into your experience without pressuring them
- Honor others' agency to respond in their own way
- Demonstrate authenticity that builds trust
- Often prompt others to share their own stories in return

Looking Ahead

In our next chapter, we'll explore how following Jesus sometimes means choosing a path different from mainstream culture—walking the "narrow way" that leads to life rather than the wide, crowded path that leads to destruction. We'll discover how choosing faith over convenience can lead to deeper joy and purpose, even when it requires sacrifice.

For now, remember Jesus' encouragement that you are "the light of the world." The choices you make, the actions you take, and the life you live can illuminate paths for others who might be searching for hope and meaning in a confusing time. You don't need to be perfect, famous, wealthy, or powerful to let your light shine. You simply need to live with integrity, allowing God's love for creation and people to shine through your ordinary, everyday life.

As you go through this week, look for small opportunities to let your light shine a little brighter. Notice the ripple effects of your positive choices. Pay attention to doors that open for deeper conversations. And remember that when many small lights join together, they can illuminate even the darkest spaces with hope and possibility.

Family Discussion Questions:

1. When have you seen someone's actions inspire others to make positive changes? How did they share their values effectively?

2. What creation care practices in our family might be noticeable or interesting to others? How could we share these practices graciously if asked?

3. What's one area where our family's "light" could shine more brightly in caring for creation? What practical step might we take this week?

4. How does our faith motivate our environmental choices? How might we articulate this practice? How might we articulate this connection?

Teacher's Corner: This chapter addresses the important connection between environmental action and faith witness in ways appropriate for middle-grade students. For classroom application, the "Light-Spreader Journal" offers an excellent ongoing activity that helps students recognize their capacity for positive influence while building reflection skills.

Consider supplementing this chapter with role-playing exercises that allow students to practice graciously responding to questions or skepticism about their environmental choices. This approach builds communication skills while helping students articulate their values in age-appropriate ways. The emphasis on action preceding words is particularly important for this age group, which is developing its sense of authentic identity and is sensitive to perceived hypocrisy.

This chapter offers rich opportunities for faith-based educational settings to connect environmental stewardship with evangelism and witness. The "Modern Light Bearers" stories can be expanded with examples from your own faith tradition or local community, helping students see concrete models of how creation care can open doors for sharing faith in natural, non-coercive ways.

Chapter 20:

The Narrow Path: Choosing Faith Over Convenience

Two Paths in the Woods

Imagine you're hiking through a beautiful forest and come to a fork in the trail. One path looks wide, smooth, and well-traveled. You can see it stretches out before you, level and easy to walk on. Lots of other hikers are strolling along this route, chatting and moving quickly without much effort.

The second path is narrower—not tiny, but certainly less spacious. It winds uphill between tall trees and appears a bit more challenging. Fewer people have chosen this route, but those who have seem purposeful and focused. Looking closely, you notice this path leads toward a breathtaking mountain view that can't be seen from the wider trail.

Which path would you choose?

This is similar to the choice Jesus described in one of His most thought-provoking teachings:

"Enter ye in at the strait gate: for wide is the gate, and broad is the way, that leadeth to destruction, and many there be which go in thereat: Because strait is the gate, and narrow is the way, which leadeth unto life, and few there be that find it." (Matthew 7:13-14)

The word "strait" here doesn't mean straight like a ruler—it means narrow or constrained. Jesus explained that living according to God's ways sometimes means taking a path that's different from what most people choose. The popular, convenient route doesn't always lead to the best destination!

In this chapter, we'll explore what it means to choose the "narrow path" in our relationship with creation. We'll discover that while convenient consumer choices often seem easier in the moment, faithful stewardship choices—though sometimes requiring more thought, effort, or sacrifice—lead to greater flourishing for both our planet and our spirits in the long run.

The Wide, Convenient Path

In today's world, the "wide path" often looks like choosing whatever is most convenient, regardless of its impact on God's creation or future generations. This path is certainly understandable—our busy lives make quick, easy options tempting! The wide path might include:

- Grabbing disposable items instead of reusable ones because they're faster
- Driving short distances that could be walked or biked because it's quicker
- Choosing whatever is cheapest without considering how it was made
- Tossing things in the trash rather than figuring out if they can be recycled, repaired, or repurposed
- Running the air conditioner or heater at maximum settings rather than adapting clothing or activities to weather conditions
- Buying new items whenever something breaks instead of attempting repairs

Twelve-year-old Marco observed this pattern in his own life: "When I really started paying attention, I realized how often I choose things just because they're easy. At lunch, I'd grab a juice box with a plastic straw instead of filling my reusable water bottle. After school, I'd ask for a ride to my friend's house two blocks away instead of walking. None of these choices seemed like a big deal individually, but they added up to a pattern of always taking the convenient route without thinking about the consequences."

The wide path is appealing because it's smooth in the short term—it requires less planning, effort, and often less immediate expense. But like a road that leads away from a beautiful destination, these seemingly small choices can gradually distance us from the life of faithful stewardship God designed us for.

The Narrow Path of Faithful Stewardship

The "narrow path" Jesus described isn't narrow because God wants to make life difficult! Rather, it's narrow because it requires intentional choices that might not align with what the majority of people around us are doing. This path is marked by thoughtful consideration of how our actions affect

God's creation, other people (both now and in the future), and our own spiritual health.

Walking this narrower path might look like:

- Planning ahead to bring reusable items rather than relying on disposables
- Allowing extra time for walking, biking, or public transportation when possible
- Considering the whole "story" behind products—how they were made, by whom, and with what environmental impact
- Learning proper recycling guidelines and composting methods, even though it takes more effort than just throwing everything in one bin
- Adapting to seasonal temperatures with appropriate clothing, selective heating/cooling, and adjusted activities instead of maintaining one constant indoor climate year-round
- Developing basic repair skills or finding repair resources in your community

Thirteen-year-old Sophia's family chose the narrower path regarding transportation: "Last year, my parents decided we would try to use our car only for trips over two miles. For shorter distances, we walk or bike. At first, it was really hard—we had to wake up earlier for school and plan our time differently. Sometimes we get wet in the rain or sweaty in the summer. But after a few months, it started feeling normal and even fun! We notice so many more details about our neighborhood now, we've met more neighbors, and we all feel healthier and more connected to our community."

The narrow path often requires more intention, preparation, learning, and sometimes immediate sacrifice, but it leads toward greater flourishing for ourselves, our communities, and God's creation.

Activity Box: Path Reflection

Take some time to identify "wide path" and "narrow path" options in your daily life!

You'll need:

- A notebook or journal
- Colored pens or pencils

Step 1: Create two columns labeled "Wide Path (Convenient)" and "Narrow Path (Faithful)"

Step 2: Throughout your day, notice choices where you have both an easier option and a more creation-friendly but perhaps less convenient option

Step 3: Record these paired choices in your columns

Step 4: Circle the choices you currently make most often

Step 5: Star one or two "narrow path" options you'd like to try implementing this week

This exercise isn't about feeling guilty—it's about growing in awareness of how daily choices form paths that lead in different directions!

Why the Narrow Path Matters

Choosing the narrow path of faithful creation care isn't just about environmental impact—though that's certainly important! It's about aligning our entire lives more closely with God's intended design for humans as caring stewards of His world. Here are some reasons why this path, though sometimes less convenient, leads to true flourishing:

Spiritual Formation: Becoming More Like Christ

Jesus consistently chose obedience to God and love for others over personal convenience or comfort. When we make similar choices in our relationship with creation, we practice Christlike character—developing patience, thoughtfulness, self-control, and consideration for others beyond our immediate desires.

Pastor Williams explains this: "Creation care choices are spiritual formation opportunities. When you choose to repair something broken instead of replacing it, you're practicing patience. When you bike instead of asking for a ride, you're developing self-discipline. When you consider how your purchases affect people and places you'll never see, you're growing in compassion. These small daily choices shape not just our planet's future but our own souls."

Relationship Building: Creating Authentic Community

The narrow path often leads us toward deeper connections with others. Sharing rides, exchanging repair skills, borrowing tools instead of everyone owning their own, participating in community gardens—these creation-friendly choices naturally foster relationships that convenience culture often misses.

Fourteen-year-old Leila discovered this through her family's decision to live with one car: "When we decided to become a one-car family, we had to start carpooling with neighbors for some activities. At first, it felt awkward to ask for rides, but now we have these amazing conversations during our shared trips. My mom gives rides to our elderly neighbor for her doctor appointments, and in exchange, she teaches me how to bake traditional pastries from her homeland. We've built real friendships that never would have developed if we'd kept driving separately in our own little bubbles."

Creation Renewal: Healing Our Home Planet

Of course, the narrow path choices also contribute to the healing of God's creation—reducing pollution, conserving resources, protecting habitats, and addressing climate disruption. These benefits might not be immediately visible from one person's actions, but collectively, they create significant positive impacts.

Eleven-year-old Jamal witnessed this transformation in his neighborhood: "Our community decided to stop using chemical lawn fertilizers and pesticides because they were washing into our creek and harming the fish. The first summer, people complained because some lawns didn't look as perfect. But by the third year, something amazing happened—the creek had otters again! No one alive in our town remembered ever seeing otters before. Now, people are so proud of 'our otters' that no one misses the perfect lawns. What seemed like a sacrifice turned into a gift."

Countercultural Living: Standing Out for Good Reasons

Walking the narrow path often means making choices that differ from mainstream culture. This can feel challenging, especially for young people who naturally want to fit in with peers. But Jesus never promised His followers would blend seamlessly with the surrounding culture! In fact, He said:

"Ye are the salt of the earth... Ye are the light of the world. A city that is set on an hill cannot be hid." (Matthew 5:13-14)

Salt stands out because it has a different flavor than everything around it. Light stands out because it shines in darkness. When we make creation-friendly choices that prioritize faithful stewardship over convenience, we might stand out from the crowd—but in ways that can actually attract others to a better path!

Standing out by walking the narrower path can sometimes lead to good conversations, opportunities to share your values, and even inspiring others to join you!

Spiritual Practices for Narrow Path Living

Choosing the less convenient path consistently requires spiritual resources—inner strength and motivation that goes beyond just "trying harder." Throughout Christian history, believers have developed spiritual practices that help sustain faithful living. Here are some practices particularly helpful for creation care:

Gratitude: Appreciating What We Already Have

A regular practice of giving thanks for the resources, relationships, and natural beauty already present in our lives helps counter consumer culture's constant message that we need more, newer, and better things. Gratitude helps us recognize abundance where the wider culture sees scarcity.

Try keeping a creation gratitude journal, writing down three specific natural gifts you notice each day—from dramatic sunsets to the perfect design of a leaf to the refreshing taste of clean water. This practice trains your attention to value what you already have rather than always craving more.

Sabbath: Practicing Holy Rest

Setting aside regular time to rest from production and consumption—whether a traditional religious Sabbath or another designated period—helps break the cycle of constant doing and acquiring. During Sabbath time, we remember that our value doesn't come from what we produce or possess but from being beloved children of God.

Twelve-year-old Ethan's family practices a weekly "electricity Sabbath" from sunset Friday to sunset Saturday: "Except for our refrigerator and heating system, we unplug from electricity one day a week. Instead of screens and electric entertainment, we play board games by natural light, take walks, read books, and talk more. It was really hard at first—I missed my games and shows! But now it's my favorite day of the week. I feel more peaceful and connected to my family."

Simplicity: Clearing Away Distraction

The practice of simplicity involves intentionally removing excess possessions, activities, and commitments that distract us from what matters most. This doesn't mean living with nothing; rather, it means thoughtfully choosing what supports our deepest values and releasing what doesn't.

For young people, this might mean periodically sorting through possessions to donate items no longer needed, being selective about extracurricular activities to allow margin in your schedule or designating screen-free times or zones in your home to create space for other experiences.

Community: Finding Support for the Journey

No one walks the narrow path alone! Finding or creating a community with others who share your values provides encouragement, practical support, and the joy of shared purpose.

This might look like joining (or starting) an environmental club at school, participating in a church creation care team, connecting with local conservation groups that welcome young volunteers, or simply finding a few friends who also care about living more sustainably.

Project Box: Narrow Path Challenge Week

Organize a week-long challenge where you and friends or family members commit to choosing "narrow path" options in a specific area of life. Here are some challenge ideas:

- Zero-Waste Lunches: Pack meals without any disposable packaging
- Car-Free Days: Use only human-powered transportation for short trips
- Repair Instead of Replace: Fix something broken instead of buying new

- Phantom Energy Hunt: Identify and unplug devices using electricity when not in use
- Secondhand First: Commit to checking secondhand sources before purchasing new items

Create a group chat, bulletin board, or daily meetup where participants can share their experiences, challenges, and discoveries. At the end of the week, celebrate your efforts with a special gathering!

Real-Life Narrow Path Journeys

All around the world, people of different ages are discovering the joy and purpose of choosing the narrower path of faithful creation stewardship, even when it means sacrificing some convenience. Here are a few inspiring examples:

The Repair Café Movement

In Amsterdam, Netherlands, Martine Postma had a simple but revolutionary idea: instead of throwing broken items away, what if communities created spaces where people could bring their broken things and find help repairing them?

The first Repair Café opened in 2009, and now over 2,200 exist worldwide! These community spaces match people who have repair skills (electronics, furniture, clothing, bicycles, etc.) with those who have broken items. Together, they work to fix things instead of discarding them.

"Repair Cafés choose the narrow path over the convenient one," explains youth volunteer coordinator James Martinez. "It's almost always easier to throw something away and buy a replacement. But taking the time to repair items saves resources, teaches valuable skills, builds community relationships, and reminds us that we can fix things instead of just consuming more."

Youth play important roles in this movement, often partnering with older generations with repair skills to share. Fourteen-year-old Sophia discovered her passion at a local Repair Café: "I thought I wanted to be a fashion designer, but after volunteering at our Repair Café and learning to mend clothing, I'm now interested in sustainable fashion that focuses on durable, repairable garments. I'm learning both traditional techniques from elderly volunteers and modern approaches to upcycling."

The Thompson Family's Year of Living Differently

The Thompson family—parents, a teenager, and two elementary-aged children—decided to spend one year intentionally choosing the "narrow path" in four areas of life: transportation, food, energy, and purchasing. They didn't make extreme changes all at once but gradually shifted toward more sustainable choices.

For transportation, they committed to walking, biking, or using public transit for any trip under three miles. "The first month was really challenging," recalls 13-year-old Jason. "We had to wake up earlier and plan our time differently. Sometimes, we got wet in the rain or tired from biking uphill. But after a while, it just became our normal. Now I actually prefer biking to school—I arrive more awake and energized than when we drove."

For food, the family committed to eating meat only once per week and focusing on locally grown, seasonal produce. "I really missed having meat at every dinner at first," Jason admits. "But my parents found great vegetarian recipes, and now some of my favorite meals are plant-based. I'm also much more aware of where our food comes from after visiting local farms."

Their energy commitment involved keeping their home cooler in winter and warmer in summer, adapting their clothing and activities to seasonal temperatures instead of maintaining one constant indoor climate. Their purchasing pledge required checking for secondhand options before buying anything new.

"The most surprising outcome," shares Jason's mom, "wasn't just the environmental impact of our changes—it was how much closer we grew as a family. When we spend more time doing things together, we're more engaged with our local community, and we have a shared sense of purpose. What started as sacrifices for the planet's sake have become lifestyle choices we genuinely prefer."

Faith Community Solar Co-op

When several churches in North Carolina realized that the upfront costs of solar panels prevented many families from accessing clean energy, they formed a cooperative to make solar power more accessible to all community members.

The cooperative uses a combination of volunteer labor, bulk purchasing, and no-interest loans to help families install solar systems. Those who can afford to pay the full cost do so, which helps subsidize systems for lower-income households. Youth groups and confirmation classes participate in installation days, learning practical skills while putting faith into action.

"Our co-op is choosing the narrow path over the convenient one," explains founder Reverend Washington. "It would be easier for each family with financial resources to install their own system and not worry about others. It would be easier for our churches to focus just on traditional ministry activities rather than organizing a solar co-op. But by taking the more challenging path of working together, we're creating something that better reflects God's vision of community where everyone's needs matter."

Thirteen-year-old Darius has participated in several installation days: "It's definitely harder than just hanging out with friends on Saturdays! We have to wake up early, and installing solar panels is physical work. But seeing the faces of families when they generate their first solar electricity—especially families who thought they could never afford clean energy—makes every sore muscle worth it."

Balancing Faithfulness and Grace

As we explore the narrow path of creation stewardship, it's important to remember that following Jesus is about both faithfulness and grace. Here are some balanced perspectives to keep in mind:

Aim for Progress, Not Perfection

No one walks the narrow path perfectly! The goal isn't flawless environmental living but rather growing consistently in the direction of more faithful stewardship. Celebrate steps forward without becoming discouraged when you fall short of ideal practices.

Pastor Kim encourages her youth group this way: "Creation care is a journey, not a destination. Every step toward more faithful stewardship matters, and God rejoices in our growth process, not just our outcomes. When you make mistakes or choose convenience sometimes, receive God's grace, learn from the experience, and continue moving forward."

Honor Different Capacities and Circumstances

People have different abilities, resources, and circumstances that affect what "narrow path" choices are possible for them. Physical disabilities, financial limitations, geographic location, family situations, and other factors legitimately influence what creation care practices are accessible.

Fourteen-year-old Zoe, who uses a wheelchair, offers this perspective: "For me, the 'narrow path' sometimes looks different than for my able-bodied friends. I can't walk or bike instead of driving, but I've found other ways to care for creation that work with my abilities—like starting a clothing repair club at school and advocating for accessible public transportation that would reduce car dependence for many people."

Extend Grace to Others

As you grow in creation-conscious living, you may sometimes feel frustrated when others don't share your commitments. Remember that each person is on their own journey, and criticism rarely inspires positive change. Instead, model joyful stewardship, share information when it's welcomed, and respect others' autonomy to make their own choices.

Looking Ahead

In our next chapter, we'll explore how salvation isn't just about individual spiritual transformation but about the restoration of all things—humans, communities, and the entire created world. We'll discover how caring for creation connects to the broader biblical story of God's redemptive work.

For now, consider what "narrow path" choices might be calling to you. Where might God be inviting you to choose faithful stewardship over convenience? What small steps could you take this week to align your daily practices more closely with your values? Remember that you don't walk this path alone—God's presence, the community's support, and the destination's beauty make the journey worthwhile, even when the path requires more effort than the wide, convenient alternative.

As Jesus reminds us, the narrow path—though sometimes challenging—leads to life in all its fullness. When we choose faithful stewardship over mere convenience, we discover a richer, more meaningful way of living that connects us more deeply to God, each other, and the created world that God loves.

Family Discussion Questions:

1. Where have you experienced the tension between convenient choices and creation-friendly choices in your daily life?

2. What "narrow path" choice have you made that initially seemed difficult but eventually brought unexpected benefits or joy?

3. Are there areas where our family might be called to choose a less convenient but more faithful path regarding creation care?

4. How might we better support each other in making creation-friendly choices, even when they require extra effort?

—

Teacher's Corner: This chapter addresses the important tension between convenience and faithful stewardship in ways accessible to middle-grade students while providing deeper ethical frameworks for parents and educators. For classroom application, the "Path Reflection" activity offers an excellent opportunity for students to develop metacognition about their daily choices without inducing unhelpful guilt or shame.

Consider supplementing this chapter with age-appropriate discussions about consumer culture and advertising. This will help students recognize how media messages often encourage the "wide path" of convenience and consumption without acknowledging longer-term consequences. This will build media literacy skills while supporting students' capacity for thoughtful decision-making.

The "Narrow Path Challenge Week" project provides an excellent opportunity for experiential learning. In educational settings, this could be adapted as a class-wide or school-wide initiative with different grade levels focusing on age-appropriate challenges. Pairing this with reflection activities helps students internalize the connection between their values and their choices, building intrinsic motivation for sustainable living practices.

Chapter 21:

Salvation and Creation: Redemption for All Things

The Big Picture of God's Love

Have you ever finished a big jigsaw puzzle? There's something incredibly satisfying about seeing all those tiny pieces finally fit together into one beautiful picture. After focusing on individual sections—maybe the sky in one corner or a flower in another—suddenly, you can step back and see how everything connects in the complete image.

Understanding God's plan for salvation is a bit like that. Sometimes, we focus so much on one piece—like how Jesus saves individual people from sin—that we might miss the breathtaking bigger picture. But when we step back to see the whole puzzle, we discover something amazing: God's salvation plan is even more wonderful and far-reaching than we might have realized!

The Bible gives us this "big picture" view in a remarkable passage from Colossians:

"For it pleased the Father that in him should all fulness dwell; And, having made peace through the blood of his cross, by him to reconcile all things unto himself; by him, I say, whether they be things in earth, or things in heaven." (Colossians 1:19-20)

Did you catch that? God's plan through Jesus is to reconcile "all things"—not just people, but literally everything in creation! The scope of salvation extends to the entire cosmos that God lovingly made. This means the redeeming love that heals human hearts is the same love that will ultimately heal forests, oceans, ecosystems, and every part of creation affected by sin and brokenness.

In this chapter, we'll explore this magnificent truth and discover how caring for creation isn't separate from our faith—it's actually part of participating in God's grand plan of redemption for everything He has made!

Beyond Sunday School: Salvation's Cosmic Scope

Many of us grow up with a simple understanding of salvation: Jesus died on the cross to save us from our sins so we can go to heaven when we die. This is absolutely true and wonderfully important! But it's like focusing on just one section of our puzzle while missing the complete picture.

The Bible actually presents salvation as much bigger than just "souls going to heaven." It's about God restoring and renewing everything that sin has damaged—including the natural world!

The Full Story of Salvation

To understand this, let's look at the whole biblical story:

Creation (Genesis 1-2): God creates a perfect world where humans live in harmony with Him, each other, and the natural environment. Humans are given the special role of tending and caring for creation as God's representatives.

Fall (Genesis 3): Sin disrupts all these relationships. Humans become alienated from God, conflict arises between people, and even humanity's relationship with nature becomes distorted. The ground itself is cursed (Genesis

3:17-18), showing that sin's effects reach beyond humans to creation itself.

Redemption (Throughout Scripture): God launches a rescue plan, ultimately sending Jesus to deal with sin and begin the healing of all that was broken. Through His life, death, and resurrection, Jesus makes reconciliation possible.

Restoration (Revelation 21-22): The story ends not with disembodied souls floating in clouds but with a "new heaven and new earth" where God's presence fully dwells with His creation again. The tree of life returns, bearing fruit and "leaves for the healing of the nations."

This complete story shows us that God never abandoned His original plan for creation—He's working to restore it! As Romans 8:19-21 tells us:

"For the earnest expectation of the creature waiteth for the manifestation of the sons of God. For the creature was made subject to vanity, not willingly, but by reason of him who hath subjected the same in hope, Because the creature itself also shall be delivered from the bondage of corruption into the glorious liberty of the children of God."

This passage beautifully expresses how creation itself is waiting eagerly for complete restoration and will share in the freedom that comes through salvation!

Thirteen-year-old Marco had a lightbulb moment when studying these ideas in youth group: "I always thought being 'saved' just meant my soul would go to heaven someday. I never realized God planned to save and renew everything He made! This makes my faith feel so much bigger and more exciting. It's not just about me—it's about God's love for the whole universe He created!"

Activity Box: Salvation Connections

This activity helps visualize the connections between human salvation and creation renewal!

You'll need:
- A large piece of paper
- Colored markers or pencils
- Bible

Step 1: In the center of your paper, draw a cross to represent Jesus' redemptive work.

Step 2: Around the cross, draw or write different aspects of creation: plants, animals, ecosystems, humans, communities, etc.

Step 3: Draw lines connecting the cross to each element, representing how Christ's redemption extends to all these aspects of creation.

Step 4: Next to each line, write a Bible verse that shows God's care for this part of creation.

Step 5: Share your diagram with family or friends and explain how salvation connects to each area!

Does Taking Care of Earth Really Matter?

Sometimes, Christians wonder if caring for creation should be a priority. After all, if God will make everything new someday, why worry about environmental problems now? This question deserves thoughtful consideration!

Participating in God's Redemptive Work

While only God can fully restore creation, He invites us to participate in His redemptive work now. Just as we don't say, "God will eventually eliminate all sin, so we don't need to resist temptation today," we shouldn't say, "God will eventually restore nature, so we don't need to care for it today."

Pastor Rodriguez explains: "When we work to heal damaged ecosystems, reduce pollution, or protect endangered species, we're not replacing God's future restoration—we're participating in it! We're offering the world a foretaste of the complete healing God will bring. It's like when Jesus healed people during His earthly ministry. Those healings didn't replace the need for His death and resurrection, but they gave people glimpses of the kingdom that was coming."

Growing in Christlikeness

Caring for creation also helps us grow more like Christ, who reconciles all things to God. When we develop habits of stewardship, compassion for creatures, and respect for natural systems, we're practicing Jesus' mindset—seeing the world as God sees it, as valuable and worthy of care.

Fourteen-year-old Sophia noticed this change in herself: "Before our church started talking about creation care, I never thought much about how my choices affected animals or plants. But as I've learned to pay attention to these connections, I've felt my heart expanding. I'm more aware of God's presence in everything around me, and I think that's helping me become more like Jesus, who noticed and cared about even sparrows and wildflowers."

Living Out Our Purpose

In Genesis, humans were given the role of caring for creation before sin entered the world. This means stewardship isn't just a response to environmental problems—it's part of our original purpose! By caring for the earth, we're living out the role God designed for us from the beginning.

Mrs. Chen, a Christian environmental educator, explains: "Being God's image-bearers means we're supposed to reflect God's character in how we relate to creation. God creates with wisdom, sustains with care, and redeems with love. When we approach the natural world with these same attitudes, we fulfill our purpose as humans made in God's image."

Seeing Salvation in Action: Signs of Renewal

While complete restoration awaits Christ's return, we can already see encouraging signs of healing in both human communities and natural ecosystems. These success stories give us hope and show what's possible when we work in harmony with God's redemptive purposes:

The Return of the Jordan River

The Jordan River—where Jesus was baptized—became severely polluted and depleted during the 20th century due to water diversion and contamination. By the 1990s, portions had become little more than a sewage ditch, with 95% of its natural flow diverted.

In recent years, however, Israeli, Jordanian, and Palestinian communities have worked together—despite political differences—to begin restoring this sacred river. Sewage treatment plants have been built, water allocations have been adjusted to maintain flow, and portions of the riverbanks have been replanted with native vegetation.

"This project shows both ecological and social healing," explains environmental minister Rabbi

Cohen. "Not only is the river ecosystem coming back to life, but the restoration work has created rare opportunities for cooperation between communities often in conflict. When people focus on caring for a place they all consider sacred, it builds bridges that politics alone cannot."

Twelve-year-old Leila visited the restoration site on a school trip: "We learned how certain fish species that disappeared decades ago are now returning to the river. Our guide explained that in the Bible, the Jordan River was a place of new beginnings—where the Israelites entered the Promised Land and where Jesus was baptized. Now, it's becoming a symbol of new beginnings again as former enemies work together to heal it. It made me see how caring for creation can also help heal relationships between people."

The Church Forest Miracle

In Ethiopia, deforestation has claimed over 95% of the country's native forests. But scattered across the northern highlands are hundreds of bright green circles of forests surrounding Ethiopian Orthodox churches. For centuries, these churches have protected the forests around them as sacred spaces, resulting in over 1,500 "church forests" that serve as islands of biodiversity in a largely deforested landscape.

In recent years, church leaders have expanded their conservation efforts, working with scientists and local communities to plant native trees, build protective stone walls around forest perimeters, and teach young people about these sanctuaries' ecological and spiritual importance.

"These forests show how faith can guide conservation," explains Dr. Wassie, a forest ecologist and church member. "Our priests teach that protecting these forests honors God's creation. Inside these sacred spaces, thousands of species survive that have disappeared elsewhere, including medicinal plants that help heal human communities. It's a living example of how salvation extends to both people and nature."

Thirteen-year-old Daniel's family participated in a church forest expansion project during a mission trip: "We helped plant trees alongside Ethiopian children our age. Their priest explained that in their tradition, these forests represent the Garden of Eden—a reminder of the perfect world God created and the restored world He promised. I thought it was beautiful how they're not just waiting for that restoration but actively participating in it through their care for these forests."

The Solar Parish Movement

In the Philippines, a network of Catholic parishes has pioneered an approach to ministry that integrates spiritual and ecological renewal. Each participating church has installed solar panels, implemented water conservation systems, and transformed church grounds into food forests that provide fresh produce for community meals.

What makes this movement special is how it connects environmental initiatives directly to the church's sacramental life. Solar power is presented as a way to honor God's light; water conservation connects to baptism; and food forests provide not just physical nourishment but ingredients for the Eucharist, with some communion bread made from wheat grown on church property.

"Our approach roots creation care deeply in our faith rather than treating it as a separate 'environmental program,'" explains Father Santiago. "When parishioners see the connection between caring for creation and central Christian practices like communion, they understand that environmental stewardship isn't optional—it's part of living out our salvation."

The movement has particularly energized young people. "Before our church installed solar panels and started our food forest, I thought religion was mostly about ancient history," admits fourteen-year-old Maria. "Now I see how our faith connects to the future and gives us practical ways to make a difference. I'm proud that my confirmation service used bread made from our own church garden—it felt like everything was connected: God, people, and creation all celebrating together."

Solarpunk: Imagining Healed Relationships

Throughout this book, we've explored the Solarpunk vision, which envisions communities where humans live in harmony with nature using creative technologies, cooperative social structures, and sustainable practices. This vision resonates deeply with the biblical picture of salvation as the healing of relationships between God, humans, and the natural world.

Both/And, Not Either/Or

One of Solarpunk's core insights is that we don't have to choose between human well-being and ecological health—these goals can and should support each other! This aligns perfectly with the biblical understanding that God desires flourishing for both people and the rest of creation.

Pastor Williams explains, "Sometimes we think that helping humans means exploiting nature or that protecting nature means restricting human development. But God's redemptive plan isn't an either/or proposition—it's about restoring the right relationships between all parts of creation. When we design communities that allow both people and nature to thrive, we align with God's vision for a restored creation."

Practical Examples

Solarpunk communities demonstrate this integrated healing through designs like:

- **Edible Landscaping**: Public spaces planted with fruit trees and vegetables that provide both environmental benefits (habitat, carbon capture, stormwater management) and human needs (nutritious food, especially for those with limited resources)

- **Healing Architecture**: Buildings designed to improve human health (with natural light, clean air, and access to nature) while also functioning as living systems that capture energy, purify water, and provide habitat

- **Restorative Technology**: Innovations that simultaneously heal damaged ecosystems and meet human needs, like living machines that purify wastewater while creating beautiful, productive wetlands

Eleven-year-old Aiden saw this integration at an urban farm in his city: "Our class visited this amazing farm built on what used to be an abandoned lot full of trash. Now it has gardens, chickens, rainwater collection systems, and solar panels. The farmers explained how the same systems that grow healthy food also create habitat for pollinators, build healthy soil that captures carbon dioxide, and provide jobs for people who had trouble finding employment elsewhere. It showed me that when we do things God's way, everyone and everything benefits!"

Personal Stories: Experiencing Integrated Salvation

Around the world, people are discovering how caring for creation connects to their spiritual journey. Here are a few inspiring examples:

Miguel's Healing Garden

After struggling with depression and addiction, seventeen-year-old Miguel found healing through a church-based rehabilitation program that included tending a recovery garden. As his hands worked in the soil, something unexpected happened—his spirit began to heal, too.

"Working in the garden became a form of prayer for me," Miguel explains. "Each day, as I watered plants and pulled weeds, I could see God's redemption happening—both in the garden and in my life. The garden was once neglected and full of trash, kind of like my life had been. But with consistent care and God's help, both were being transformed."

Miguel is now fourteen months sober and leads garden therapy sessions for other teens in recovery. "When I help a younger kid plant their first seed or harvest their first tomato, I'm sharing the healing God gave me. The garden taught me that God's salvation isn't just about getting to heaven someday—it's about new life beginning right now, both for me and for the piece of creation I'm caring for."

The Chen Family's Climate Witness

When the Chen family learned how climate change disproportionately affects vulnerable communities, they saw a connection to Jesus' command to love their neighbors. As a way of living out their faith, they decided to reduce their carbon footprint.

Thirteen-year-old Sophia recalls: "We started with simple changes—eating less meat, walking more instead of driving, installing better insulation in our house. But what began as environmental actions became spiritual practices that changed how we see everything. We're more grateful for what we have, more aware of our connection to people around the world, and more intentional about our choices."

The family's choices have created opportunities to share their faith in unexpected ways. "Our neighbors often ask why we make these choices that sometimes seem inconvenient," shares Sophia's mom. "That opens doors to talk about how our faith in Jesus motivates us to care about how our actions affect others. We've had deeper spiritual conversations through our climate witness than we ever did by just inviting people to church."

Pastor Williams' Watershed Revelation

When Pastor Williams first proposed a creation care ministry at his rural church, he encountered resistance. "Some members worried this was a distraction from 'real' spiritual work like evangelism," he recalls. "But then we organized a cleanup day at the creek running through our property, and something unexpected happened."

As church members pulled shopping carts and tires from the creek, an unhoused man emerged from the woods. He'd been living alongside the creek for months and was curious about what they were doing. When the church members explained they were cleaning the creek because they believed God cared about both people and creation, the man was moved to tears.

"That man, Michael, told us he'd felt worthless and forgotten by society—like the trash in the creek," Pastor Williams shares. "But seeing people care for this forgotten waterway helped him believe that maybe God hadn't forgotten him either. That day, we connected Michael with housing resources, but more importantly, he reconnected with his faith."

The experience transformed the congregation's understanding of creation care. "Now we see that caring for our watershed and caring for our human neighbors aren't separate ministries—they're interconnected aspects of the same Gospel," explains Pastor Williams. "Michael still helps with our creek cleanups, but now he also leads some of our other outreach efforts. His story reminds us that healing often happens holistically—restoration for both people and the places they inhabit."

Project Box: Salvation Scrapbook

Create a visual record of places where you see God's restoration happening!

You'll need:

- A scrapbook, notebook, or digital collection
- Camera or smartphone
- Art supplies for adding notes and decorations

Step 1: Throughout the next month, take photos of places where you see signs of renewal or healing—both in nature and in human communities. This might include:

- A formerly polluted area being cleaned up
- Native plants returning to a restored habitat
- Community gardens bringing people together
- Renewable energy installations
- Historic buildings being preserved and repurposed
- Damaged relationships being reconciled

Step 2: For each photo, write a brief reflection on how this example connects to God's big picture of salvation.

Step 3: Add Bible verses that remind you of God's promises to restore all things.

Step 4: Share your scrapbook with others as a way of spreading hope!

Living in the "Already-But-Not-Yet"

As Christians, we live in what theologians call the "already-but-not-yet" time—after Christ's first coming but before His return. Salvation has already begun, but it's not yet complete. This creates a creative tension in how we approach creation care:

"Already" Perspective: Hopeful Action

Because Christ has already come and begun the work of reconciliation, we can act with hope, knowing that our efforts to heal creation align with God's purposes. Every restored ecosystem, every carbon-reducing initiative, and every species protected from extinction matters—not because these actions will perfect the world, but because they participate in and point toward God's ultimate restoration.

Fourteen-year-old Emma's science teacher helped her class understand this concept: "When we restored the native plant garden at our school, Ms. Chen compared it to how doctors treat patients. A doctor doesn't think, 'Why bother treating this person since they'll eventually die someday?' Instead, they provide healing now, even knowing it's temporary. Similarly, we care for creation now to provide healing that points toward God's eventual perfect restoration. Our work matters even if it's not the final solution."

"Not Yet" Perspective: Humble Dependence

At the same time, we recognize that complete restoration awaits Christ's return. This keeps us from either despairing when our efforts seem inadequate or becoming prideful when they succeed. The "not yet" reminds us that while our work matters, ultimate salvation comes from God, not human effort alone.

Pastor Garcia explains: "Understanding the 'not yet' aspect keeps us balanced. We work diligently for creation's healing without placing an impossible burden on ourselves to 'save the planet.' We know that, despite our best efforts, perfect restoration awaits Christ's return. This frees us to act faithfully without being crushed by the weight of thinking everything depends solely on us."

This balanced "already-but-not-yet" perspective shapes how we approach creation care—with both purposeful action and patient hope, knowing that our small efforts connect to God's cosmic plan of reconciling all things to Himself through Christ.

Looking Ahead

In our next chapter, we'll explore how salvation isn't just an individual experience but a communal reality. We'll discover the concept of "green communion"—how caring for creation can strengthen community bonds and how communal approaches to environmental challenges reflect the biblical vision of salvation as creating a restored people, not just rescued individuals.

For now, remember the breathtaking scope of God's redemptive plan—not just saving human souls but reconciling "all things" to Himself through

Christ. When you help restore a damaged ecosystem, reduce pollution, or protect vulnerable creatures, you're not just doing "environmental work." You're participating in the grand story of salvation, offering the world glimpses of the complete restoration God will bring when heaven and earth are made new!

As you go through this week, try to notice signs of God's redemptive work in both human communities and natural systems around you. Where do you see healing beginning, even if it's not yet complete? How might God invite you to participate in His work of reconciling all things to Himself? Remember that in God's big picture of salvation, caring for creation isn't an optional add-on to faith—it's part of living out the full, beautiful story of redemption that includes the entire world God loves.

Family Discussion Questions:

1. Where have you recently seen signs of healing or restoration in nature or human communities?

2. How does understanding salvation as including "all things" (not just human souls) change how you think about caring for creation?

3. How could our family participate more fully in God's work of reconciling all things to Himself?

4. How might caring for creation provide opportunities to share God's love with others who might not otherwise be interested in faith conversations?

Teacher's Corner: This chapter addresses important theological connections between salvation and creation care in ways accessible to middle-grade students while providing deeper theological frameworks for parents and educators. The "already-but-not-yet" tension offers a balanced approach that encourages environmental engagement without either despair or unrealistic expectations.

For classroom application, the Salvation Connections activity provides an excellent opportunity for students to integrate biblical literacy with ecological understanding. Consider expanding this into a more comprehensive project where students research specific ecosystems and identify both signs of damage and signs of renewal, connecting these observations to theological concepts of fall and redemption.

The case studies of integrated salvation-creation initiatives (Jordan River restoration, Ethiopian church forests, Solar Parish Movement) can be used as launching points for research projects that explore how faith communities worldwide connect spiritual practices with environmental stewardship. This approach helps students recognize creation care as an authentic expression of faith rather than a secular concern grafted onto religious traditions.

Chapter 22:

The Green Communion: Salvation as Communal Restoration

The Table of Sharing

Have you ever been to a potluck dinner at church? Everyone brings something different—casseroles, salads, bread, and desserts—and when it's all arranged together, there's an amazing feast with more than enough for everyone! This simple community meal perfectly illustrates something profound about God's vision for His people and creation.

In the book of Acts, we discover how the earliest Christians lived after Jesus ascended to heaven:

"And they continued steadfastly in the apostles' doctrine and fellowship, and in breaking of bread, and in prayers... And all that believed were together, and had all things common; And sold their possessions and goods, and parted them to all men, as every man had need." (Acts 2:42-47, KJV)

Imagine that! These first believers didn't just gather for worship once a week and then return to their separate lives. They shared life together, sharing meals and possessions and ensuring everyone's needs were met. This wasn't just a nice idea; it was how they understood salvation itself.

Beyond Individual Salvation

Many of us have grown up thinking about salvation primarily as an individual matter—Jesus saving each person, one by one. While your personal relationship with God is absolutely essential, the Bible shows us that salvation is even bigger and more beautiful than that!

Pastor Rivera explains: "When we look at Scripture carefully, we see that God isn't just saving individual souls—He's restoring all of creation and forming a new community that reflects His love. It's like the difference between rescuing a single fish from a polluted pond versus cleaning the entire pond so all fish can thrive together."

The Bible uses many communal images to describe salvation: a body with many parts working together (1 Corinthians 12), a building made of many living stones (1 Peter 2:5), and a great feast where many gather at one table (Revelation 19:9). These images show us that while salvation begins with individual hearts turning to God, it doesn't end there—it extends to restore our relationships with each other and with all creation.

Ecological Salvation: The Earth Needs Restoration Too

When the Bible talks about salvation, it includes the natural world! Romans 8:19-22 tells us that *"the creation waits in eager expectation"* and that *"the whole creation has been groaning"* for redemption. These verses reveal that God's salvation plan extends to forests, oceans, animals, and ecosystems—not just human souls.

Think about it this way: When sin entered the world through human disobedience, its effects touched everything—human hearts, relationships, societies, and even the physical world. So, when God brings restoration through Jesus, that restoration extends to everything sin has damaged!

This understanding changes how we view environmental care. Creation care isn't just a nice add-on for Christians who happen to like nature—it's an essential part of participating in God's redemptive work. When we plant trees, clean rivers, reduce waste, or protect endangered species, we join God's "Green Communion" of restoration.

Activity Box: Restoration Mapping

Draw a simple map of your neighborhood. Mark places that seem healthy and flourishing with green. Mark places that need restoration with red. These might be natural areas that need cleaning, community spaces that need care, or places where people are struggling. Discuss with friends or family: What would restoration look like in each red area? What small steps could you take to participate in God's restoring work in these places?

From Scarcity to Abundance: The Economics of God's Kingdom

One of the most counterintuitive aspects of God's kingdom is how it approaches resources. Many of our world's economic systems are built on the assumption of scarcity—there's not enough for everyone, so we must compete to get our share. But God's economy works differently!

Consider how Jesus frequently demonstrated abundance in His ministry:

- Turning water into wine—not just a little, but 120-180 gallons! (John 2:1-11)
- Feeding 5,000+ people from a small boy's lunch (John 6:1-14)
- Teaching that giving generously leads to receiving abundantly (Luke 6:38)

Sharing doesn't make us poorer in God's kingdom—it makes everyone richer! Conventional economics seem to make this impossible, but Jesus repeatedly demonstrated it. When resources are hoarded, they stagnate. When they're shared, they are somehow multiplied.

Pastor Kim describes it this way: "God's math is different from our math. In our calculations, five loaves - 5,000 people = not enough. In God's calculations, five loaves + God's blessing + sharing = abundance for all with baskets leftover! The miracle wasn't just that Jesus created more bread;

it was that He showed us a new way of relating to resources and to each other."

Solarpunk Communities: Models of Shared Abundance

Around the world, communities are beginning to experiment with living out these biblical principles of communal restoration and abundance. Often called "Solarpunk" communities, they combine sustainable technology with cooperative economics and care for creation. While not always explicitly Christian, many of these communities embody biblical values that reflect God's vision for a restored community:

Community Gardens: In Detroit, Michigan, church congregations have transformed vacant lots into productive gardens where neighbors grow food together. The harvest is shared among participants, and the extra is donated to local food pantries. These gardens not only provide fresh food but also restore relationships between neighbors who might otherwise never interact.

Tool Libraries: In Portland, Oregon, a neighborhood has created a "library" where people can borrow tools instead of each household purchasing their own rarely used items. This reduces waste and consumption while creating community connections as people share knowledge and resources.

Repair Cafés: In Uppsala, Sweden, volunteers with different skills gather monthly to help neighbors fix broken items—from toasters to bicycles to clothing. This practice honors the biblical principle that resources should be maintained and restored rather than discarded while also creating meaningful relationships across generational and social divides.

Thirteen-year-old Sofia experienced this firsthand: "When my family joined the community garden at church, I was just expecting to learn about plants. But I've gained so much more! I've become friends with elderly neighbors who teach me their growing techniques, and I've learned that I have things to contribute, too—like showing them how to create social media accounts to share garden photos. We're all different ages and backgrounds, but everyone's gifts are valued."

Living Out Green Communion in Daily Life

How can we participate in God's communal restoration right where we are? Here are practical ways to begin:

In Families:

- Share meals together regularly, inviting others who might be alone
- Make decisions that consider impacts on others and on creation
- Practice gratitude that recognizes all good things as God's gifts to be shared
- Repair and maintain possessions instead of quickly replacing them

In Churches:

- Create systems for sharing resources among members (meal trains, clothing exchanges, tool sharing)
- Make church property available for community needs (gardens, meeting spaces)
- Practice inclusive worship that celebrates the gifts of all members, regardless of age, background, or ability

- Include creation care as part of discipleship and mission

In Communities:

- Support local businesses that practice fair trade and environmental responsibility
- Advocate for policies that protect vulnerable people and ecosystems
- Participate in community cleanup and restoration projects
- Choose cooperative solutions over competitive ones when possible

After studying these principles, Pastor Williams' congregation transformed their approach: "We realized we had a large building that sat empty most of the week while community groups struggled to find meeting space. Now, our church hosts a food co-op, adult education classes, a repair café, and community meetings. Our members volunteer alongside non-church neighbors in these initiatives. We're not just talking about God's kingdom—we're demonstrating it tangibly by sharing what we have."

The Ultimate Restoration

While we work toward restoration in our communities today, we also look forward to the day when God will complete the work of making all things new. Revelation 21-22 gives us glimpses of this ultimate restoration—a renewed creation where God dwells with His people, where death and tears are no more, and where the "tree of life" provides healing for all nations.

The amazing thing is that we don't have to wait passively for this future—we can participate in it now! Every act of sharing, every garden planted, every relationship reconciled, and every ecosystem restored becomes a preview of God's coming kingdom.

As you go through your week, look for opportunities to join in God's work of communal restoration. Remember: salvation isn't just about individual souls being rescued—it's about a whole new way of living together with God, each other, and all creation in harmony and abundance!

Looking Ahead

In our next chapter, we'll explore God's magnificent vision of "a new heaven and a new earth" and how Solarpunk ideals reflect aspects of this ultimate divine renewal. We'll discover how hope for the future can inspire action today!

Family Discussion Questions:

1. How have you experienced the difference between scarcity thinking (there's not enough) and abundance thinking (God provides enough to share)?

2. What's one area of creation (a natural place, animal species, or ecosystem) that you feel especially called to help restore?

3. How might our family share more of what we have with others? What practical steps could we take this week?

4. In what ways could our church or community better reflect the "Green Communion" we've discussed?

Teacher's Corner:

This chapter addresses the theological concept of salvation as extending beyond individual souls to communities and creation. This holistic understanding helps students connect their faith with contemporary environmental and social concerns while maintaining biblical integrity. The metaphor of communion provides a familiar religious practice through which to understand broader theological concepts.

For classroom application, the Restoration Mapping activity offers a concrete way for students to apply these concepts to their immediate context. This can be expanded into service-learning projects where students identify needs and develop and implement small-scale restoration initiatives.

The chapter intentionally balances theological principles with practical examples, helping students see how abstract concepts translate into real-world action. This approach supports cross-curricular learning that bridges theological concepts with science, social studies, and civic responsibility.

Chapter 23:

Thy Kingdom Come: Envisioning a New Heaven and New Earth

The Promise of Complete Renewal

Have you ever built something with blocks or LEGO bricks, only to have it knocked down? When that happens, you have two choices: you can either start over with something completely different, or you can rebuild—perhaps making it even better than before. When God looks at our broken world, He doesn't throw it away to start over. Instead, He promises something far more remarkable—to renew and transform everything into something more beautiful than we can imagine!

In the very last book of the Bible, the apostle John describes an extraordinary vision:

"And I saw a new heaven and a new earth: for the first heaven and the first earth were passed away; and there was no more sea." (Revelation 21:1, KJV)

This verse doesn't mean God will destroy everything and create an entirely different universe. The word translated as "new" in Greek is kainos, which means "renewed" or "fresh"—like when spring brings new life to plants that seemed dead in winter. God plans to transform our current world into something wonderfully renewed, healed of all damage, and freed from all corruption.

Dr. Martinez, a biblical scholar, explains: "Think of it like the restoration of a beautiful old painting that's been damaged. The restorer doesn't throw away the original and paint a different picture—they carefully remove the dirt, repair the tears, and bring back the original beauty, perhaps even more vivid than before. That's what God promises to do with our entire universe!"

What Will the Renewed Creation Be Like?

The Bible gives us glimpses of what God's renewed creation will be like, and it's more amazing than any fantasy world in books or movies! Here are some of the wonderful promises we find:

"And God shall wipe away all tears from their eyes; and there shall be no more death, neither

sorrow, nor crying, neither shall there be any more pain: for the former things are passed away." (Revelation 21:4)

"The wolf also shall dwell with the lamb, and the leopard shall lie down with the kid; and the calf and the young lion and the fatling together; and a little child shall lead them." (Isaiah 11:6)

"And he shewed me a pure river of water of life, clear as crystal, proceeding out of the throne of God and of the Lamb... and on either side of the river, was there the tree of life, which bare twelve manner of fruits, and yielded her fruit every month: and the leaves of the tree were for the healing of the nations." (Revelation 22:1-2)

Twelve-year-old Noah shares his thoughts: "When our Sunday School teacher described the new earth, with animals living peacefully together and no more sadness or pain, I asked if it would be like the Garden of Eden. She said it would be even better—because this time, there would be no possibility of another Fall. God will make everything perfect forever! That makes me excited about the future."

Already But Not Yet: Living Between Two Worlds

Here's a fantastic truth that Christians throughout history have understood: While the complete renewal of creation will happen in the future, we can experience and participate in glimpses of God's kingdom right now! Theologians call this living in the "already but not yet"—God's kingdom is already breaking into our world but not yet fully realized.

Jesus taught us to pray: *"Thy kingdom come, Thy will be done, on earth as it is in heaven"* (Matthew 6:10). This prayer isn't just about a future hope—it's about asking God to bring heaven's reality into our present world!

Pastor Williams uses the following analogy: "It's like when a new president is elected but hasn't yet taken office. Technically, the old administration is still in charge, but everyone knows a new day is coming, and preparations for the transition are already underway. Similarly, though sin and death still influence our world, King Jesus has already won the decisive victory through His resurrection, and

His followers are ambassadors of His coming kingdom."

When we:
- Plant trees and care for ecosystems
- Build communities based on sharing rather than greed
- Create beauty through art, music, and poetry
- Work for justice and reconciliation
- Share God's love with others

...we're not just doing nice things. We're actually participating in God's kingdom work—giving the world a foretaste of the complete renewal that God has promised!

Thirteen-year-old Elena experienced this after a tornado devastated her Oklahoma community: "When everyone came together to rebuild—churches, schools, even people who didn't know each other before—I saw something I'd never noticed. Mom explained that when we help rebuild after disasters, we're practicing for our future job as part of God's creation-renewal team. We're not just fixing things temporarily; we're rehearsing for the big restoration God will complete someday."

Activity Box: New Earth Vision Boards

In small groups, create "vision boards" of what aspects of God's renewed creation you most look forward to. Use magazines, drawing materials, or digital tools to collect and create images representing what the Bible describes about the new heaven and new earth. Include both the physical aspects (like peaceful animals or healing trees) and relationship aspects (like peace between people and God dwelling with humans).

After creating your vision boards, discuss which aspects of God's renewed creation we can participate in bringing about even now. What small actions could help make our world more like your vision board images?

Solarpunk: Practicing Hope Through Imagination

Have you ever noticed that working toward something you can't picture is hard? That's where imagination becomes so important! Throughout history, God has used visions, dreams, and imagination to help people see beyond current reality to what could be. The biblical prophets often vividly described their visions, helping people imagine God's promised future.

In our time, a movement called Solarpunk serves a similar purpose. Solarpunk artists, writers, and designers create visions of a hopeful future where humans live in harmony with nature, using clean energy and sustainable practices. These aren't just fantasy pictures—they're visual prayers saying, "This is what we hope the world could become!"

Solarpunk images often show:

- Cities integrated with nature, with gardens on every rooftop and trees lining the streets
- Communities powered by renewable energy like solar and wind
- People from different backgrounds working together cooperatively
- Technology used to heal rather than harm the earth
- Beautiful, practical designs that benefit both humans and ecosystems

While Solarpunk visions aren't identical to biblical descriptions of the new earth (only God can create that perfect renewal), they share important values that align with Scripture: care for creation, justice for all people, beauty, abundance, and hope for the future.

Fifteen-year-old Zoe, who loves art, explains the connection: "In my art class, we studied Solarpunk imagery and compared it with Bible passages about the new earth. Our teacher pointed out that both show harmony between people and nature, communities sharing resources, and technology being used to help rather than exploit. I created a drawing that combined Revelation's Tree of Life with solar-powered buildings. It helped me see how we could work toward some aspects of God's promises even now."

Not Just Wishful Thinking: Hope Based on God's Promises

Some people might dismiss visions of a renewed earth as unrealistic fantasies. "The world has always had problems," they might say. "Things will never really change." But Christian hope is different from mere optimism or wishful thinking!

Our hope for creation's renewal is based on God's character and promises, not on human ability. The same God who raised Jesus from the dead promised to make everything new! This gives us a unique kind of confidence—not that humans can perfect the world through our own efforts, but that God will complete the good work He has begun.

Pastor Garcia explains the difference: "Optimism says, 'Things will probably get better because people are basically good.' Biblical hope says, 'Regardless of how things appear, God has promised renewal and has proven His power through Christ's resurrection.' One depends on human potential, and the other rests on God's faithfulness. That's why Christians can remain hopeful even in the most difficult circumstances."

This hope isn't passive—it motivates action! We can work confidently in the present because we trust God's promises about the future, knowing our efforts aren't in vain. As Paul writes in 1 Corinthians 15:58, after discussing resurrection hope: "*Therefore, my beloved brethren, be ye stedfast, unmoveable, always abounding in the work of the Lord, forasmuch as ye know that your labour is not in vain in the Lord."*

Living Today in Light of God's Tomorrow

How should we live now if we believe God will renew all things in the future? Here are practical ways to align our lives with God's coming kingdom:

In Your Personal Life:

- Practice resurrection hope by repairing and restoring things rather than discarding them
- Create beauty through art, music, gardening, or other creative expressions
- Make choices that reflect care for creation, like reducing waste and conserving resources
- Learn skills that will be valuable in God's renewed world—growing food, building community, creating beauty, and promoting healing

In Your Family:

- Talk about God's promises for the future and how they give us hope today
- Work on family projects that restore or beautify your home or neighborhood

- Share family resources generously, practicing the abundance of God's kingdom
- Celebrate signs of renewal and restoration when you see them

In Your Community:
- Participate in or start community gardens that transform unused spaces into places of beauty and food production
- Support clean energy initiatives that reflect good stewardship of God's creation
- Help restore damaged ecosystems through tree planting, stream cleanups, or habitat protection
- Create community spaces that bring people together across differences, reflecting the unity of God's kingdom

Fourteen-year-old James shares how his family lives this out: "After studying Revelation in youth group, my parents decided our family needed to practice 'new creation living' now. We transformed our yard into a wildlife-friendly garden that also grows food for us and our neighbors. Dad installed solar panels, and Mom started a neighborhood tool-sharing program. They say it's not about being perfect environmentalists—it's about practicing the habits we'll need as citizens of God's renewed world."

Balancing Future Hope with Present Action

As we look forward to God's promised renewal, it's important to maintain a healthy balance. Some Christians focus so much on the future that they neglect their responsibilities in the present world. Others become so consumed with current problems that they lose sight of God's ultimate promises.

Biblical wisdom guides us between these extremes. We work diligently for restoration and justice in the present world, knowing that these efforts matter to God and serve as signposts pointing toward His coming kingdom. At the same time, we recognize that complete renewal depends on God's work, not our own efforts.

Dr. Williams offers this perspective: "Think of it like planning a wedding. The engaged couple works hard to make preparations—choosing rings, planning the ceremony, and preparing their home together. These preparations are important and meaningful! However, the actual marriage relationship is much better than all those preparations. Similarly, our current efforts toward justice, sustainability, and beauty are important preparations for God's kingdom, but the fullness of that kingdom will far exceed anything we can accomplish on our own."

God Will Dwell With Us

Perhaps the most wonderful promise about the renewed creation is not about what will be different but about Who will be present:

"And I heard a great voice out of heaven saying, Behold, the tabernacle of God is with men, and he will dwell with them, and they shall be his people, and God himself shall be with them, and be their God." (Revelation 21:3)

The greatest joy of God's renewed creation will be a direct, unhindered relationship with God Himself! Just as God walked with Adam and Eve in the Garden of Eden before sin created separation, God will dwell directly among His people in the renewed creation.

This is the ultimate fulfillment of Emmanuel—"God with us." Jesus came as Emmanuel in His first advent, making a way for us to be reconciled to God. In the new creation, that presence will be complete and permanent!

Pastor Kim reflects: "Sometimes we focus so much on the physical aspects of the new creation—no more death or pain, beautiful environments—that we miss the most amazing promise of all: God Himself will live among us! Every time we experience God's presence in worship or prayer now, we get a tiny foretaste of that ultimate reality."

Looking Ahead

In our next chapter, we'll explore what it means to live as "new creations" in Christ even now. We'll discover how God is growing us like precious seeds in His garden, developing our unique gifts and calling as we participate in His work of renewal.

Family Discussion Questions:

1. What aspect of God's promised renewal gives you the most hope or excitement?

2. How does believing in God's ultimate renewal of creation change how we approach environmental challenges today?

3. How could our family better reflect God's "new creation" values in our home or neighborhood?

4. How might remembering God's promises help us when we feel discouraged about problems in the world?

Teacher's Corner:

This chapter addresses the theological concept of cosmic redemption—God's plan to renew all of creation—while making these complex eschatological ideas accessible to young readers. The "already but not yet" framework helps students understand their role in God's unfolding kingdom work without either minimizing the reality of current problems or placing unrealistic expectations on human efforts.

The Vision Board activity engages visual and kinesthetic learners in concretely imagining biblical promises for classroom application. This can be expanded into a cross-curricular project with art and science classes, where students could explore both the scriptural descriptions and ecological principles that might characterize a renewed creation.

The chapter intentionally connects traditional Christian eschatology with contemporary environmental ethics, helping students see faith-based reasons for creation care without falling into either apocalyptic fatalism ("the world will end anyway") or secular utopianism ("humans can perfect the world"). This balanced approach supports healthy ecological discipleship within an orthodox Christian framework.

Chapter 24:

Faith in Bloom: Living as New Creations

God's Living Garden

Have you ever planted a seed and watched it grow? There's something almost magical about how a tiny, seemingly lifeless seed transforms into a vibrant plant with leaves, flowers, and fruit or new seeds. A single sunflower seed, smaller than your fingernail, can grow into a towering plant over six feet tall with a face full of seeds—each capable of growing into another sunflower!

This miracle of growth and transformation is one of God's favorite ways to help us understand how He works in our lives. Throughout the Bible, God uses gardens, seeds, plants, and harvests as pictures of spiritual life. Jesus told parables about seeds and soil. He compared God's kingdom to a mustard seed that grows surprisingly large. He described Himself as a vine and His followers as branches.

These aren't just nice nature comparisons. They reveal something profound about how God sees us and works within us. As the apostle Paul writes:

"Therefore, if any man be in Christ, he is a new creature: old things are passed away; behold, all things are become new." (2 Corinthians 5:17, KJV)

This verse tells us something amazing—when we come to Christ, we don't just get slightly improved or patched up. We become entirely new creations! Just as a sprouting plant looks nothing like the seed it came from, our new life in Christ transforms us from the inside out.

God's Garden of Souls

Pastor Martinez, who maintains a community garden alongside his ministry, explains: "God isn't running a factory, producing identical followers on an assembly line. He's tending a garden filled with incredible diversity. In my garden, I grow tomatoes, zucchini, peppers, herbs, and flowers—each needing different care and contributing different gifts to the garden. Similarly, God cultivates unique spiritual growth in each person while ensuring we all reflect His character."

The Bible confirms this garden perspective in many places. Isaiah 61:11 says: *"For as the earth bringeth forth her bud, and as the garden causeth the things that are sown in it to spring forth; so the Lord GOD will cause righteousness and praise to spring forth before all the nations."*

Just as a garden contains enormous diversity—flowers, vegetables, trees, and herbs of countless varieties—God's spiritual garden includes people of every nation, culture, personality, and gift. Yet all are nourished by the same Son, watered by the same Spirit, and rooted in the same Father.

Thirteen-year-old Maya discovered this during a church retreat: "Our youth leader gave each of us a different seed to plant—some got flowers, others vegetables, and mine was a little tree! She explained that just as each plant grows at its own pace and in its own way, our spiritual growth is unique too. We shouldn't compare our growth to others, but trust that God is growing something beautiful in each of us."

The Growth Cycle of a New Creation

Just as every plant goes through stages of growth, our spiritual lives also develop through a beautiful process. Let's explore these stages, which often overlap and repeat throughout our lives as we continue growing in different areas:

Redemption: The Precious Seed

Before a seed can grow, it must be selected, saved, and protected. In ancient times, farmers carefully selected the best seeds from each harvest and preserved them to plant the following season.

"For all have sinned, and come short of the glory of God; Being justified freely by his grace through the redemption that is in Christ Jesus." (Romans 3:23-24)

These verses tell us that though sin had damaged all of humanity, God didn't discard us. Instead, through Christ's sacrifice, He redeemed us—literally "bought us back" at great cost, like a farmer investing in precious seeds for next year's garden.

Pastor Williams explains: "The word 'redemption' comes from the marketplace, describing the purchase of something valuable. When Jesus redeemed us through His sacrifice, He was essentially saying, 'These lives are precious to me. I see their potential. I'm willing to pay the highest price to reclaim them from sin and death.'"

God sees the potential in each of us, not just what we are now but what we can become in Him—just as a gardener envisions the magnificent plant a tiny seed will become in the future.

Twelve-year-old Jackson reflects: "When my mom explained redemption using seeds, it finally clicked for me. She showed me our family's seed collection and explained how carefully they save seeds from the best plants each year. It helped me understand that God chose me not because I was already perfect but because He sees what I can become through His care."

Repentance: Preparing the Soil

Every gardener knows that the soil must be adequately prepared before planting. Hard, compacted soil must be broken up, rocks and weeds must be removed, and sometimes, the pH needs to be adjusted or nutrients added.

In our spiritual lives, this soil preparation is called repentance:

"Repent ye therefore, and be converted, that your sins may be blotted out, when the times of refreshing shall come from the presence of the Lord." (Acts 3:19)

The word "repent" literally means to turn around or change direction. It's like a gardener turning over soil that's been facing away from the sun, exposing it to light and air. When we repent, we turn away from sin and toward God, allowing Him to remove the "rocks and weeds" hindering our growth.

A seminary professor and avid gardener, Dr. Chen, shares: "Many people misunderstand repentance as just feeling bad about yourself. But true repentance is actually hopeful and forward-looking! It's saying, 'This way isn't working; I'm turning toward something better.' Every spring, when I turn over my garden soil, I'm filled with anticipation for future growth. That's the spirit of true repentance—looking forward to new life."

Baptism: Being Planted with Christ

Once the soil is prepared, seeds must be buried—placed in a dark, humble place where transformation can begin.

"Know ye not, that so many of us as were baptized into Jesus Christ were baptized into his death? Therefore, we are buried with him by baptism into death: that like as Christ was raised up from the dead by the glory of the Father, even so we also should walk in newness of life." (Romans 6:3-4)

Baptism beautifully pictures this "planting" stage of our spiritual growth. Just as a seed must be buried before it can sprout, in baptism, we identify with Christ's death and burial—the necessary prelude to resurrection life.

Pastor Rivera explains using a seed demonstration: "When I teach about baptism, I bring in bean seeds and clear cups with soil. We plant the seeds and discuss how they must be 'buried' before new life emerges. The seed doesn't stay in the ground—that's not the end of the story! But the burial is a necessary part of the transformation process."

Fourteen-year-old Sophia shares her baptism experience: "When I was baptized last summer, our pastor explained that going under the water symbolized being buried with Christ, and coming up represented new life. I remember thinking about how a seed has to be completely surrounded by soil to grow properly. It helped me understand that following Jesus isn't just adding Him to my life—it's about becoming something completely new."

Activity Box: Seed Starting

Materials needed: Small pots or cups, potting soil, various seeds (flowers, herbs, vegetables), water, labels

1. Fill your containers ¾ full with moistened potting soil

2. Plant 2-3 seeds in each container at the depth recommended on the seed packet

3. Label each container with the plant name and today's date

4. Water gently and place in a warm, sunny location

5. Check daily, keeping the soil moist but not soggy

6. Journal about what you observe each day, comparing the growth stages to spiritual development

What do you notice about how different seeds germinate at different rates? How might this relate to how people grow spiritually at different paces? How does caring for these seedlings help you better understand God's care for you?

Receiving the Holy Spirit: The Living Water and Sunshine

Even the best seeds, planted in perfectly prepared soil, cannot grow without two essential elements: water and sunlight. In our spiritual growth, the Holy Spirit provides both these life-giving necessities:

"Then Peter said unto them, Repent, and be baptized every one of you in the name of Jesus Christ for the remission of sins, and ye shall receive the gift of the Holy Ghost." (Acts 2:38)

Just as water softens the seed coat and activates growth processes within, the Holy Spirit softens our hearts and activates new life within us. And just as sunlight provides energy for plants to grow and produce fruit, the Holy Spirit energizes our spiritual growth and fruit-bearing.

Pastor Kim says, "When I water my garden on a sunny morning, I often think about the Holy Spirit's work in my life. Water makes nutrients available to the plant, just as the Spirit makes God's truth alive to us. Sunlight gives energy for growth, just as the Spirit empowers us to live out what we believe. Without water and sunlight, plants wither, and without the Holy Spirit, our spiritual lives stagnate."

Thirteen-year-old Elijah noticed this connection during a drought: "Last summer, when it barely rained, our garden struggled even though the sun shone every day. Dad installed a drip irrigation system, and the plants bounced back in just a week! It made me think about how I need both kinds of spiritual nourishment—not just learning about God (sunlight) but also prayer and worship time to connect with Him (water)."

The Seasons of Spiritual Growth

Just as plants move through predictable stages of development, our spiritual lives progress through recognizable seasons. The amazing thing is that God knows precisely what each season needs and provides it perfectly:

Seedling Stage: Tender Beginnings

When we first come to faith, we are like tender seedlings—full of potential but vulnerable. During this stage, we need protection, basic nourishment, and simple care.

New believers often experience rapid, visible growth as they discover foundational truths about God. They may experience strong emotions and dramatic changes as their new life emerges. Like seedlings stretching toward the light, new believers naturally reach for God with enthusiasm.

Pastor Williams advises: "Just as young plants need protection from harsh conditions, new believers need a supportive community and basic spiritual disciplines—regular Bible reading, prayer, and fellowship. Simple, consistent care during this stage builds strong roots for later growth."

Growing Stage: Developing Strength

As plants develop beyond the seedling stage, they grow deeper roots and stronger stems. This often means less visible growth above ground for a time, as energy goes into establishing a strong foundation.

Similarly, maturing believers may experience seasons when growth feels slow or even dormant, but important development is happening beneath the surface. During these times, God often strengthens our character, deepens our understanding, and tests our commitment.

Sixteen-year-old Thomas shares: "Last year, I went through what our youth pastor calls a 'root-building season.' My faith didn't feel as exciting as when I first believed, and I wondered if something was wrong. Then I realized that just like my dad's apple trees, which spent years developing roots before producing much fruit, God was helping me build a stronger foundation to support future growth and fruit."

Flowering Stage: Discovering Your Gifts

One of the most beautiful phases in a plant's development is flowering, when its unique colors, fragrances, and forms are finally expressed. Some plants flower quickly, while others take years or even decades (like century plants, which bloom only once after many years of growth).

In our spiritual journey, the flowering stage represents discovering and expressing our unique spiritual gifts, calling, and purpose. This often happens gradually as we experiment, serve, and learn where our passions and abilities can best contribute to God's kingdom work.

Pastor Garcia observes: "Just as flowers serve different purposes—some attract pollinators, some become food, some simply bring beauty—God designs each person with unique gifts that contribute to the whole garden. The body of Christ needs all our different 'flowers' to function properly."

Fruiting Stage: Reproducing and Nurturing Others

The ultimate purpose of a plant's growth is to produce fruit containing seeds—ensuring the next generation can grow. Mature plants don't just take in nutrients for themselves; they produce food for others and seeds for future plants.

Spiritually mature believers similarly focus increasingly outward—nurturing newer believers, serving others, and reproducing their faith in the next generation. This doesn't mean they stop growing, but their growth now nourishes others.

Fifteen-year-old Leila recognized this in her grandmother: "My grandma has been a Christian for over 60 years, and she's definitely in the 'fruiting stage.' She mentors younger women at church, teaches children, and sometimes even helps pastors with their sermons! But she still gets excited about learning new things in her own Bible study. She says spiritual growth never stops—it just includes more people as you go."

Communities as Diverse Gardens

While individual spiritual growth is essential, God's ultimate design is for communities of believers to grow together, creating diverse "garden ecosystems" that reflect His creativity:

"For as the body is one, and hath many members, and all the members of that one body, being many, are one body: so also is Christ." (1 Corinthians 12:12)

Just as the most resilient and productive gardens contain many different plants working together—tall sunflowers provide shade for lettuce, marigolds repel pests from tomatoes, and clover fixes nitrogen in the soil—healthy faith communities include people at different growth stages with complementary gifts and perspectives.

Pastor Martinez's church demonstrates this principle: "We intentionally nurture intergenerational relationships in our congregation. Our seniors mentor young adults, teenagers help children, and middle-aged members support elderly folks. We've also embraced cultural diversity, learning from members with African, Asian, European, and Indigenous backgrounds. Like a diverse ecosystem, we're more resilient and fruitful together than any of us could be alone."

Thirteen-year-old Zoe observed this during her church's community garden project: "Different families adopted garden sections, growing vegetables from their cultural backgrounds. Korean families grew special greens, Mexican families planted chiles and tomatillos, Italian families grew tomatoes and basil, and my Nigerian family contributed amaranth and special squashes. At harvest time, everyone shared and traded. Our youth pastor said it perfectly represented how the church **should** work—everyone contributing their unique gifts and everyone benefiting from the diversity."

Nurturing Your Growth

Just as plants need ongoing care throughout their lifecycle, our spiritual growth requires continuous nurturing. Here are practices that help us flourish at every stage:

Daily Spiritual Disciplines:

- Reading Scripture (providing direction like a plant's genetic code)
- Prayer (connecting to God, like roots connect to soil)
- Worship (turning toward God, like plants turn toward the sun)

Season-Specific Growth Supports:

- Community support (like trellises that provide structure for climbing plants)

- Testimony sharing (cross-pollination that spreads growth)
- Serving others (distributing nutrients throughout the whole garden)
- Rest and sabbath (the dormant seasons that prepare for new growth)

Pastor Kim encourages families: "Pay attention to which growth stage each family member is in and provide appropriate support. New believers need simple, clear teaching. Growing believers need deeper challenges and opportunities to discover their gifts. Mature believers need chances to mentor others while continuing their own growth. When we recognize these different needs, everyone can flourish."

Looking Ahead

As we conclude our journey through this book, the final chapter will offer a vision for moving forward with hope and purpose. We'll explore practical ways to spread the vision of faith-centered sustainability to others and how we can create a brighter, greener, faith-centered world.

Family Discussion Questions:

1. Which stage of plant growth (seedling, growing, flowering, or fruiting) best describes your spiritual life right now? Why?

2. What "spiritual nutrients" do you need most in this season of your growth?

3. How has God used different people—like different types of plants in a garden—to help you grow spiritually?

4. What unique gifts or perspectives do you contribute to our family's and church's "garden"?

Teacher's Corner:

This chapter uses the extended metaphor of gardening to make the abstract concept of spiritual formation concrete and accessible for young readers. The plant growth analogy provides a developmentally appropriate framework for understanding spiritual maturation while honoring individual differences in growth patterns and expressions of faith.

The seed-starting activity offers a hands-on, object lesson for classroom application that reinforces the chapter's key concepts. This can be expanded into a longer-term project where students observe plant development over weeks, journaling connections between plant growth and spiritual development at each stage.

The chapter emphasizes individual growth and community interdependence, helping students understand personal faith development within the Christian community. This balanced approach supports healthy spiritual formation that avoids individualistic isolation and community-dependent faith that lacks personal ownership.

Conclusion:

Walking Forward in Light and Truth

The Journey Thus Far

Throughout this book, we've explored how Biblical teachings align beautifully with Solarpunk ideals of hope, sustainability, and community. We've discovered that caring for creation isn't just a modern environmental concern—it's a sacred responsibility given to humans from the very beginning. We've learned that the Bible offers wisdom not just for our spiritual lives but for how we live with each other and with the natural world God created.

From the Garden of Eden to the New Jerusalem, Scripture shows us that God cares deeply about our relationship with the Earth. Jesus' teachings on simplicity, generosity, and loving our neighbors provide a foundation for sustainable living. We've explored practical ways to apply Biblical principles through renewable energy, wise resource management, community-building, and creation care.

As we conclude our journey together, let's consider how to move forward with hope and purpose, putting these principles into action in our everyday lives.

A Prayer for Hope and Action

Pastor Williams shares this prayer that beautifully captures the balance between trusting God and taking action:

"Heavenly Father, Creator of all things, we thank You for the incredible world You have made and entrusted to our care. Give us eyes to see its beauty and wisdom to understand our role within it. Fill us with hope that comes not from human achievement but from Your promises and presence.

As we face challenges in our world, keep us from both despair that paralyzes us and pride that thinks we can save the world without You. Instead, guide our hands to work, our minds to create, and our hearts to love in ways that reflect Your character and purposes.

Help us to be faithful in small things and courageous in larger ones. May the seeds we plant—both literal and figurative—grow into gardens that nourish bodies, communities, and souls. Through Jesus Christ, who reconciles all things in heaven and earth, Amen."

This prayer reminds us of an important truth: Christian hope isn't passive waiting—it's active anticipation. When farmers plant seeds, they trust God for sunshine and rain, but they don't just sit back and wait for harvest. They prepare soil, pull weeds, and tend their crops. Similarly, our hope in God's promises should motivate us to participate in His work of renewal, starting right where we are.

Thirteen-year-old Emma reflects: "After our youth group studied this material, I realized I had been thinking too small about my faith. I thought being a Christian was just about going to heaven someday. Now I understand that God invites me to join His work of healing and renewing the world right now! That's both exciting and a little scary—but mostly exciting."

The Call to Action: Living With Purpose

So, what does it look like to live out these principles in your daily life? Here are some practical ways to begin, organized into different areas of impact:

Personal Choices

Every day, we make dozens of small choices that either move us toward or away from the Biblical vision of faithful stewardship:

- **Simplify**: Jesus taught that "*a person's life does not consist in the abundance of their possessions*" (Luke 12:15). Consider areas where you might simplify—fewer but higher-quality belongings, less screen time, more meaningful activities.
- **Reduce Waste**: When we waste resources, we dishonor the Creator who made them. Look for opportunities to reduce waste through composting, recycling, repairing items, and choosing products with less packaging.
- **Practice Sabbath**: Set aside regular time for rest, prayer, and enjoying creation—without consuming or producing. This ancient practice is revolutionary in our always-busy world!

Twelve-year-old Miguel made this change: "I used to ask for lots of plastic toys for birthdays and Christmas. After learning that those toys often break quickly and create pollution, I started asking for experiences instead—like fishing trips with my dad or art classes. I've discovered that I remember and value these experiences much more than I ever did the toys!"

Family Actions

Families have unique opportunities to nurture sustainable values and practices:

- **Garden Together**: Even a few containers on a windowsill can teach valuable lessons about food, patience, and care. Growing food connects us to God's provision in tangible ways.

- **Cook and Share Meals**: Preparing and sharing food is a biblical practice that builds relationships while developing practical skills. Try making meals from scratch using local, seasonal ingredients.

- **Make Homes More Sustainable**: Involve everyone in projects like setting up rain barrels, starting a compost pile, or making your home more energy efficient.

The Anderson family shares their experience: "We decided to have a 'creation care' family meeting each month. Everyone brings one idea for how our family can better care for God's world. So far, we've started composting, replaced most of our light bulbs with LEDs, walked to nearby places instead of driving, and started a small vegetable garden. Our kids actually remind us when we forget these practices!"

Activity Box: Family Sustainability Challenge

Create a friendly family competition to see who can come up with and implement the most creative sustainability idea in one month. Categories might include:

- Most creative reuse of something that would have been thrown away
- Most water saved
- Most energy conserved
- Most nutritious food grown

- Most neighbors involved in a community project

Award simple prizes like choosing a family activity or being exempt from a chore. The real prize? Discovering how creativity and care for creation can go hand in hand!

Community Engagement

Biblical faith has always been lived out in the community, not just individually:

- **Join or Start a Group**: Connect with others interested in faith-based environmental stewardship at your church or in your community. Working together multiplies your impact and provides encouragement.
- **Support Local Businesses**: When you purchase from local farmers, craftspeople, and independently owned businesses, you strengthen your community while often reducing your environmental impact.
- **Share Resources**: Tool libraries, community gardens, carpooling, and skill-sharing groups embody the early church's practice of having "all

things in common" (Acts 2:44) while reducing unnecessary consumption.

Spreading the Vision: How to Inspire Others

As you begin living out these principles, others will naturally become curious about your choices. Here are ways to thoughtfully share this vision with others:

Live It First, Talk About It Second

The most powerful testimony isn't what we say but how we live. As Francis of Assisi reportedly said, "Preach the gospel at all times; when necessary, use words." When you joyfully live out creation care and sustainable practices, others will notice—and some will ask why.

Find Common Ground

When discussing these ideas with others, start with the values you share. For example, you might begin with Biblical stewardship with fellow Christians. With non-religious friends, you might connect around caring for future generations or appreciating nature's beauty. Finding common ground builds bridges for meaningful conversation.

Invite Rather Than Impose

Nobody likes being lectured or made to feel guilty. Instead of telling people what they "should" do, share your own journey and invite them to consider similar steps. "I've been learning about..." or "I've been trying this..." opens doors that "You should..." often closes.

Use Stories and Examples

Jesus taught complex principles through stories and everyday examples that people could relate to. Similarly, sharing specific examples and personal stories about creation care often communicates more effectively than abstract concepts or overwhelming statistics.

Pastor Kim reflects: "I've found that gardening provides endless opportunities to naturally discuss Biblical principles. When neighbors admire our church's community garden, I can share God's first instructions to humans to tend and keep the earth, Jesus' parables that used agricultural examples, and how growing food together builds community. These conversations happen organically—no pun intended!"

Vision for the Future: A Brighter, Greener, Faith-Centered World

As we conclude, let's imagine together what our world could look like if more people embraced this Biblical vision of faithful stewardship and sustainable living:

Renewed Churches

Imagine churches whose buildings and grounds demonstrate creation care through native landscaping, community gardens, renewable energy, and efficient resource use. Beyond their physical spaces, these faith communities would model sharing economies, intergenerational learning, and practical love for both neighbors and creation.

Dr. Martinez envisions: "Churches could become neighborhood resilience centers—places where communities gather not just for worship but for learning practical skills, sharing resources, and working together toward local solutions. When storms or other challenges come, these churches would already have the relationships and systems in place to help their communities weather difficulties."

Thriving Communities

Imagine neighborhoods where people know each other's names, share tools and skills, grow food in front yards and community spaces, and collaborate on local projects. These communities would embody the early church's example of mutual care while creating more resilient local systems.

Healed Landscapes

Envision landscapes where human activity enhances rather than degrades natural systems—where regenerative agriculture builds soil health, native plants support biodiversity, clean energy replaces pollution, and design works with natural patterns rather than against them.

Hearts Aligned With God's Purposes

Most importantly, imagine more people discovering that caring for creation isn't separate from spiritual life but an integral part of following Jesus—that loving God and loving neighbor extends to loving and caring for the world God made and all who dwell in it.

Fifteen-year-old Leila shares her vision: "I dream of becoming an engineer who designs buildings that work with nature instead of against it. I want to help churches and schools create spaces that teach people about God through their design—using natural patterns, conserving resources, and creating beauty that points to the Creator. My faith and my future career aren't separate—they're totally connected in caring for God's world!"

Starting Where You Are

This vision might seem overwhelming. How can one person or family make a difference when the challenges are so enormous? Remember the mustard seed Jesus described—the tiny seed that grows into a large plant where birds can nest (Matthew 13:31-32). Great changes often begin with small, faithful actions that grow beyond our imagination.

You don't need to do everything at once. Start with one change, one practice, or one conversation.

Then add another and another. Like seeds taking root and growing, these small beginnings can produce fruit beyond our expectations when we offer them faithfully to God.

Pastor Williams offers this encouragement: "Throughout history, God has used ordinary people willing to take extraordinary steps of faith. Noah built an ark when there was no sign of rain. Abraham left home without knowing the destination. Ruth gleaned in fields as a foreigner. Mary said yes to God's unexpected plan. The disciples left their nets to follow Jesus. In each case, one faithful step led to a world-changing impact. Your steps toward faithful creation care and sustainable living—however small they seem—matter more than you know."

A Final Word of Blessing

As you go forward from these pages into your daily life, may you walk with both deep roots in Biblical truth and wide branches reaching toward God's vision for a renewed world. May you find joy in caring for creation, wisdom in living sustainably, and purpose in joining God's restoration work.

Remember that you're not alone on this journey. Throughout the world, others are taking similar steps—planting gardens, building communities, seeking simplicity, generating clean energy, and caring for both people and the planet as acts of faith. Together, our individual efforts create something beautiful that reflects God's character and purposes for the world He loves.

May your faith bloom brightly as you live as a new creation in Christ, participating in His ongoing work of making all things new!

Family Discussion Questions:

1. What practice or idea from this book most inspired or challenged you? Why?

2. What's one step our family could take this week to better care for God's creation?

3. How might caring for creation and living sustainably become a natural expression of our faith rather than an "extra" thing we do?

4. Who could we share these ideas with, and how might we do that respectfully and effectively?

Teacher's Corner:

This conclusion synthesizes the book's key themes while providing practical next steps for application. The emphasis on starting with manageable actions helps prevent students from feeling overwhelmed by environmental challenges, while the vision casting provides motivational direction for long-term engagement.

The Family Sustainability Challenge could be adapted as a classroom or school-wide initiative for classroom application. Students could form teams to implement sustainable practices at school, documenting their process and results to share with the broader community.

The conclusion intentionally balances theological foundations with practical action, helping students connect faith principles with everyday choices. This integrated approach supports the development of an environmental ethic that is deeply rooted in faith rather than merely adopted from secular environmentalism while still finding common ground with wider sustainability efforts.

Bibliography

Biblical References

All biblical quotations are from the Bible's King James Version (KJV).

Books and Academic Sources

Anderson, J. (2020). *Watershed Discipleship: Reinhabiting Bioregional Faith and Practice*. Cascade Books.

Bahnson, F., & Wirzba, N. (2018). *Making Peace with the Land: God's Call to Reconcile with Creation*. InterVarsity Press.

Bouma-Prediger, S. (2019). *Earthkeeping and Character: Exploring a Christian Ecological Virtue Ethic*. Baker Academic.

Brown, W. P. (2018). *The Seven Pillars of Creation: The Bible, Science, and the Ecology of Wonder*. Oxford University Press.

Chen, E. (2022). *Divine Patterns: Theological Reflections on Quantum Physics and Creation*. Fortress Press.

DeWitt, C. B. (2011). *Earthwise: A Guide to Hopeful Creation Care*. Faith Alive Christian Resources.

Hayhoe, K. (2021). *Saving Us: A Climate Scientist's Case for Hope and Healing in a Divided World*. Simon & Schuster.

Martinez, J. (2019). *The Garden of God: Toward a Human Ecology*. Catholic University of America Press.

Middleton, J. R. (2014). *A New Heaven and a New Earth: Reclaiming Biblical Eschatology*. Baker Academic.

Moo, D. J., & Moo, J. A. (2018). *Creation Care: A Biblical Theology of the Natural World*. Zondervan Academic.

Sleeth, M. (2019). *Reforesting Faith: What Trees Teach Us About the Nature of God and His Love for Us*. WaterBrook.

Snyder, H. A. (2011). *Salvation Means Creation Healed: The Ecology of Sin and Grace*. Cascade Books.

Wassie, A. (2019). *Sacred Forests: Ethiopia's Church Forests Preserve Community and Biodiversity*. University Press of North America.

Wright, N. T. (2017). *Surprised by Hope: Rethinking Heaven, the Resurrection, and the Mission of the Church*. HarperOne.

Articles and Papers

Chen, R. (2021). "Biomimicry as Creation Care: Learning from God's Design." *Faith and Science Journal*, 43(2), 118-132.

Garcia, M. (2020). "Early Christian Communal Practices as Models for Sustainable Living." *Journal of Religion and Society*, 18(3), 201-215.

Henderson, J. (2023). "Mathematical Patterns in Creation: A Christian Perspective on Tesla's Work." *Perspectives on Science and Christian Faith*, 75(1), 45-57.

Kim, S. (2022). "The Liturgy of Creation: Connecting Sacramental Practices to Environmental Stewardship." *Worship and Ecology*, 29(4), 312-325.

Martinez, R. (2019). "The Garden as Theological Metaphor in Contemporary Environmental Ethics." *Studies in Christian Ethics*, 32(1), 40-55.

Rodriguez, A. (2021). "Redemptive Ecology: Creation Care as Participation in Christ's Reconciliation of All Things." *Evangelical Review of Theology*, 45(2), 143-156.

Thompson, E. (2020). "The Divine Economy: Biblical Principles for Sharing Resources Sustainably." *Faith and Economics*, 76, 23-42.

Washington, J. (2022). "Church Forests of Ethiopia: Models of Faith-Based Conservation." *Journal of Religion and Environmental Conservation*, 15(3), 178-192.

Williams, T. (2018). "From Garden to Garden: Eden and New Creation as Frameworks for Christian Environmental Ethics." *Theology and Science*, 16(4), 391-408.

Organizations and Initiatives Referenced

Eden Reforestation Projects. (n.d.). Retrieved from https://edenprojects.org/

Faith in Place. (n.d.). Green Team resources and training. Retrieved from https://www.faithinplace.org/

Green Churches Network. (n.d.). Helping churches care for creation. Retrieved from https://greenchurches.org/

A Rocha International. (n.d.). Christian conservation organization. Retrieved from https://www.arocha.org/

Solar Parish Movement. (n.d.). Integrating renewable energy into church communities. Retrieved from https://solarparish.org/

The Evangelical Environmental Network. (n.d.). Creation care resources for Christians. Retrieved from https://creationcare.org/

Community Initiatives and Case Studies

Detroit Urban Farming Initiative. (2019). Community impact report of urban gardening projects.

Ethiopian Orthodox Church Forest Protection Program. (2020). Conservation outcomes in church-protected forests of northern Ethiopia.

Jordan River Rehabilitation Project. (2021). Collaborative restoration efforts and ecological outcomes.

New Harmony Sustainable Community Design. (2018). Architectural and social planning documents.

Repair Café International Foundation. (n.d.). Community repair initiatives. Retrieved from https://repaircafe.org/

The Green Belt Movement. (n.d.). Community tree planting and environmental conservation. Retrieved from https://www.greenbeltmovement.org/

The Watershed Discipleship Alliance. (n.d.). Bioregional faith communities. Retrieved from https://watersheddiscipleship.org/

Scientific and Technical Resources

IPCC. (2022). Sixth Assessment Report on Climate Change: Impacts, Adaptation and Vulnerability. Intergovernmental Panel on Climate Change.

Mollison, B., & Holmgren, D. (1978). *Permaculture One: A Perennial Agricultural*

System for Human Settlements. Transworld Publishers.

Wohlleben, P. (2016). *The Hidden Life of Trees: What They Feel, How They Communicate—Discoveries from a Secret World*. Greystone Books.

Additional Sources Consulted

Berry, W. (2010). *What Are People For?: Essays*. Counterpoint.

Francis, Pope. (2015). *Laudato Si': On Care for Our Common Home*. Vatican Press.

Krueger, F. (n.d.). National Religious Partnership for the Environment. Retrieved from https://www.nrpe.org/

McKibben, B. (2007). *The Comforting Whirlwind: God, Job, and the Scale of Creation*. Cowley Publications.

Wilson, E. O. (2006). *The Creation: An Appeal to Save Life on Earth*. W. W. Norton & Company.

Note: *While every effort has been made to cite all sources referenced in this book accurately, some explanations and examples represent composite accounts based on multiple real-world examples or* *pedagogical illustrations designed to make concepts accessible to young readers. Personal anecdotes from children and families have been anonymized and, in some cases, represent composite experiences to protect privacy while illustrating important concepts.*

Tracy Taylor

www.ingramcontent.com/pod-product-compliance
Lightning Source LLC
Chambersburg PA
CBHW030507080526
44586CB00011B/104